E. M. Murray
342. Morningside Road.

D1630085

Scotland Bitter-Sweet

James Drawbell

Scotland
Bitter-Sweet

Macdonald · London

Copyright © James Drawbell, 1972

First published in Great Britain in 1972 by
Macdonald and Company (Publishers) Ltd,
St Giles House,
49–50 Poland Street,
London W.1

Printed in Great Britain by
Redwood Press Limited
Trowbridge, Wiltshire

SBN 356 04165 4

Acknowledgements

The author and publishers would like to thank those who have given permission for quotations from the following works.

George Allen & Unwin, Ltd: *Scotland under Mary Stuart* by Madeleine Bingham

BBC Publications and John Murray (Publishers) Ltd: *Civilization* by Kenneth Clark

William Blackwood & Sons Ltd: *The Outgoing of the Tide,* from *The Watcher by the Threshold,* by John Buchan

Cassell & Co. Ltd and the author: *Breaking Out,* Volume Two of *Life is a Four Letter Word,* by Nicholas Monsarrat

Sean Day-Lewis and the *Daily Telegraph*

Faber & Faber Ltd: *The Fiddler,* from *The Turn of the Day,* by Marion Angus

Hodder & Stoughton Ltd: *The Courting of T'nowhead's Bell* by J.M. Barrie

Address on *Courage* and *The Entrancing Life* by J.M.Barrie

Sir Compton Mackenzie and Chatto & Windus Ltd: *My Life and Times, Octave Nine*

John Murray (Publishers) Ltd: *The Little Tinker,* from *Seen and Heard,* by Jane H. Findlater.

A.D. Peters & Co.: *My Scotland* by A.S. Macdonnell

For Lily Mackenzie

I

1

It must have started to snow in the late afternoon. When I woke I could see the flakes swirling in the glow from the street lamps. I couldn't see the lamps themselves for I was two floors up in the hotel, and from the pillow my eyes saw only the outer darkness and the confetti of snow in the misty light.

I was glad I hadn't drawn my curtains, and I lay there for several lazy minutes enjoying the satisfaction of my own comfort in contrast with the winter world outside. The traffic below was constant and rhythmic. It must be getting on for rush hour.

An hour before, I had kicked off my shoes and dropped on to the bed, pulling the coverlet around me. I wasn't twenty-one any more, I had told myself. The fitful sleep of the over-night train journey, and the busy morning in this cold, numbing city in January, had tired me. Aware of the other commitments still to come — pleasant in themselves and gladly chosen, but lowering the resistance when capsuled into a single day and night — I had slipped up to my room to get off my feet. I should have come by plane, I thought, but winter air travel has its own hazards. And one of them was now demonstrating its menace and its magic outside my window.

I got up, leaving the room in darkness, and went over to look out. My room was on the corner, above the Waverley steps, and instantly the long, flat perspective of Princes Street stretched out below me to the distant West End. It was brilliantly lighted, like a stage. The lighting seemed to come from some new, imaginative contrivance of lamps attached at regular spaces high up on Princes Street's long single side of buildings. It suffused the stage with a bright illumination, thrown along and across the whole street, somehow avoiding within its range any suggestion of shadow.

The shadow began on the opposite side, the gardens' side. Here the street fell away into blackness, blotting out what in daylight is the haunting miracle of Auld Reekie's skyline with its gardens and green slopes climbing to the blue-grey castle, its silhouetted line of old buildings, its near-by hills — almost part of the city — its immense sky changing hour by hour in the luminous northern light. All this grandeur that I had so often enjoyed, looking up from the platform of Princes Street, had disappeared in darkness.

But the side of Princes Street on which one usually turns one's back to enjoy the opposite view was now a theatrical setting of unexpected splendour. The radiance gave the hurrying bent figures the sharpness of spotlighted actors. The lighted cars and buses, whether streaking away to the west or coming towards me, accented the lines of pleasing perspective. The pinkly-tinted shop windows were fuzzy blobs of candy floss. The snow was everywhere, swirling, softening, drifting down on to the stage as in some new and oversized ballet of *les patineurs.*

Could this be the same famous street that so many inhabitants, particularly the women, now constantly deplored, longing aloud in their precise Edinburgh tones — the very antithesis of sentiment — for the good old days of the lovely stone shops, deprecating the modern glass-and-concrete multiple stores (but shopping there); regretting the vanished tea-rooms with their vast plate-glass windows, where once one devoured delicious cakes, and gossiped; hating the hustle and the hordes of tourists who hide it completely in the summer? And remembering with longing the peaceful Saturday mornings in the sunlight of a different Princes Street when they met their friends, lingered with them on the pavement like burghers in an old print, and compared complacent notes about the affairs of their comfortable middle-class existence.

I shared some of their nostalgia. It is always a Scottish belief that the past is preferable; almost all Scottish aspiration springs from history rather than from prophecy or anticipation. On my occasional visits north I had tried to keep in line with my deprecating friends when I described the famous shopping centre of Edinburgh as being indistinguishable from Middlesbrough or Leeds. The glory had departed. Any city was just like another. I knew it to be nonsense. I had only to look out of the window of the Scottish Liberal Club to see the castle rising out of its jagged rock and reaching for the sky. The shopping side did not matter, did not exist.

Until now. The tiredness had gone out of me, vanquished by the fantastic spectacle. I had a special place, of course, a ringside seat, but Princes Street that night, at that time, from almost any vantage point, must surely have been entrancing. Well, perhaps not to the thousands of people on the street itself, slithering or pushing against the snow or waiting coldly for the buses of what must be one of the worst services in Britain. They are never there when you need them, and seem to suffer from bad drivers or faulty clutches, or both, that jerk passengers into each other's laps, throw them across the bus, or land them – as I have been landed – flat on the floor. The people have learned on boarding to reach out instantly for a firm rail or a friendly hand (readily extended) before the bus literally 'takes off'; and on leaving to shuffle warily, eyes and hands alert, towards the quivering so-distant exit.

It is some indication of the reality of their suffering that I could even then give them a thought, although fleeting and almost indifferent in the light of the pleasure I was experiencing. For this place, glimpsed from my eyrie, was a gay new entertainment. Not new in the structure of its setting or in the scenery and props, or even in the words and music. I knew the show by heart from my infrequent visits and the early life I had lived in Edinburgh, but this time I was seeing it under new management, or I was sitting in the gallery instead of the stalls. Or a different director was letting himself go, someone who had done a musical on ice, and knew what to do about snow and lighting when he had ad lib quantities of both.

This was the Edinburgh the summer visitor never saw. There were no tourists on stage. No seekers of tartan souvenirs. No strangers from foreign parts ferreting out proof of their family's vague or distant attachment to some Highland clan so that they could return home in triumph to Toorak or Tennessee. This was the Scotland not of the improbable postcards with their eternal blue skies, green glens, heather-covered mountains, shaggy cattle, a hundred pipers an' a' that. This was the Scotland where the Scots lived, every day of their lives, left to themselves, thank God, in these winter months of iron cold and snow and damp and mist and wind and rain.

At the moment, from where I stood sheltered and warm, the watcher in the wings, it looked like the only place that anybody in their senses would ever want to be. For what other reason would I quit my

3

home in its softer southern clime to come up here for only a day and a night in the heart of winter?

Well, there were other reasons for me, less romantic perhaps, but none the less beguiling, and I was cramming as many of these as I could into the twenty-four hours I had permitted myself to be here. The foolish contradiction of man: Return to your birthplace, fall in love with it again — summer or winter — savour it in silent soliloquy for a brief moment, and then depart.

I reminded myself of some of the reasons as I turned reluctantly from the window and switched on the light. It was five o'clock. Tea time. Down in the warm golden lounge of this comfortable hotel the cups and saucers would be tinkling. The waiters, some known to me years ago, would be serving the special blend of tea you get only at this hotel and its sister hotel at the other west-end of Princes Street. They won't tell you how they contrive its particular flavour — the softer water of Edinburgh may have something to do with it — but even as I thought of it my palate relaxed in anticipation.

I went into the bathroom and splashed some cold water over my face. I brushed my hair, pulled my tie into place, shook out my sleep-tousled trousers, pushed my feet into shoes. I was ready for my date with a pot of that delicious tea. For my date too with the unknown young man to whom I had spoken on the telephone that morning.

2

It was warm and cosy in the lounge, with only a sprinkling of people comfortably settled. I chose a table where I could keep my eye on the entrance, gave my order to an old friend whose feet, like those of most waiters, were giving him hell, and went through to the front hall to get the *Evening News*. I peered through the revolving door at the snow. It was certainly coming down. My visitor would be late.

So I made myself comfortable. I had my first cup of tea and looked again at his letter. It had arrived at my Sussex home a few days before and when I read it I passed it over to Sheila with the satisfied comment: 'Scotland still breeds them!'

I judged it to be the letter of a young man, and a young man who seemed to know what he wanted to do. It said:

'Dear Mr Drawbell,

'Beginning in March, Scotland will have its own monthly magazine of the theatre. I am writing to ask whether you would consider lending your support to this venture by contributing an article for our initial issue.

'The aim of *Scottish Theatre* will be the promotion and development of the theatre – both professional and amateur – in Scotland. The magazine will include articles of general interest to theatregoers and to those actively involved in the theatre; a "Profile" each month of a well-known figure in the Scottish theatre; a comprehensive review of professional productions in Scotland; special sections devoted to amateur and student drama; and many other features.

'*Scottish Theatre* will be entirely independent. It will be produced by a group of professional journalists – all working on a voluntary basis. The thinking behind the magazine is that if Scotland can support an International Festival of Drama, seven professional repertory companies, a festival theatre, and a thriving little theatre and amateur movement, Scotland can also support a magazine to cater for this specialized, but growing, market.

'The subject of your article would be of your own choosing. It need not be related directly to the *Scottish* theatre, but should be an opinion piece – naturally the more thought-provoking if not downright provocative, the better.

'I very much hope that you will be able to support in a practical way a publishing venture which will be unique in Scotland.'

Young enthusiasm is sweet music to someone who has sought out young enthusiasm and been surrounded by it most of his life. There were phrases in the letter written out of youth and, I was sure, limited experience, that could not be more provocative – 'Scotland can also support a magazine for its theatre lovers....'

Could it indeed? I wondered. Did Scotland want to do any such thing? Did Scotland give much of a damn about its theatre; and would it care any more for a magazine about it?

Four years before, when I had opted out of the day-to-day grind of my publishing life, and expected to live in semi-retirement, writing an occasional book, playing golf, and seeing more of my grandchildren, I had been lured back for a short time to Edinburgh by one of the nicest

5

men in the Scottish theatre, and one of its most accomplished actors. Tom Fleming, the newly-appointed director of a new Edinburgh Civic adventure at the Royal Lyceum Theatre, invited me to help him in his relations with the Press and to give him the benefit, if I could, of my awareness of the public and its responses.

I had held him off for a time, pleading that the theatre was not my game, but finally agreed to join him for a limited time. It would be an interesting experience and help me to play myself in to the life of the Scotland to which I was ultimately planning to return. I feared it would be an uphill job. I didn't altogether believe the reports that Scotland was experiencing a wide cultural renaissance. I guessed from my newspaper experience that some of the critics reporting the Edinburgh Festival were as interested in their yearly safari to the Scottish capital as in the Festival's activities themselves. Journalists are only human, and if the lengthy columns in the world's press sometimes gave the impression that something more than terrific was happening in Scotland, one had learned to take enthusiastic reporting with a degree of wariness. Who wouldn't want to go on a free visiting trip to the Cannes Film Festival every May in spite of its many deplorable offerings?

My friends in Edinburgh had warned me that while the Festival hullaballoo was just tolerable for three weeks in the year, the normal climate of cultural interest settled in depressingly soon afterwards. The normal climate, I gathered, was cool and apathetic. That unique spectacle and common unifier, 'that mixture of sentimentality, militarism and bogus history – the Edinburgh Tattoo', as Stuart Hood described it, was out of sight for another year and Edinburgh largely returned to its peace and quiet, its cultural indifference.

I hadn't found it altogether like that. There was a small hard core of devoted theatregoers, which included all ages of men and women. They were very much in a minority, but their dedication was encouraging and unmistakable. Sometimes they were a huddled handful in the vast theatre which Tom Fleming had the awful responsibility of filling, and the sight was a dismal one. The Lyceum, a 'commercial' theatre of the past where great plays had been put on by great players; where saccharine-sweet musical comedies and glamorous stars had brought out regular, eager, expectant queues; where famous repertory companies like the Macdona Players and the Graham Moffatt company had entertained another generation with Shaw and Barrie, was facing – like most theatres outside London, which still kept the theatre alive through vigorous commercial competition – not only the moment of truth but the hours and days and weeks of a seemingly certain lost fight.

The bingo fans everywhere were taking over the cinema and the theatre. The discotheques were luring the predictable young. Television, the Frankenstein of the modern entertainment world, gave you everything from soap suds to soap opera at the turn of a switch and in your own warm sitting room, with a drink by your side and a tray of food in your lap.

No wonder the theatres in the provinces were suffering. Unless there was an absolutely super play, either prior to being played in London, or immediately after, with popular stars, what citizen in his right senses would go out into a cold winter night like this to see a company that was being subsidized out of the rates or from the depthless cornucopia of the Arts Council?

Well, some people would, as I had discovered. As the writer of this letter also knew. And as some of his close friends also believed, who were willing to work for nothing to produce a theatre magazine to express their common faith. I could tell from the letter that its writer didn't feel he was fighting for a lost cause. His appeal had confidence in it, and resolution. He meant to make a go of it.

I had known I was coming up to Edinburgh, but doubted if time would give me the chance of meeting him. But this was exactly the kind of fighting Scot I wanted to meet, so that morning I had altered some plans and phoned him at his office. Could he come and have a cup of tea with me on his way home and before I went on to my other engagement?

He could. I liked the sound of his voice as I had liked the sound of his letter. Young, as I had thought, and eager; but firm and confident. An old head on young shoulders, I guessed. I wanted to see what made Kenneth Roy tick.

And as I looked up, there he was weaving his way between the tables towards me. A waiter was following at his heels, anxious to take the young man's snow-dusted raincoat from him before the snow was scattered on the carpet. Kenneth Roy had come right through from the front door, his coat still on, not wanting to prolong my waiting. He was tall and too thin ('a bundle of bones' we used to say in Scotland), and somewhere in his early or mid-twenties. Even so, there were touches of grey in his unruly dark hair, falling forward over his forehead and his lean face in the style of Robert Burns. It made his head appear bigger. He smiled straight at me. But it was a shy smile, coming from his eyes rather than from his mouth. It was only a little later that I saw he was unnecessarily shy of smiling widely because of a few teeth which could be made good — and which he meant to make good, no doubt, when he could find time to get round to it. So he was aware of himself, and his shortcomings. Good. It figured, as the Americans say; and that's the way I like them.

He ran a quick hand through his hair and the snow drifted on to his shoulders. His other hand held on to a brief case, the bulky kind of the worker, not the slim black leather wafer of the high executive.

The waiter managed to get the raincoat off him as Kenneth Roy reached my table.

'Sorry I'm so late,' he said, shaking my hand.

'I expected it. What a night.'

'I had to walk from Castle Street.'

I caught the waiter's eye before he got away.

'Fresh tea,' I ordered, and taking a quick look at the cold young man: 'And two large whiskies. OK?'

'Wonderful,' he agreed, and folded himself into the chair beside me with a satisfied sigh.

I was thinking of the thin raincoat.

'You must be frozen.'

'No, not really. I actually ran most of the way, so I'm not as cold as some of them out there.'

'A drop in your tea will do you good.'

'That's a great idea. Thanks for thinking of the whisky.' He was relaxing, thawing out, reassured by his welcome. I wonder what he had expected. He must have had some varied encounters in the course of persuading people about his project.

'And we've got to celebrate the magazine,' I said casually.

He laughed. It was a laugh with a bit of a crack in it.

'Celebrate! If you only knew!'

The waiter came with the tea. The whisky in the glasses matched the golden warmth of the room.

'Oh, I know all right.' I tipped some whisky straight into his hot tea. 'It's tough at the beginning. I've been through it.'

'Haven't you just!'

I liked the slightly Scots-American expression, today's idiom of journalism and the theatre. The right mixture. It had also the right inflexion of acknowledgement towards the old hand. He'd done his home-work on me.

8

'You've always got to celebrate,' I assured him. 'The beginning as well as the achievement. Nothing's any use if it isn't fun. Here's to it!'

We raised our glasses slightly over the white tablecloth, the shining silver, the thin china, and drank. It was a beginning, and any young man with guts deserves to be cheered on his way. It would be uphill enough for him. I knew what it was like at twenty-four, which was his age, with plenty of ambition, not much money, and the flutterings in the stomach.

'Celebrate!' He repeated the word with relish, bemused by it. He sipped his whisky happily.

He had caught on. I had guessed right, supplying him with the beginnings of a new doctrine. Brought up the hard way in dear old Calvinistic Scotland, he was too young to have worked abroad, probably hadn't been out of Scotland, hadn't had the opportunity or the disadvantage (you make it what you want) of a university, and was hell-bent on carving out his career, standing up for his beliefs, and always leading with his chin. It was written all over him. The breed apparently didn't change in this strange, dour, enchanting bloody country. Nor the complexities of living in it. I indulged my older man's privilege of weighing him up, confident that I wasn't a hundred miles out in my surmises. I knew him of old, as I had known my chums in this same city so many years ago; as I knew myself. He had all the lessons to learn, except the important one of believing in himself. He was making my day.

'You mentioned Castle Street?' I murmured.

'Where I work. The Scottish Council.'

'The Arts Council?'

'Good Lord, no!' He spluttered his whisky. 'That's strictly for the academics.'

I had been right about the university. He wouldn't have a chance with the Edinburgh Establishment. In Scotland it's almost as bad as England. If you didn't go to Daniel Stewart's, or George Watson's, or the Royal High, or one of the other well-known Edinburgh schools, you really belonged to that old-fashioned (I had thought outmoded) mould of Scots boy who made good by his own efforts. I had come across it when I was roped in to help the Edinburgh Civic Theatre, and so became part of the social life of the city. Continuing contact only emphasized that nothing had changed, except to become more so. There were so many Scots, and Scottish habits and institutions, that had become Anglicized in their outlook that sometimes I thought I was back in London. You conformed in this homeland of mine, or you stagnated. Or you became one of the forty thousand men and women each year who emigrated from it.

Forty thousand. Almost exactly the same annual number as left their Auld Scotland the year I did, more than forty years before. Scotland has no shame. I had thought for a time that she was living in the past. '*On* the past,' I was corrected by Bob Daw, a nineteen-year-old Dundee sub-editor on the London *Daily Mail* who had fled his first job in the north; and who filled me in before I returned to it. 'It's a great country to be born in and to come back to, but a hell of a place to work in.' He couldn't have been far out. All my Scottish friends had gone to one of the famous schools, had lived in Edinburgh most of their lives, and envied me the life I had had the good fortune to enjoy away from it. They did not know that often I longed to be there in Edinburgh with them.

Tom Wilkie-Millar, who is a doctor and knows his Scots and his Scotland, amplifies Bob Daw's belief. 'For a man with ambition, there are few great heights he can reach here. If you're in something peculiarly Scotch, say like shipping, then fine! The Clyde's the home of shipping. The sky's your limit. The same with whisky. But in most other businesses, if you really want to go to town, the big opportunities lie outside Scotland. You have to get out. Unless, of course, you recognize that it's the only place to live. As so many of us do.'

These thoughts flickered through my mind in the few seconds while I watched Kenneth Roy dab at the whisky he had spilled on his sleeve with a spotlessly clean handkerchief. Item: there was a wife in his life; perhaps children. Almost certainly. A vital, creative person like Roy seldom dodged the human relationships. In his rage to live he embraced every responsibility, instinctively banking on his own ability and confidence to be able to cope, never counting the cost.

That was how I read him, but I wanted to hear more from himself.

'You've taken something on,' I said.

I wanted to lead him gently on to his ideas about his magazine, not bludgeon him with questions which might be misconstrued as criticism. The merest prompting, a suggestion rather than an interrogation, and the other person is often released from himself. Once, caught in a traffic jam in London, I only had to say through the taxi window to my driver, 'It gets worse every day'; and in the next ten minutes to Victoria I heard his life story, his views on the bloody public, and his earthy solution for what should be done with single-passenger cars in London.

And, thrown in for good measure, a spiel about the stupidity of people who don't realize that a taxi driver can take them more quickly to their destination through side streets instead of sticking to the jam-packed main routes. 'The silly bleeders think I want to make the journey longer! They don't realize. I know all the short ways. I got my living to make! It pays me and saves them if I get there quicker. They're all nuts!'

Kenneth Roy responded carefully. He knew already that I was interested in his project, and sympathetic. I had written the article he wanted and it was going to appear in the first issue. But he was conscious, I thought, of his youthful over-enthusiasm, and its dangers.

'Oh, I know we've got problems,' he said slowly. 'Money, the right kind of editorial, willing people to help.'

I remembered the words of his letter.

'But you've got them?'

'Oh, yes; they're all pals of mine who feel as I do about the need for the magazine. I'm lucky.'

'They love the theatre?'

'I suppose you can put it that way. Yes. There's a lot of enthusiasm.'

'But not an awful lot of Scottish theatre?'

He said quickly: 'Not as much as there should be. But what there is has plenty of life in it. And there'll be a lot less if somebody doesn't stir it up all the time.'

'What's really prompting you?' I asked. 'Nationalism or theatre?'

He laughed openly, his sensitive guard over his smile forgotten.

'Oh, I see the way you're thinking! SNP and all that. Up with the claymores and to hell with the English!'

'Well, I wondered.'

I signalled to the waiter for refills of whisky. I liked him. There was humour in him and fire in the belly, and he was his own man's man. I suspected he hadn't a clue about the enormity of his task, but if his courage was the courage of ignorance – as once my own had been; as once Orson Welles's had confessedly been when, at the age of twenty-five, he produced, directed and acted in his epic film *Citizen Kane* – it was still courage. His own.

'Of course there's a bit of nationalism in it,' he said. 'Naturally. But the priority is theatre. The title *Scottish Theatre* doesn't mean it's going to be parochial. Look at your own piece.'

My own piece was an article about *Hair,* the hippie musical that had just started to galvanize London, its implications, and the audience

11

reaction to it. I wanted to learn about the Scotland of today. I had done it deliberately to see if Kenneth Roy would drop dead and funk publishing it. After all, this was still the country of John Knox. He was so sure of himself and his readers-to-be that he was pushing the *Hair* piece into the first number, to be followed by an article by Kenneth Tynan.

Roy went on: 'Anything about the theatre will be printed. The theatre anywhere. It's *Scottish Theatre* because it's done in Scotland and we want the Scottish theatre to flourish. But there's no "wha's like us!" Very much to the contrary. But we do want our own theatre to be alive and kicking.'

'And not only through Scottish writers and Scottish actors?'

He said soberly: 'We haven't got a sufficiency of either to have an exclusive Scottish theatre. Not yet anyway.'

I suggested: 'But you must be having a pretty hard time getting the magazine off the ground.'

'It's not so easy.'

The typical Scots answer.

'What about the finances?'

'It's not really the expensive venture it seems. Twenty-four pages; not one of your great big glossies.'

'Monthly?'

'Oh, yes. A quarterly would be no good: not enough continuity: and a weekly is out of the question. It would be all wrong anyway.'

I visualized it: 'With no photographs; too expensive. Except perhaps one on the cover?'

'That's it to a tee!' He laughed: 'You might have been in on the planning! The cover is a two-coloured standard design, only the colour changing – and the photo on it – each month.'

All the trimmings of economy.

'Selling for what? Two bob?'

'Half a crown. Not through the bookstalls. No middleman. By direct subscription. The rep. theatres will boost it, the theatre clubs, actors, writers, journalists. It's *their* magazine. Our interests are identical. You know.'

He had his head screwed on. He knew what he wanted to do and the true way to do it.

'We've worked out the figures,' he went on, 'and we've got a good local printer who'll do it at our price.'

I wondered what sort of circulation he was hoping for.

'A thousand?' I guessed. Were there a thousand dedicated theatre-goers left in Scotland?

'I think we can do between twelve-fifty and fifteen hundred.' He crossed his fingers. 'If we give them the right stuff.'

Watching him, and remembering his letter to me, I hadn't any doubt that he'd give them the right stuff.

'Provocative was the word you used.'

'All the way,' he enthused quietly. 'Not just for the sake of it, but because plain hard speaking is what is needed, and what a Scottish audience appreciates.'

All fifteen hundred of them, I thought. I remembered the circulation figure of the last magazine I had ever had anything to do with. I remembered the name of the man, Victor Goldsworthy, who had come up from the works at Watford and laid the slip of paper on my desk. With silent relish. The figure of the printing run was just on three million. And that was a weekly. We had both looked at it for a moment, and then he had said: 'A bit different from when we started, isn't it?'

At his words, a whole decade of hectic effort with incredibly enthusiastic young people had filled my mind. What had that thought to do now with Kenneth Roy embarking on his adventure and relishing in anticipation his audience of fifteen hundred? Everything. I had never thought, at my beginning, that I would influence a weekly public of three million people. I had begun as modestly as he, perhaps even more humbly, for he at least was starting as a magazine owner, and I never achieved that. It was all behind me; it was all ahead of him. For me there could be no further surprises; for Kenneth Roy, it was an uncharted future.

I think I had wanted to see what he was made of because I wanted to be reassured that there were young men like him still in Scotland, ready to stake their belief in themselves. There was nothing wrong in him beginning at the top, running his own magazine; that's the right way to begin.

But I wondered where the initial capital had come from. It's all very well to work for nothing, but right at the start there's a printer to be assured that his printing will be paid for, promotion expenses to get the thing known, office stationery and postage. Money of some kind is needed to get a venture like this off the ground. Not the millions of pounds that you need in Fleet Street, but some small change.

'Is there a good fairy helping you?' I asked him.

'Not really. A few well-wishers have pitched in. Also one department store owner, entirely out of the goodness of his heart. Scottish Television — our biggest supporter so far — has taken a whole series of page ads in advance. Ads, by the way, are coming in well. So are the promises of subscriptions. The rep.theatres will show our posters.'

'You didn't need to find a sponsor?'

He eyed me carefully.

'What sort of sponsor?'

'Somebody with real money. Someone as concerned as you about the theatre, to shoulder a bit of the burden.'

'In what way?'

'To cover you for a year. The first year's the worst, you know.'

'You mean, having a hand in it?'

'No, not necessarily. Just putting up the lolly.'

'What kind of bloke?'

'Someone with a name. A name in Scotland that's respected. Wouldn't that help?'

He said slowly: 'Don't you think that sooner or later he'd want to have a hand in running it?'

I laughed: 'And you wouldn't want that?'

'What do *you* think?'

'I think you'll manage without him.'

'Oh, we'll manage.'

'Here in Edinburgh?'

'Actually from Inverkeithing.'

It had been the town of his address.

'From your own home?'

'Oh, yes.'

'No office?'

'It isn't necessary. We all work in Edinburgh and can meet in the city at lunch, or over dinner at one of our houses. And we've already got correspondents resident in all the areas where there's a theatre — rep. or otherwise.'

He had it all worked out.

'But why Inverkeithing?' I asked. 'Why do you live there?'

I had forgotten that the new Forth Road Bridge made Inverkeithing, and all the Fife towns just across the river, the new bedrooms of Edinburgh. The old romantic but slow river ferries had gone for ever.

'It's cheaper,' he said simply.

He did not tell me then, nor was it from him that I learned later that he had bought a house at Inverkeithing for £4,000 that would have cost over £5,000 in Edinburgh. And that he travelled to Edinburgh daily, not over the road bridge by car (because he didn't own a car), but by train to save money. Nor did he tell me then that his first baby boy was only nine months old and that Margaret, his wife, as dedicated to his aims as Ken himself, would manage their home, their child, and the whole correspondence connected with *Scottish Theatre,* and the comings and goings of the little team of young men and women setting out to tell Scotland about its own theatre.

'Were you born in Inverkeithing?' I asked him.

'No; in Falkirk.'

'Well I'm damned!' I exclaimed. 'That's my home town.'

'I know,' he said. 'We're both Falkirk "bairns".'

The town of Falkirk, mid-way between Edinburgh and Glasgow, part of the highly concentrated industrial belt that runs across the centre of Scotland, has an aggressive motto that declares: 'Better meddle with the de'il than the bairns of Falkirk.' You'd have more of a chance taking on the devil than a Falkirk native. It was a fighting town. I had spent my childhood there, in grim days when it took all a grown man's stamina to keep going in the conditions of almost continuous unemployment. You learned from infancy to be tough, to stand up for yourself. Evidently, even in the new affluent conditions that now flourished in Falkirk, the old instinct to take on the world wasn't dormant.

It had been worth coming up to Edinburgh to meet Kenneth Roy, although that's not what I had come for. He had been a niggling reminder in my brain that there still was enterprise and talent about; and old habits and instincts in me died hard. All my life I had dealt with people. You can be misled by a persuasive letter, or a voice on the telephone, or by both. But it had been my job to find young men who had started with me from scratch, and had become by their own efforts prominent newspaper and magazine editors; and young women who had got to the top of their special ladders: fashion-trenders, novelists, illustrators.

Some of them had started as tea boys or copy typists in the office pool. They had achieved their ambition by the essential stuff they were made of, their readiness to learn, the hidden quality of steel that must be in everyone who succeeds – and the something in their eyes that could flash you a clue. My part had been to spot the likely ones, to work them gradually into the scheme of things and to test them with all the challenging, impossible tasks. Ambition isn't enough. Enthusiasm isn't enough. The real professional is the man with the know-how and the guts. My fun had been the privilege of throwing them the world they wanted, and had earned.

I'd certainly have taken a chance on the young man sitting with me drinking tea and whisky. He was embarking on an adventure in terrain where the going would be tough all the time. He certainly hadn't chosen the easy way to easy money. I wished I were staying longer in Scotland to find out more about my own country of today, and its new generation of people. I knew them well enough from my own time, but I had often wondered from afar what had happened to them in the years between. It might be worth while to wander about and have a look at them.

As we talked, I got a little more from him about his own background. He hadn't gone to my school in Falkirk. He had attended the Denny High, hated it, and left when he was fifteen. He couldn't get into journalism fast enough. So he began, as I began (as the lucky ones in life begin), by knowing what he wanted to do. This is almost the greatest advantage in life. You just equip yourself for the ride. He took a course in shorthand and typing at Skerry's in Glasgow and began typing cinema notes for the *Falkirk Mail.* The paper subsequently collapsed. These things happen. My own first Chief Reporter dropped dead in the office soon after he gave me a job. I always wondered if my inadequate shorthand had something to do with it.

And now I thought I saw under the Robert Burns hair tumbling over his brow the smouldering eye of the crusader as well as the journalist. Was he a reformer, a tilter at windmills? His theatre magazine might be a piece of sheer masochism, mixed up with the usual narcissism of journalism. Whatever he was, he was going to be a handful, yet his progress up to this moment in the N.B. lounge seemed normal enough for a young man in a hurry. He had gone to work on the *Greenock Telegraph,* where he met the managing-director's personal secretary. Ken and Margaret were the same age, nineteen. Together they acted in amateur drama. Their first play was *Quiet Wedding;* she played the bride, he the bridegroom. Off-stage as well as on-stage, they became engaged.

From there, at twenty, to the *Glasgow Herald,* 'where I learned to write'. I liked to hear him say that. There's always a paper you work with, or a presiding genius of one man, from whom you learn. Not always 'how to write', for that writing urge is there from the beginning, but how to use words properly, how to condense, how to discipline yourself. How to make a story or an article come alive for the reader. He was there two-and-a-half years, and then he and Margaret got married.

I wondered why he had joined the Scottish Council, to do its publicity work. It is one of these establishments designed to further Scottish trade, a formidable task in the conditions of the country and the limited aid it receives. And now I understood why he had to find a new outlet for his energies, for the things he had to say. He wanted to run some show of his own, the mark of a born editor. His first letter to me had been a request, yet in its form it was almost an admission. In making clear his needs, he revealed his own capacity.

I had taken up a lot of his time, and he had abundantly rewarded me for the whisky and the tea. I think we could have gone on talking. But he had to get home across the Bridge to a young wife and a new baby, and all the problems that engulfed his life; and I had to give myself the pleasure of sitting alone a little longer, turning it all over in my mind, before going up to my room to change and put on a black tie.

I saw him to the front door of the hotel and out into the Edinburgh night. It had stopped snowing, the traffic had died away, Princes Street was comparatively empty.

It was only when I turned back into the lounge that a question which I had meant to ask Kenneth Roy came sharply at last to the front of my dull brain. Why hadn't the Scottish Arts Council, with so much public money available to spend on the development and encouragement of the Arts, come forward to help this lone adventurer and his voluntary team with the finances of their magazine, *Scottish Theatre?*

Had Kenneth Roy been too foolish, or too independent, not to seek aid from the people most able and surely most willing to help?

3

Two hours later I was getting into a taxi at the hotel entrance. My destination, the Adam Rooms of the George Hotel, was only a step or two away, just far enough to get some fresh air into my lungs. Normally I would have walked. Edinburgh is a quiet city in the evening, a delight to walk through, and this was the quietest of times: when people are already in their homes or comfortably settled in cinema or theatre. Or bingo hall. But although the snow had gone, swept off the street by wind or rain or earlier traffic, the chill struck at me through my thin evening clothes. I played it safe and took a taxi.

'But go the long way,' I suggested to the driver.

'The long way?'

He was quite right to turn round and have a good stare at me. There is only the short direct way from the N.B. Hotel to the George, quarter of a mile away. You'd have to make an effort to lengthen it. Which is just what I wanted him to do.

I hadn't a route in mind, so it must have been instinct that made me say: 'Turn up the Bridges, then into Chambers Street. You can get into the Meadows from there, can't you?'

'Oh, ay,' he said cautiously.

'You know that road that goes along through the Meadows – the Jaw Bone Walk?'

'And on to Toll Cross?'

'That's it. Well, we can then go down Lothian Road and come into the West End of Princes Street.'

His engine was gently revving, his foot ready to press down on the accelerator. A line of unwanted taxis stood against the kerb just beyond the Waverley Steps. His luck was in; he must have thought he had landed a nut case.

But he had the pawky Scottish sense of humour.

'You're wanting a bit of a hurl then?'

'That's the idea.'

'What about coming back through Auchtermuchty?' he asked.

I laughed. This was my man. It was a joke a much older generation would have made; this was a man of between forty and fifty. It showed the unchanging thinking, but more importantly to me it revealed the age-old Scottish attitude of man to man. In this country some things persisted.

I knew exactly how to answer him.

'Or Kirriemuir. I could take in J.M. Barrie's birthplace.'

'Ay, and a grand nicht for it!'

As he turned the cab slowly away from the hotel to go to the corner for the Bridges, I said through the window: 'But come back along Princes Street after Lothian Road, and then go up to the George by any street you like.'

'Ay, that's what I was thinking you'd want, sir.'

The 'sir', too, was uttered in the traditional way. In the Scotland of my day men used the word as the Americans do. Not the address of a servant to a master, but the conversational respect of one man offered in equality to another. I have never heard the word used as the Scots and Americans use it anywhere else in the English-speaking world. It recognizes similarity between men, not difference: the equivalent perhaps of the French 'monsieur'. He had not used it till that moment when he acknowledged me as one of his own. I might still be a nut case wasting money wandering about Edinburgh in his cab, but I wasn't the alien he had at first thought me to be.

His modern taxi turned on its tight lock as we headed round for the traffic lights. It reminded me of something.

'So all the old Rolls-Royces have gone?' I said.

He was listening with his left ear cocked, his eye on the street. But I could see his face smile with understanding. There was a time when almost every taxi in Edinburgh was a sleek black Rolls. They were one of the sights of the city. Someone must have had a contract (was it a firm called Croall?) for all those second-hand cars, but they looked shining new, and they were a grand sight. No one ever used them of course. No one used a taxi in a city where you could walk almost anywhere to your appointment in a few minutes, or board a tram. You had to be in a desperate hurry to take a taxi. Distances were nothing in a city like this. Even the roundabout route I had chosen for my journey now would be covered in ten minutes at the most, and I still wouldn't be late at the George Hotel.

He said: 'That's going back a while.'

'Ay,' I said. 'Before you were born.'

'No, not exactly. My faither drove one. My first hurl in a car was a Rolls Royce!'

I always have luck with my taxi drivers.

'There's no' many can say that!' he laughed.

'Especially round about 1930.'

He stayed silent. He had pulled over to our left side and was cruising along. He knew I was in no hurry and had my own reasons.

'What's it like?' I asked.

'In Edinburgh?'

You didn't have to spell it out to this man. 'I mean, nowadays.'

He glanced briefly back at me, and then gestured his left hand at the deserted streets.

'Deid.' Then after a pause; 'Oh, it's a bit better than it was. And in the summer wi' a' the visitors, there's plenty doing. But this is a deid

19

toon for six months in the year. No life in it at all.'

Once more, he was the Scot I had always known. You asked him something and he answered straight out. I had been brought up that way, and plenty of trouble it had got me into in various places in the world where people were used to saying one thing and thinking another.

'But there's more work than there was surely?'

'Not so much here. Further west. Falkirk, Grangemouth, Glasgow. There's a lot o' new industries, but not much here.'

I thought of some of the things I had heard and read in the newspapers about Edinburgh. The wrangling over an Opera House that had been suggested years before and still hadn't happened. The interminable discussions about a ring road. The city's airport at Turnhouse which, after nearly a quarter of a century of the Edinburgh Festival that brought people from all over the world, still wasn't an international airport capable of taking the jets. From the air its small control tower and assembly buildings looked like something out of the early movies. As you came down to land you thought the pilot must have made a mistake.

'But it's a lovely city,' I said.

There were always the compensations.

'Oh, ay. It's a bonnie place.'

But it sounded as if he meant that beauty by itself wasn't enough, and I knew we should lapse into silence.

4

We turned right, into Chambers Street, just before the University. It was a short street, both shorter and wider than I remembered. Perhaps the darkness had something to do with it.

I don't know why I had impulsively chosen this street. And yet as we crawled up into it and came upon the great dark pile that was the Museum, the memories stirred in me, and I knew again that it always hurts to come back.

It always hurts to come back. It's not that you're coming back to something new or strange. It's that these are the things you've been carrying with you in your mind for most of a lifetime far from home. I hadn't had a home in Edinburgh to come back to for a long time, but all the associations of boyhood lay in wait for me in this city at the most unexpected corners.

And this big ugly building was one of them.

'Could you stop for a minute?' I asked the driver.

If we had been in New York a printed card facing me in the cab would have given me his name. Paulus Karnowictz, or something similar. With his photograph attached, just like a police 'Wanted' notice. And I'd have been calling him Paul. But the Scot taking care of me was probably Jock MacPherson or Alex Ferguson. And in this single journey, I'd never know, and we'd certainly never be on first-name terms. This wasn't New York, where once my young daughter, setting out alone to make a career, had been seen weeping silently by the taxi driver taking her back to her lonely hostel. He had stopped his cab, discovered that this was her first step into life, an ocean away from home, and taken her into a drug store, given her coffee, and eased her homesickness. But my Edinburgh driver had the instinct to know that I was on some kind of pilgrimage, however strange or impulsive. His car had almost come to a stop anyway. He had sensed my interest.

I got out. He cautioned wisely: 'It's gey nippy.' And I acknowledged his concern with a nod and walked up the long steps in the darkness to the big front doors.

The first time I had come here was with my mother. I had begun stamp collecting, and she knew that in this building there was a fabulous array of glass trays that you slid towards you from a cabinet, and there before your very eyes was everything you had ever seen in a stamp catalogue. It was long before the days of all the gay stamp series of today, these gorgeous birds, these sporting events, these Christmas cards in miniature. It was almost better then. You could keep track. Your eyes could rest on the riches, contented; not be distracted by the mountainous temptations that now confront, and surely confuse, the young collector. My mother had been very patient: the white swan that represented Australia, the bearded old man from Austria, the cross on the red background that was Helvetia. Then, although she knew I hadn't a mechanical instinct in my make-up, she had taken me into the big hall where all the marvels of machinery, secure in immense glass cases, could be moved into action by the pressure on a button. If I had no mechanics, I had at least the sense of magic in me, and imagination stirred as wheels revolved, pistons went up and down, complicated arrangements of iron arms and legs contorted themselves. The wonder of course was that it was my finger making it all happen; and it is only long afterwards that you understand that this is what your mother was doing for you.

I discovered the Museum through her, and much later I was there one thrilling Saturday evening when the alarm was sounded because some suffragettes were in the building. My memory is that one or several of the glass cases were smashed, and everybody in the place was hustled towards the exits. Alas, my mother wasn't there on that occasion. She might have deplored the destruction, but she heartily approved the cause, and was herself a quietly ardent suffragist. After her experience with my father, whose own strongest personal preference was for the golden stream of whisky which could be bought for twopence a glass, I could understand her enthusiasm for feminine freedom.

She was not with me that time, because I was out of boyhood, with my own young friends, and beginning to find my own knowledge of the world. We were probably in the Museum that Saturday evening because it was free, and we had no money to go elsewhere. I wondered as I stood in the darkness how many youngsters today, with their riches and their privileges, would opt for the Edinburgh Museum on a Saturday night.

Across Chambers Street, almost opposite the Museum, was another institution that had played its part in my upbringing; Heriot-Watt College. There, during the winter months, I attended various evening classes, trying to improve my French and my shorthand. And not far away, in this same neighbourhood, the Edinburgh College of Art had had to suffer my other free evenings and my other extravagant hopes. Education has always played an important part in Scottish life. It is a faith instilled into one, as potent as the country's religion. The two merge beautifully together into a single credo: salvation and reward through trial and effort.

Attending evening classes was a way of life for young men and women. I was no exceptionally industrious boy pushing to get ahead; I was in the company of thousands of others like myself, in all the towns and cities, seeking the knowledge that would enable us to justify our belief in ourselves. We all had our private, reticent Scottish faith which we intended would one day make its impact on the world. In the world of my boyhood it was no deprivation to spend evenings and spare time in study. It was a way of life. There were in any case few entrancing social alternatives, and there was no money. We started, in summer, planning what we should be involved in at schools in the winter

22

evenings to come.

It was strange, or perhaps not, that I should have chosen now to come to this part of Edinburgh to pass a little time on my way to the George Hotel. I looked at the Heriot-Watt buildings whose rooms, unlike the Museum, were alight, where another generation was going through an experience similar to my own.

I remembered the face of a girl from the past. I went down the steps to the waiting driver, who had come out of his cab to swing his arms back and forth round his body for warmth. I could see his breath, white in the night cold. He held the door open for me.

'And now for the Meadows, eh?'

He hadn't forgotten my mention of the Jaw Bone Walk. The Meadows are a large undulating tract of green land on the south-west fringe of the city. There is a stretch near the Royal Infirmary, flat enough for a large cricket space. On summer evenings medical students played there in their white flannels, and coloured students seemed to be in the majority. There was no racial question then in Edinburgh, as there is none today. Edinburgh Infirmary was a popular training institution with Indians, not only because it was the best in the country but also because it was cheap to live in Edinburgh. I can remember being in the Meadows watching cricket, on the very first evening that Summer Time was introduced, in May 1916.

The ground rises gently towards Bruntsfield, where there is a pitch-and-putt golf course. There are several paths, and one motor road runs through and connects both the south side and the Marchmont residential district with the city. The Jaw Bone Walk (the jaw of a whale arched across the path) leads towards this from the Infirmary, a stone's throw away from where we stood now, and crosses the motor road and goes on up to Bruntsfield links.

It is only a few minutes from the Heriot-Watt College in Chambers Street, and if I used to arrive for classes too early by chance, or more often by choice, I would walk down towards the Jaw Bone Walk to meet my fellow student coming from the Bruntsfield end. We'd then walk back to the college together.

Sometimes I'd meet her quite soon on my mission; sometimes, and more frequently, I'd get across the motor road and well towards the pitch-and-putt course before we met. I did not do this because it was dark in the Meadows and the girl might be apprehensive. I did it because I wanted to be with her as long as possible. She had crossed the dark Meadows many a time without my escort, both coming and going

23

to the college, although frequently I travelled back the whole way with her.

I cannot remember that anyone in that day and age was afraid of what might happen to a woman in the darkness of a public place in Edinburgh. I cannot remember that women themselves were given to much concern about their safety. It wasn't 1972. No girl I ever knew was learning karate, or being taught that a kick in a man's crotch was the quickest way to cool his ardour. I never knew a member of what we still believed to be the fair sex who was an adept at a knock-out blow delivered by her shoe or her knee.

No one stuck to the main, well-lighted streets and avoided the quiet and pleasant places of the city because of the likelihood of getting your teeth kicked in, your dress ripped off, or your wallet stolen. So it was a dull, safe place to drag out your life in? To me it was the grandest place on earth. I loved it then and still do, and all the people I have met in different parts of the world, and who know it, have spoken of it as I do. You made your own pleasures with your own kind. There were no discotheques then, no gambling casinos, no night clubs. The place is full of them now. No young person in our crowd had a car in which to risk the lives of half a dozen others after a gay alcoholic party.

It was, unfortunately, the world of your elders which you followed without question, and it – or we – could be faulted. The young rebellion that must have been in all of us was muted, or sublimated, or churched out of us, or held at arms length, to break out in later life no doubt, in savage bursts of God-fearing guilt and money-grubbing activity far from home and respectability. But it was the only way of young life we knew, and we certainly made the best of it. There were decorous dancing classes, and whist drives, and the evening classes I've mentioned, and singing after supper in each other's homes. And in summer we played golf on the Braid Hills or did a fifteen-mile trek on a Saturday or Sunday across the Pentland Hills, or watched the Hibernians or the Hearts, the local football idols. In all our diversions we were as mixed in our company as are the boys and girls of today; but most of us were sexually inhibited or sexually ignorant. We knew, by hearsay, the horrors of veneral disease and through personal fear the oft-repeated dictum that if you masturbated you would go mad.

It was a law-abiding city, and we were all law-respecting youngsters. To fall foul of the law in any way would have been a social disgrace and a personal nightmare. Edinburgh is still in general much the same in this respect and its people appear to be almost as well-behaved as in my day.

24

The young are as uninhibited as in any other city, but cleanliness is still a virtue. So is love of education. The very long-haired young men are still an exception in this city, to be civilly tolerated. I imagine that Scottish self-respect, that inner image of himself in any Scot, stopped the hippie advance somewhere about the Borders. The young of both sexes are not behind in wearing the way-out clothes of their day, but they wear them in the main as decoratively as they do the kilt.

There must have been a time between the wars, perhaps nearer to the Second World War, when the social life of the capital loosened its strings somewhat, and a sensational local scandal boiled up around the goings-on at a well-known club. I have heard so many different versions of the tale on my rare visits that it wouldn't be possible for me now even to guess at the nature of the cesspool, which seemed to involve call-girls and goodness knows what else. But it must have caused a mighty bother in this city of the good, for it is still brought up in conversation, if not exactly with bated breath then certainly with a whisper in the voice that implies something like Sodom and Gomorrah.

To reach the Jaw Bone Walk, my cab had had to take a longer, round-about way than the straightforward short walk that used to bring me quickly here from the Heriot-Watt; but there was no mistaking the arched bones at the end of the long dark path, or the roadway leading upwards from it towards Bruntsfield.

I got out.

'Just another minute or two,' I said to my indulgent driver, 'and then we're on our way.'

'Take your time,' he said. 'I've got all the time in the world.'

But I hadn't. I had allowed myself just enough time to come on this capricious jaunt, brief enough in space, timeless in experience; but I had my date at the George Hotel, a date with plenty of latitude in it, but an important rendezvous just the same. And I did not mean to be late.

I crossed the quiet road, empty of any kind of traffic in spite of the changing red, green and amber lights, undreamed of – and unnecessary – in my youth. A few yards towards Bruntsfield and I was in the shadows of another lifetime. The path was still and quiet, and completely deserted.

I stood still and listened. There was no need for me to pretend that I could hear the tapping of a woman's shoes on the surface. There was no one there. But I remembered that tapping of many another dark evening as she came towards me, the signal that we would be joined together in a minute or so and then, with our arms linked (not hand-in-hand as young people walk with real intimacy nowadays), head for our class in French or our discussion at the debating society.

What on earth did we debate? Keir Hardie and Socialism? Bernard Shaw? Feminism? Likely as not. But I cannot remember one of the subjects of the many that must have been flung across the room at the Heriot-Watt; or a single other person there.

How much had happened in my life since those tapping heels were a reality out of the night, and not only a memory. I wondered what had become of the callow young man who had stretched forward with such eagerness to the sound. What had happened to him? Where, along the trackless road of time, had he ceased to be? I should never again in this life be able to catch a glimpse of him. Or of her.

It always hurts to go back. Sometimes you don't even have to go back to be hurt.

I shivered slightly as I stepped into the cab.

'I'll get you there in a couple of shakes,' my new friend said, closing the door on me. 'An' see that you get a good glass of whisky as soon as you're indoors.'

'Ah,' I promised him. 'that'll be ready and waiting for me.'

II

1

The idea had come from Lord Cameron. He had found a willing aide in Alastair Dunnett, the editor of *The Scotsman.* And Alastair, a master at organizing, had undertaken the pleasant spade work of bringing to reality an unusual birthday party for Sir Compton Mackenzie.

That cold January night in Edinburgh was the last night of Monty Mackenzie's eighty-fifth year. When midnight chimed he would be entering the eighty-sixth year of his incredibly crowded life, still embarked on his ten-volume autobiography, *My Life and Times* (published by Chatto & Windus), *Octave Eight* of which was already completed. Eighty-six of his old friends, one for every year of his life, had united to be his hosts in the Adam Rooms of the George Hotel that evening.

'There'll be drinks and supper,' Alastair had told me on the phone weeks before, 'and we'll probably even bring in the actual birthday with the midnight chimes. Monty and Lily are delighted with the idea, and want you and Sheila to be here.'

Nothing could have kept me away, but it wasn't on for Sheila. She had had a serious spinal operation three months before, and was still pulling out of it. In time she would make her own remarkable recovery, but that time was not yet. So I was on my own. But not for long. The company was still arriving as I handed over my coat: some old familiar, well-liked friends, some faces as alien to me as mine was to them. I was still a transient on the Edinburgh scene.

My long exile had made me a half stranger to the city and deprived me of contacts that might have led to precious friendships; but in late years we had come back more frequently, eventually buying a small property in North Berwick near the sea, twenty miles away from the city, against the day of our ultimately living there. I had formed a surprising number of agreeable new associations and renewed old ones who were there to make one feel again at home.

Compton Mackenzie was one of the old ones, in every sense of the word. He was nearly twenty years older than I, but never once in our long association had I thought of him in that way. Monty is ageless. He has carried the bright spirit of youth with him throughout his long life, and although that night he did not remain standing but sat just inside the large room to receive his friends, we all knew that it was the sensible thing to do for a man conserving his energies for the amount of work he still poured out of himself. All his life he has been a worker, all his life he has had to work to earn his keep; most of his life he has been wracked with pain — the disabling pain of neuritis and the other ailments that overwork and passionate advocacy of causes bring in their trail.

There is no suggestion of any of this in the early novels that first made him famous; but the later volumes of self-experience are charted with the bouts of pain which laid him low but never kept him down. Or idle. He worked through them, or was invalided out of the Dardanelles campaign in the Great War, or suffered in silence. His 'asides' about his pains in these books are frequent, but so casual that you realize he is unaware he is writing about self-pain and might just as well be saying 'I started the new novel on Saturday' for 'I started the new novel during another bad bout.' It is the work that counts; the other is the incidental intelligence about the background condition in which he worked. Both are important; but they are a completely professional observing, part of the job. There is no note of self pity; at one time he worked through a period of six months without the sight of one eye, and not a friend was told about it.

When he wrote *Sinister Street,* in 1913, I was a schoolboy and at once became a Mackenzie devotee. I waited with impatience for *Guy and Pauline* and *Sylvia Scarlett.* Then, after the Great War, I was in Canada and the United States, and my reunion with the literary idol I had never met was delayed until 1927. By that time I was the editor of a London national newspaper, and I was able to express my admiration for his work and the pleasure he had given me in concrete form. I bought for serialization in my paper Compton Mackenzie's new novel about the theatre, *Rogues and Vagabonds,* so that a million other people could share my pleasure. Afterwards he wrote a weekly column for me about books, and although our friendship was never close at that time, it was continuous and we somehow kept on the same track. Both of us spotted Hitler for the menace he was, and with a small group of other journalists, writers, one particularly notable politician, and two highly intelligent soldiers, Liddell Hart and General Fuller, did our best to warn the nation of the nightmare to come. Both of us were keen on encouraging and discovering literary talent and had a hand in finding that young woman of particular promise, Monica Dickens, the great grand-daughter of you-know-who.

I published her first manuscript, *One Pair of Hands,* a work which indicated exceptional ability. She was then only twenty-three, and when she hit the jackpot I urged her to lay off for a while until she knew what it was she wanted to do with her special gift, and never at any price to become one of those novel-a-year lady writers. She was probably too young and too full of the thrust of life to know what I meant. Anyway, she never followed that particular piece of advice, and her books poured steadily out, winning a large audience for her and a comfortable income.

The modern generation knows Compton Mackenzie best as the author of that robust piece of humour, *Whisky Galore,* and the film that followed it. But Monty's activities could fill pages of *Who's Who* instead of the column-and-a-bit he prefers to contain his many exploits. He has fought for Scottish autonomy, run a war-time Intelligence Service, was Rector of Glasgow University, and he has been Governing General of the Royal Stuart Society.

It is in the nature of things that he should have written *On Moral Courage* in 1962, for a year later, at the age of eighty, he began *Octave One* of his autobiography with the publicly avowed intention of completing the life with a volume each year for the next eight years. Nothing has prevented him from carrying out his purpose, the volumes have come along as promised, and the final one — making ten in all and not eight — has just been published as I write these words on Monty's eighty-eighth birthday, 17 January 1971.

Mackenzie, who never kept a diary except for one brief period in his life, relies on his own tenacious memory, a mountain of correspondence and documents, and an energy that is boundless. His method is to work mostly in bed during the day, leaving his evenings for television programmes as diverse as Hughie Green and *The Power Game,* and to talk and eat with his friends. Monty does most of the talking; his friends prefer it that way. The rich experiences of his long and active life roll out of him with quiet gusto, his comments and judgements on people, however discerning and on target, are always tinged with a kindly and understanding humour.

You find this humour in all his *Octaves.* There is impatience at human stupidity, annoyance at the follies of people in high places; but all the time there is the civilized man, with deep humility in him, able to take life as it comes. And to give it.

In these happy evenings in Drummond Place, the dining-room is a pleasant place. Monty's ginger cat — now, alas, no longer with us — sat in his own chair at the table and was fed tit-bits. A person's name crops up in the talk, and Monty, a born actor, imitates the character in voice and gesture. A story to accompany the imitation is at once produced; no, not just a story — a whole background of history and detail about the person and the circumstances of some crazy adventure in which he has been involved.

Monty sits on a rubber ring during dinner to ease the strain on his spine, and on the same rubber ring when he holds court in the big book-filled room with his friends clustered about him. He is a complete entertainment, talking quietly, easily, his keen eyes, that have seen so much of life, lighting up at some particular story that sends us into hoots of laughter.

But those 'keen eyes' of his are deceptive if you do not know that one of them has ceased to function and the sight of the other is imperilled. The final *Octave* was a race against time. 'My one eye has been growing more and more tired all the time,' he confessed, 'and the job of consulting old letters and papers a growing fatigue and irritation. Indeed, I might have found it impossible to continue without the help of my beloved Lily to whom I was married in 1965.'

Yet at eighty-nine, this gay young trooper is still lashing out in all directions. Can he ever grow old? He remembers with pleasure a BBC discussion about age in which he took part with Harold Nicholson, as long ago as 1952. Nicholson recollected that Monty Mackenzie believed that old age did not make everything different. Nicholson considered it 'the greatest of human tragedies'. Monty suggested that there were few physical disadvantages: What did it really matter if a person could walk two miles an hour instead of four? Monty noticed no difference in his memory, character or creative powers.

Mackenzie was then going to be seventy in nine months' time. Harold Nicholson was four years younger. Monty's later comment, at eighty-seven, was: 'I find now that I forget people's names occasionally and, more regrettably, owing to my wretched eyesight, people's faces, but mercifully my power to concentrate on work in hand has not in the least diminished.'

His actual writing is made easier for him by Lily, who has secured a specially light and boldly-writing pencil. On the large-page pad on which he now writes, he is just able to see the words, and their size ensures that neither they nor the lines run into each other and scramble.

He is not, I should say, afraid of the future. The completely blind writer, James Thurber, came to Scotland to investigate the Loch Ness Monster. He spent two grand evenings at 31 Drummond Place.

And of that visit, Mackenzie says: 'His courage in bearing his blindness is an inspiration. If ever I become completely blind I shall try to be as brave as Thurber.'

2

His wife Lily was standing beside him now in the gaily-lit room, the well-loved Lily of all of us. She shields, guards, guides; sees that he is fed carefully and well, types for him, looks after the masses of correspondence and the thousands of documents that are channelled into his work. Monty must be a difficult, sometimes contrary, devil to have to look after. Like Churchill, he wants to go on all night. He goes to bed late, sleeps late, wakes hours after Lily has been on deck handling all the affairs of the house, launches himself fresh and lively into a new chapter of his current book.

How does she cope with this man, completely in love with life, full of drive, dedicated to his purpose, and yet as skittish and mischievous as a schoolboy? Lily's sister coped before her. Chrissie MacSween was Monty's secretary for many years. The eldest daughter of Malcolm MacSween, of Tarbert, Harris, she devoted her life to him. Monty's wife, Faith, died after fifty years of their happy marriage. Two years later he married Chrissie, on whom he had leaned for so much help. A year later she was dead. That was in 1963.

Two years passed and Monty and Lily MacSween, the younger sister, were married. She too is a true daughter of the Isles. Dark eyed, dark haired, utterly dazzling, with Highland blood in her and Highland devotion and Highland laughter. You cannot know her and not love her. I have the same slender but completely unbreakable bond with Lily as I have with Monty. And with Lily it was born out of laughter.

I had not met her when, on one of my first flying visits back to Edinburgh (it must have been about 1966), I telephoned Monty. Lily answered and we fixed up for me to drop in and have a drink with them two or three evenings later. At the appointed time I was on the doorstep.

It certainly didn't look like being a party. The street was deserted, and there was no car near the Mackenzie entrance. Fine, I thought: a quiet drink with Monty and his new wife. Nothing could have pleased me more. But even the Mackenzie house, now divided into flats like most big houses — even in Edinburgh's elegant New Town — had only a few lights showing.

I searched for the bell push; rang. Long, long pause. I rang again. Nothing happened. I was living at such a stretch at that time that I could easily have made a mistake about the arranged time or the day. I tried one last ring.

Someone else was living at stretch. For Lily, so recently wed and taking up the literary burden where her sister had left off, life must indeed have been hectic. On that particular day, I learned later, everything had gone haywire. Then the door opened, reluctantly, as though the person behind it was hoping the caller had gone away. And, as they describe these things in the books of today, there was this dark, unbelievable chick looking out at me with questioning dark eyes.

'What about my drink?' I queried.

She stared at me. Then suddenly she dissolved into laughter, gay, free, unabashed.

'You're Jimmy Drawbell!' she exclaimed.

We looked at each other. I knew what had happened all right.

'I'd forgotten all about you!'

Our laughter grew. There was something so ridiculous about our situation. The deserted street, the obviously deserted Mackenzie house, the utter absence of anything resembling festivity where a drop of festivity had been promised, appealed to the comic in both of us. Then she leaned forward in greeting to make up for her forgetfulness, a touching gesture, and we held each other up and exploded. In that moment life had gently slapped us both into place and this should always be an occasion for merriment.

Presently, wondering what the devil was going on, Monty shuffled into the range of light, wearing bedroom slippers and his cosy, quilted evening jacket. He was rightly indignant. Hughie Green and his *Opportunity Knocks* was just about due on television, and Monty wanted to relax after a hard day.

'Have a whisky and stay on to watch with me,' he invited.

It wasn't on. Unlike Monty, I can't take Hughie Green. But I went in with them, gulped a spoonful of whisky, promised to come back another night, and left – to Monty's great relief, I am sure, and to Lily's laughing farewell.

'We'll make up for this,' she said.

There was nothing to make up for. I wouldn't have blotted out a minute of such a meeting, for it was an occasion of instant recognition, often better by far than the long build-up into what is known as 'old friend'-ship. I know it was the same with Lily. She recalled it afterwards in a letter from Pradelles.

The Mackenzies summer (and work) in France; winter (and work) in Edinburgh. If this sounds as if they had got life the wrong way round, I can only say that I cannot imagine a better design for living. It is one we hope to make for ourselves. We don't want to spend summer in Scotland, with all its tourists. We want to enjoy its homely comfort on nights like this January night of Monty's birthday party. Summer is completely summer in the south; winter is completely winter in Scotland. I don't want to avoid winter; I like it. Equally, I want to swim every possible day in summer, and you can't always do that in Scotland.

Is it immodest – then so be it! – to quote this paragraph about myself from Lily's letter, if it lights up what I called just now the instant recognition of our meeting?

> 'I have last week finished reading your book *The Sun Within Us* and now I understand very clearly why you gave me the impression on our first meeting (!) of being one of the sunniest people I have ever had the fortune of meeting. Thank you so much for such enjoyable reading, brimful of the joy of life.
>
> 'When I told Monty I was going to write to you to say how much I enjoyed your book he nearly fell off his chair with pleasurable shock, and added, "Well, he'll know you're not just an autograph hunter."
>
> 'Work goes on at top speed but this *Octave* is a killer as it covers what must have been the busiest year of his life. The

amount of paper available is TOO much — a hindrance more than a help. However he keeps well but I have to curb a tendency to overstrain himself at times.'

3

'I was born a Scotsman,' said Sir Walter Scott, 'and a bare one. Therefore, I was born to fight my way in the world.'

He spoke for most of us. All through our history poverty has been a malaise affecting large areas of the land, sometimes the whole of the land. There is nothing picturesque or noble about poverty, and the poverty of Scotland's cities and countryside in the old days was good enough reason for so many men and women to get up and go. They are no longer going in such large numbers to Canada and Australia and South Africa, and those other distant lorelei lands that were then part of our Empire, but many are still going there, and others are finding a more rewarding living nearer home, in England.

It would have been difficult to associate poverty with that well-dressed successful group of men and women met together that evening to honour Monty Mackenzie, to show their affection, and wish him well in his future years. They seemed not only to have the privilege of Monty's friendship, but something also of that social and inherited privilege which is so often a political bone of contention.

Most of these friends were firmly established people, but they had come to know each other, and to be present together, through many vicissitudes of life and some strange and trying journeys. Not all, like Scott, had been born 'bare', but most of them had had to fight their way in the world.

Scotland is anything but a feather-bed country. It is too small, and in many places too barren, for life here to be rich and profligate; and its people are like a smallish family, always aware of how its relatives live. Of course there is privilege, as everywhere; but in Scotland there is not much mystery about how the other half live. They all live much the same.

It is this commonalty of frugal living, carefulness, and devoted endeavour to succeed that makes men understand each other. Historically, Scotsmen are bound together in the traditions of their fighting past against 'the English'; emotionally, they have been shaped by the Church, an inborn love of family and country, and the unpretentious school – although there are now some pretentious schools on the English model. Economically, the majority of Scots go through the same mill.

They are nearer a true democracy, in personal relationship, than any other people I know. I did not know how much their outlook had been affected or changed by the mass media, operating mostly from London, but I had been made more curious over my tea and whisky with Kenneth Roy, himself so bare, and beginning. Now, accompanying the pleasure of good food, drinks and chatter, I was aware that my affection for my people and country had a new alertness in it.

'Born to fight my way.' Certainly Alastair Dunnett, one of the most influential men in Scotland, had not reached his editor's chair in *The Scotsman* the easy way. He had not begun his life as a journalist but on a high stool in the Glasgow office of the Commercial Bank of Scotland, at the age of fifteen. Bare enough, as Scott would have put it.

There was no one to pave his way to the top except himself. But the Mactavish in his name wasn't there just for decoration. He looked every inch a Mactavish, dark, with concealed determination, and Highland; yet with a pawky wit, and a flair for journalism that had made him impatient with the bank and could not be tucked away and forgotten in its vaults.

It had to break out; and it was typical of his background, and his yearning, that he set out to produce a magazine for Scottish boys. Sick of the bromides of English public school life in all the boys' weeklies from London, he struck out on his own, or rather with an equally adventurous friend, Jimmie Adam, to give the youth of Scotland a new literary diet. He was fed up, he once said, with the legend that no British schoolboy could hope to be a hero unless he'd been a fag and a fourth-former in his day, with plenty of high-class japes. 'The bad yins of these tales were coarse errand lads usually discovered twisting the arms of small boys, although these villainies were mere by-products of the major crime of working for a living.'

Jimmie Adam and Alastair were the babes in the wood of publishing. They hadn't a hope of succeeding against the big commercial combines who flooded the juvenile market, and although their publication had the stirring title of *Claymore,* which would appeal to any young Scot (and did appeal in ever growing numbers), their small savings, thrown heroically into the venture, were insufficient for the long running fight to stave off inevitable disaster.

In my book, *Time On My Hands* (published by Macdonald in 1968), I told how their one-room office was, unknown to their landlord, also their living quarters, kitchen and bedroom. A few friends helped them with the editorial content of *Claymore*, but in the main the work was done by themselves. They slaved at the job, were often hungry, and always overtired. And their defeat and disappointment did not deter them. They knew where they were going, and in time both reached their heights.

Alastair had been educated at Hillhead High School, Glasgow. Lily MacSween, before she became Lady Mackenzie, was a school teacher, and since her marriage (and in spite of all her work for Monty) had become a trained hair-dresser and now owned her own fashionable salon in their big basement flat at Drummond Place. Eric Linklater, whose noble forehead glistened under the bright lights, was a private in the Black Watch in the 1914–1918 war. He was severely wounded when a German bullet ripped through his steel helmet, tore open his head in one place, and decided to come out in another. Unable to handle his emergency field dressing, he clamped the whole envelope containing it over the wound and clapped his helmet on top. Two operations just saved his life, leaving him with a scarred head and, unbelievably, the helmet with the hole in it. Surely one of that terrible war's most precious trophies.

I don't know if Jock Cameron (the Honourable Lord Cameron, and one of Monty's closest friends) had had it rough in his youth, because this was my first meeting with him, and one I enjoyed because of his welcome to me, and the breadth of his learning and humour; but he certainly was a fighter. He was in the Great War when he was eighteen, in the RNVR. And back again in the RNVR, from 1939 to 1944. He was then forty-four, mentioned in despatches, and awarded the DSC.

He had read a recent article of mine in *The Scots Magazine* on the need for a more up-to-date approach to tourism in Scotland, and being himself involved in the work of the Edinburgh Festival, came across the room to discuss it with me. We stood against the long table, a drink in our hands, and I liked his wise eyes, the creases in the weather-beaten face ready to deepen in a smile, the quiet, sure manner that spelt knowledge of men and the world. And although he politely concentrated on me, and missed nothing, I liked also the way – like a journalist – his searching legal eye missed nothing either of the people about us or their movements in the room.

I have sometimes wondered what it must be like to be a Judge, and to know not only what law is, but the type of men who break it, and why. To sit in judgement on your fellow beings, aware that there but for circumstances, or the quality of the blood passed on to you, or the environment in which you were raised, or – most of all – but for the Grace of God, you might have been one of the unfortunate ones, or the unhappy, or the downright damned, must be a sobering and intriguing speculation. They should be able to write good books, these judges and lawyers, and generally do (Norman Birket's was a classic); but doctors write better ones. There is no question of judging the guilty or the innocent with them; their clients are only the frightened and the dying, and it is too serious with one, and too late with the other, to be in any doubt. The judgement must be sure, and mostly independent of a jury.

I wondered where Jock Cameron got his weathered face from, and then remembered the RNVR, and that I had heard his hobby was sailing. You have to get away from sinning humanity sometime! He mentioned his connection with the Edinburgh Festival; many of the people in that room sat on committees or advisory boards concerned with the social and artistic welfare of Scotland. His aim was to bring about all-round improvements and so perpetuate the value of the Festival, loved, suspected, disregarded by many of the locals, who still thought it an alien intrusion for a limited faction of Edinburgh people.

I had concerned myself in my article about that holy of holies, the Castle Tattoo. Other people had criticized it on artistic and cultural grounds. I had dared to have a go at it, not so much because of its nature (predominantly military) which year after year scarcely altered, and was enormously popular, but because of one damnable feature of its organization.

'I expect you don't like what I said?' I asked Jock Cameron.

'I think you have a very good point,' he replied. 'We're very aware that the whole Festival might get into a rut, and this is what we are most anxious to avoid. Coming only once a year, without the constant spur of criticism keeping us on our toes, we don't want to fall asleep for eleven months, and then just repeat ourselves. This is the real danger. A prod like yours lets us see ourselves from the outside.'

The Tattoo, display of kilted troops and pipers, marching and manoeuvring on the open esplanade in the shadow of the Castle, and functioning in floodlight as the summer evening closes over Edinburgh, is a 'must' for visitors, who imagine this is the true Scotland. It has become almost the cornerstone of the Festival, and is the one entertainment that even the local malcontents approve of. Its drawing power packs the terraced seats.

So it happens to be also one of the most uncomfortable to watch. Apart from the weather, and particularly the cold on many evenings, which causes the horde of blanketed and be-rugged spectators ascending the High Street to look like an Arab tribe in flight, the seating arrangements are atrocious. On hard bare wooden planks are marked very small sitting places for which thousands have to pay handsomely. This is one of the most expensive and uncomfortable entertainments in the Festival. Some of it is worth the money, some of it not. None of it is worth the quite unnecessary discomfort. The organizers boast that eight thousand people are jammed into these benches at one go. They should be ashamed of it. Seven thousand (or even less) with room to sit decently and move their limbs would make for a happier arrangement, although a few bawbees might be lost.

I took three German friends one cold evening. I paid £3 for the four seats. We were placed next to the so-called Royal Box, where a few favoured people sat in comfort. My friends looked at the marked bench with the numbers of our places. Their surprised eyes caught mine.

'We are to sit here?' one murmured politely.

It was going to be more than a tight squash. I saw that before we tried to squeeze ourselves into the allotted spaces. I tried to make it easier by going in first and pressing myself as closely as I could against the man already sitting in the farther space. He couldn't be budged. He was himself telescoped into his neighbour, and had probably been hoping that we wouldn't arrive so that he might relieve the pressure on his own bones.

Fifteen bob a seat for this, I thought. But I mentioned to my guests that you couldn't get a place for this great spectacle for love or money. They were still polite, but sceptical and uncomfortable. They loved the massed pipers – who wouldn't? – but we saw them sideways. We couldn't sit straight up, squarely in our places. We had to manoeuvre ourselves half-sideways, part of our rumps on the seat, part off.

We stuck it for nearly an hour, and by then we knew we had seen all we wanted. Almost by common accord we reached our decision.

'Do you think it would be discourteous to leave now?' asked one of my German guests. 'I ache a little.'

Discourteous? People were leaving the esplanade in droves by then, all nationalities. We mingled with them, glad to stretch our legs, to move the stiffness out of our backs.

I thought, as we went down the hill, that with a little rearrangement, and the sensible sacrifice of some of the takings, how utterly different it could have been. I was even prepared to go again another evening, taking three small children to see the pipers, and discovered that there was no reduction in prices for children (for what is an essentially children's show), and I felt that someone had got his priorities all wrong. I don't know what is done with all the Tattoo money, but surely a little less revenue and much truer hospitality to the visitors should be the order of the day. But you get this uncomfortable feeling with the Edinburgh Festival all the time; it's only once a year; let's cash in while we can.

4

There was not much serious talk that evening. It was a time for gaiety between old friends. The moving about from table to table, hailing, or being hailed, constantly joining forces with different groups of people, made for idle and diverting gossip and affectionate recollection.

I managed to get Monty to myself only for a brief period and he told me something about the *Octave* on which he was working. In 1946 he was sixty-three, and it was then that, at the invitation of the Indian Government, he wrote the story of India's achievement in the Second World War. To do so he had toured every battleground between Tunis and Hong Kong. Listening to him, even through the chatter of that crowded room, was like being apart with him in his home, against the cosy background of books. His words formed themselves easily, as always, either as he had already set them down for the record, or as he was rehearsing them in his mind for *Octave Nine*. 'El Alamein from the air was a huge wilderness of sand on which the military operations were still intagliated – gun pits, shell craters, slit trenches, wire entanglements, tank traps, and even the tracks of lorries. I say "even", but it's not so remarkable, for as you know the tracks of Roman chariot wheels are still to be seen in the crusted Libyan soil.

'The harbour at Tobruk was full of sunken ships; there were 132 of every nationality. The whole area was a scene of complete desolation, covered with smashed planes, tanks, lorries, petrol tins, guns, and endless piles of barbed wire.'

The others in the room had drifted away from us and he went on to tell me of the happy atmosphere on the ground, the camaraderie of the Mess, where after dinner he exchanged experiences with kindred spirits and had a wide-awake ear for a story, recounted amidst much laughter, which he described as 'one in which Boccaccio himself would have rejoiced'.

It concerned a Scottish officer, called X, who was captured with his own and other armoured cars in one of our minefields during the retreat from Bir Hakeim. They tried to clear a way through, but night fell and in the morning they were overtaken by the German tanks and shot to pieces. X lay down pretending to be dead, and managed to escape being taken prisoner.

The retreat had long swept past, when he wandered on across the desert and finally reached Buk Buk. Here he undressed on the beach and enjoyed a good swim, and lay sunbathing on the warm sand. He fell fast asleep. When he woke he found himself in the middle of a German bathing party.

Nobody had paid any attention to his sleeping figure and if he hadn't picked up his clothes and tried to make off he might have bluffed it out. He was caught and taken along with other prisoners to the cage.

He was the last man in the line. Noticing an empty cookhouse by the gate, he slipped aside into it. Here he pulled a blanket over himself and lay down in a corner.

At nightfall a guard party came into the cookhouse for a game of cards. One of the players, feeling chilly, spotted the blanket in the corner and X was revealed. He was hauled up before the German commandant and told that if he tried to escape again he would be shot.

Back he went into the cage. In a thoroughly depressed mood he started fiddling with the padlock of the gate when the sentry had passed by. Mackenzie chuckled as he said, 'It was nervous fidgets.' To his amazement the padlock opened. The hook had not caught when the key was turned. He slipped out quickly and this time he managed to reach our lines.

It would be enough to leave the story there. But one wants to go on listening to Monty for ever. The sequel to the story is equally amusing. X was given a Military Cross for the escapes and sent to recuperate at a rest camp near Suez. Here there were a number of Wrens who slept in tents in a wired-in enclosure, known naturally as the Aviary.

One night, coming back from a gay party, the companions of X challenged him to demonstrate his skill at escaping by getting in and out of the Aviary. He took on the bet and when he got over the wire he saw a Wren sitting outside her tent in the moonlight. She had been to a party, too, and was thinking about love, a Jessica without a Lorenzo. And suddenly Lorenzo appeared.

They talked for some time and then she invited him into the tent she shared with fourteen other Wrens, all of them respectably fast asleep. When the time came for X to leave his Wren and make his way carefully out of the tent, one of the sleepers woke up and seeing a male shape profaning the sanctity of the tent, screamed a shrill alarm. X dashed out and hid in a slit trench, but there he was discovered, and barely escaped a court-martial. He was let off with a reprimand.

But I like Monty best when he is talking of his childhood. I know no one who can so evoke the ectasies and terrors of those early days when we were all beginning to realize something of the world about us. He regrets that there is little left of that early world and is nostalgic for the childhood he knew, remembering an old milestone that said 'London 4 miles; Hounslow 7 miles', the old London cries about lavender and cherries, the chimney sweeps and their May Day dance along the street – 'In wicker-cages covered with leaves,' he says, his remarkable mind still with them. I knew nothing of that in my Scottish boyhood, but I shared Monty's fear – as so many children did – of the many gypsy caravans and their threat to our young lives that we should be kidnapped into one of them and ourselves turned into gypsies. 'They stained our bodies with walnut juice!' he laughs now, but it was no laughing matter in infancy. It was a fearsome possibility if we did not watch out.

He was picking at a petit-four while he talked to me. He has, even at his age, an incredibly sweet tooth. And an equally incredible longing for the sweets of other days. In a previous *Octave,* he told a story about a visit he made to the Fry's chocolate factory in Bristol and of telling the manager about the wallflower creams of his boyhood, made by Rowntree.

The manager said doubtfully:

'I think you're mistaken – I don't remember any essence of wallflower; rose, violet, but not wallflower.'

'I know I am right,' said Monty, but left it at that.

'About a fortnight after we got back home, I had a letter from the manager to say that I had been right. He had found an almost empty bottle of wallflower essence. There was enough to make two pounds of wallflower-flavoured chocolate creams. He was sending me those two pounds and hoped they would bring back the memory of those days at Scarborough nearly fifty years ago. And as I ate them I was back in the spa, watching the fireworks and chewing Rowntree's chocolate creams with the unspoilt palate of a thirteen-year-old.'

Sweets are a thing with Monty, much to the impatience of the BBC, who on one occasion were reluctant to do his broadcast on the subject. But it proved a great success, bringing in many letters. One was from an old lady of seventy-five, saying: 'I went back to school again and bought some of the sweets you mentioned. "Satin Pralinès" were my greatest joy. Thank you for giving me back a vivid day of my childhood.'

5

I wandered across the room to sit for a time with Fanny and Willie MacTaggart. Willie had already made it known publicly that he would soon be resigning from the Presidency of the Royal Scottish Academy, which he had graced for the past ten years, and while we were talking about this and the physical relief it would afford him, I could feel, even before he spoke of it, that he was unwell.

The demands of his office, the many calls on his time and energy, and the high standards he required of himself in his painting, had tired him. I understood and was full of sympathy for him. Willie is a deeply sensitive man for whom you instinctively desire a happy welfare. I knew how concerned Fanny must be. He was sleeping badly, and work had gone stale on him. When you resign from some high office like Willie's, it is both a relief and a landmark.

Then his face lit up with a quiet pleasure when Fanny told me the nicest thing I had heard that evening. A very sensible young woman (I don't think she was one of our present company) had recently been invited to launch a ship. After the splashing of the champagne against the hull, and the jolly-making, there came the usual occasion of a presentation for her services. Usually this is a piece of jewellery of the lady's choice. But this young woman wanted no jewellery.

'I want a painting by Sir William MacTaggart,' she declared. 'And I know the one I want. It's in the RSA.'

So off they had all trooped to Princes Street, into the famous building, and watched with joy a red sticker being pasted on the frame of the picture.

'Wasn't she an unusual girl?' said Fanny, her eyes on Willie.

'And a very fortunate one,' I said.

I knew Fanny was glad to tell me the story, and in the re-telling of it, she was subtly nursing Willie.

His kind eyes, that had made so much of the colour he enjoyed in nature, were even quieter than usual. They looked at me across the table and smiled again, but the modest man who is Willie MacTaggart was withdrawn a little behind them. And as I had wondered about the Judge in our gathering, so now I speculated, while still talking with them, on the personal problem of a world-famous painter, his work on show everywhere, bought by the Tate, the Arts Council, the Contemporary Art Society, the public galleries of the United States, Australia, Edinburgh, Glasgow, and all the others.

What did a tired great artist do for a break? How did he refresh himself? Go off with a sketch book and some pencils and a rucksack into the blue yonder and recapture his youth and its ardour? Willie was sixty-six. It was the heart of winter. A long life of endeavour and success lay behind him, and for a brief spell, as happens to all men who tear their guts out, he had worked himself too hard. He would come back fighting again after some rest and change. It must have happened to him before. It happens to most creative people, to Scotsmen particularly I think. There is always in their make-up the puritan drive to excel and over-extend themselves.

I had watched it in others: I knew it to be a fault of my own. Better people than I had gone through the turmoil. Walter Scott, whose moving hand on a table by the window, writing, writing, endlessly writing, had been observed with astonishment by a neighbour across the street; Barrie, whose constant headaches drove him into isolation, even from his bewildered and concerned closest friends; Burns, who accomplished so much, with the help of liquor and love, in the face of religious bigotry, grinding poverty, and the ill-health that killed him at thirty-eight. And the many known and unknown others.

There were times in my own life when I had hated the sight of a typewriter and never wanted to touch one again. It was hard for me to imagine that an artist could ever feel like that about canvas and colour. Surely there was no more rewarding medium to work in? But the viewer sees only the beauty of the finished work, none of the toil behind it, or the artist's intention, often frustrated. It was all right to go round an exhibition and see Willie's pictures; or stand near the one in

43

his house which is Fanny's special favourite, and be at peace with the completed work. You would have to be an artist to know what went into the achievement, and the other many years of achievement.

The Scots have another battle to fight, that of never showing. You never reveal your feelings publicly, and seldom privately. It is a second nature to them.

What would Willie really do to help himself until nature reasserted itself? In a larger city like London you can hide, escape, be unavailable to your friends, forget your commitments. I couldn't see it being done in Edinburgh, a small city where you are at the top of the tree, a public celebrity enjoying in your sixties the success you had trained and worked for, and where you live continually in the lap of your own circle.

Scott Fitzgerald, his mind at the end of its tether, had once fled New York for some unknown town in the middle-west, rented an anonymous room, and holed up for weeks, freed from all responsibility and commitment. No family, no friends, no enemies, no letters, no bills, no phone calls. Nothing. It may have delayed but did not prevent the crack-up which ultimately overtook him. But then Fitzgerald was a wild young Irish-American, unstable and volatile in spite of his brilliance, who had written his death warrant long before with his drinking and dissipation. He was his own special case.

Willie MacTaggart was a very different type. He would sit it out. The winter would ebb, spring would come, and then summer, both seasons beckoning to a man who had painted all his life. Time and rest and release, and Fanny, would work their own way towards recovery.

The trouble with success was the demands it made on you. What did you lose on the way to gaining so much? Willie was a thinking, feeling, involved man. Monty Mackenzie was the same kind of warm, friendly person, but there was a brittle enduring quality in him that had been his salvation through many illnesses for eighty-nine years; this sixty-six-year-old friend seemed to me at this moment just a little more vulnerable.

I noticed his empty glass.

'Another drink, Willie?' I suggested, half-rising to go for it.

He shook his head and made a small gesture with his hand on the table.

'I'm fine, Jimmy, thanks. No more tonight.'

Fanny said: 'It doesn't soothe him, like it does some people and send them to sleep.'

Willie knew himself. Within months, it is pleasant now to record, he was back in his studio painting again, taking life in his stride; within a year the principal galleries and exhibitions of the world were hanging on their walls brilliant new MacTaggarts.

The artistic genius of Willie was in his family, but it had skipped a generation. His father was Hugh MacTaggart, engineer and managing-director of his own well-known firm which still operated at Loanhead, near Edinburgh. His grandfather was William MacTaggart, RSA. Two of his beautiful beach scenes, in the Scottish tradition of painting, are in the National Gallery. Willie had known what he wanted to do from the start. No engineering for him. He studied at the Edinburgh College of Art, and abroad, and by the time he was nineteen he was a professional member of the Society of Scottish Artists.

My friendship with Fanny goes back to 1936, and then she was only a voice on a telephone. Fanny is Norwegian, the daughter of a general, and herself a Knight first class of the Order of St Olav, Oslo. She had always been involved in writing and journalism, and in 1936 she was in the South of France. So too was Mrs Wallis Simpson, soon to be married to the Duke of Windsor; and I, like all other newspaper editors throughout the world, was seeking contact with people who could help me in our chase for information. My search led me to Fanny Margaretha Basilier. And Fanny's soft voice on the continental telephone was kind and understanding.

Fanny remained a voice. I did not meet her then, or even immediately afterwards. But one evening in Edinburgh, just thirty years later, at a party at the home of Sir James Miller, I met Fanny for the first time. Her delighted laughter when we were introduced recalled for me the bygone tinkling over the continental telephone. In fact, she had married Willie MacTaggart soon after that telephone talk and came to live in Edinburgh.

Her name on our own telephone list comes directly next to Lily Mackenzie's. Today, just before typing these lines I dialled an Edinburgh number. When a woman's voice answered, I said at once 'Lily?' I had dialled the wrong number. 'No,' said the voice, 'This is Fanny!' And once more, the laughter.

I was grateful to James Miller for bringing us together. He himself is an example of the Scot who, when he goes for the top, double-tops it. He is the only man who has been Lord Provost of Edinburgh and Lord Mayor of London. Not even Dick Whittington could do that. There were other prominent Scotsmen at Monty's party who had married women from foreign countries: David Talbot Rice, a Vice-Principal of Edinburgh University and Professor of Fine Art, had a Russian wife, Tamara. The boss of the Arts Council in Scotland, Ronald Mavor, was married to a Dane, Sigrid. It was a cosmopolitan gathering, all bound together in their affection for Monty: Sir Fitzroy Maclean and Lady Maclean (Fitz, as Alastair Dunnett called him, is popularly known as the Balkan Brigadier). He was head of the military mission to Tito's Jugoslav partisans, and at that time was a Lieutenant-Colonel. He had resigned from the Diplomatic Service in 1939 and enlisted as private in the Cameron Highlanders. You may have seen him, with others, on television in late February, 1970, when they received their long-delayed decorations from an official Yugoslav delegation to London.

Monty has friends in every walk of life. To look round the room was to see something of the world of Scottish achievement and adventure. There was Lord Wheatley, a Judge of the Court of Session, and his wife Nancy, a great warm-hearted kindly Glasgow soul, completely unspoilt, completely natural. I admire her, feel mothered and protected in her presence. I describe her deliberately as 'a Glasgow soul', for Glasgow is the friendliest city in Scotland, her people welcoming, hospitable, uninhibited, outrageously unaware (if not openly derisive) of different social levels. The Glasgow family (and I mean the whole people as a family) is something unique, with its own distinctive sense of humour, its readiness to laugh at itself, its joy in life – and how grim that life can be for many Glasgow people – its immediate embracing of the stranger into its own kind of living.

Each recognized face in that festive room lit up a personality and a background: James Robertson Justice, the actor of picturesque renown, who has twice been Rector of Edinburgh University, who lived in Sutherlandshire where he flies hawks as a hobby, has acted in innumerable films, and dismisses himself in Who's Who as 'Career undistinguished but varied, comprising some three score jobs in different parts of the world'; Katie Macpherson, who runs the airport on the sands at Barra (where once Monty lived), talking down the planes and keeping everything right; Elspeth McIntyre, a Highlander who is the widow of the late David McIntyre, VC; Betty Constable Maxwell, the unmarried elder sister of Mrs Chalmers Davidson. Chalmers Davidson is an Edinburgh doctor and his wife is Ursula Constable Maxwell. Whenever I go to a party in Edinburgh, or for a drink to someone's house, I always hope to meet the sisters, or at least one of them. They seem to be related to everybody in the British nobility. They are cousins of the Duke of Norfolk and of the Lovats; an ancestor was Sir Thomas More who was canonized. But first and always they are nice women who make you feel at home. I remember sitting in a corner with one of them for a long time talking about a character called Jock Munro. It was she who told me Jock Munro was dead.

'He was always talking about you,' she told me.

'We worked together in London.'

'I know. I had the feeling that he depended on you a lot.'

That was news to me. How little we really know about one another.

6

And there was also with us one of Edinburgh's most remarkable young women, Alastair's wife, Dorothy Dunnett. Catching her eye across the room, I remembered a day when the Dunnetts were far removed from this evening's gaiety.

On a sunny morning in June 1964, I was in Edinburgh. I had escaped from the day-to-day chores of my own publishing life, but I could never escape its insidious hold. I was dropping in on Alastair Dunnett at his office, and we were going to lunch together.

Alastair and I understand each other well. We have both been through all that testing newspaper experience that is like a password between men who have fought in the same battles. It has left him unspoilt with a native charm, in evidence as soon as we met. But I was instinctively aware that day of a deep preoccupation behind it.

It was still early for lunch and ordinarily we should have sat for a time and gossiped. But somewhere, hiding it well, he was on edge.

'Let's get out of the city and go to the Cramond Inn,' he suggested.

It is a favourite spot of ours, four miles out towards the Forth Bridge, on the edge of the waters of the Firth. We went down and into his car. I knew that Dorothy was about to have a baby, and remembering her previous ordeal I was almost afraid to ask the question.

But when we reached the quieter Queensferry Road, after exchanging only a few words of shop talk on the way, I said:

'Is it going to be difficult?'

'Very.'

Even that terse exchange opened the door for him; and as we continued to talk of Dorothy the tension began to go out of her husband. A little later we were sitting in the Cramond Inn bar with a whisky in front of us, and when we had got that inside us we followed it up with a very good meal: a spoonful or two of haggis as an hors d'oeuvres followed by an Arbroath smokie, that delectable fish from the east coast of Scotland. Alastair began to surface.

Thirty hours later, mother and new-born son were both doing well. They have continued to do well ever since. Yet there was a time when it seemed that the Dunnetts were likely to be childless. It was thirteen years after their marriage, and after serious gynaecological adjustments, that their first son was born. Now, five years later, they had become a happy family of four.

Dorothy Dunnett is one of the best-known women in Edinburgh. She happens also to be one of the best liked and one of the most attractive. And she must also, in spite of any impression you may have gathered from these childbirth crises, be one of the healthiest. She is certainly one of the city's most energetic citizens.

Her position as Alastair's wife imposes many obligations on her, but her 'official' side is only the half of it. She was a professional portrait painter before she married; she still is, and her work appears in the Royal Scottish Academy. She also writes historical novels. I could leave it at that. Lots of people write historical novels. But there is nobody on the writing scene quite like Dorothy Dunnett. It is this side of her life that exercises for me a compelling fascination.

She herself is slight in physique, almost fragile; her voice and her manner are gentle, certainly unaggressive; she is utterly feminine. Yet she writes like a tiger. Her fiercely masculine novels, mostly based on historical fact, brim over with vigour and vitality, unafraid of brawls, bloodshed and battles. There are great swathes of savage hand-to-hand fighting in her books, involving weapons and techniques which I have checked and found to be expert.

You turn back to the title page of one of them (they are all published by Cassell) to make sure you are reading a novel by a woman and you think: 'Hey, hey, what gives here?' What goes on behind those soft dark grey eyes, this intriguing femininity?

I still don't know. When I first met her, thinking, as all journalists do, that with one look they can get to the heart of the matter, I was floored and have remained floored ever since. I still go on hoping, of course. I know of her intense concentration, of her ability to write almost anywhere at almost any time. I know she can take almost anything in her stride. I know of her enthusiasm and her deep belief in what she writes. But the enigma that is Dorothy Dunnett, mother, housewife of a large, typically Scottish stone house in Edinburgh, painter, writer, social figure, wonderful hostess, is still for me an enigma.

One day we wandered all over her house, alive with colour, and looked at some of her paintings. There is one of her first son, Ninian, which could probably tell me more about the boy's mother than anything else. I stood looking at it for a long time, knowing something of the agony that had brought the subject into life, recognizing the love behind the painter's skill. She was silent while we gazed at it. Then she drew me gently into another large room.

It was the dining-room. Along the entire length of one wall stretched a huge, half-completed mural relief. Against a background of Wedgwood blue an assembly of white, Grecian-type figures stood out, some roughly sculpted, some finished and identifiable, some future occupants of the vacant spaces indicated by a few deft charcoal strokes. Their poses and their raiment indicated something of their character and their activities.

Here was something in keeping with Edinburgh's reputation as the Athens of the North. It was an imaginative idea, superbly executed. I was too recently returned to Edinburgh to know all the people in the frieze, but I knew some of those influential men and could guess at some of the others; most of them were friends of the Dunnetts, and one day this work would be of historic value.

On that day I had lapsed into Scots idiom: 'A' the heid yins, I see!'

We laughed together. We went along the line, Dorothy supplying me with names I did not know and quick summaries of their achievements.

'How long have you been working on this?' I asked.

'Oh, five years — on and off.'

'And how long before it's finished?'

She laughed again. She knew her own programme of work, her many commitments.

'Impossible to say, I can't get at it all the time. Maybe another five years.'

The figures from Dorothy's mural, their Grecian robes abandoned, were moving around me now in more prosaic evening clothes. We drank together, filled plates with food from the long serving table, moved from table to table, from friend to friend.

In its way this party was a typical Edinburgh social evening. They have a flavour of their own. The familiar faces were there, the faces you look forward to seeing again – and do – at other Edinburgh parties. You are aware in Edinburgh that you are always in a fairly tightly-contained community – socially, economically and culturally. It is none the less warm and reassuring for that.

It is only at Festival time, in late August and early September, that the city's social life becomes cosmopolitan and the parties sparkle with invaders from all over the world. Dorothy Dunnett during this time is on a non-stop whirl, the centre of a carousel of activity and entertaining. If she can ever write a word of her books during this period she is even more of a mystery than I imagined.

She and Alastair throw a big party in their home sometime about half-way through the Festival. It begins late to allow for the arrival of actors and musicians who have been at the Lyceum theatre or the Kings, or the Usher Hall, and is a stimulant for guests who are going on afterwards to late-night shows. This is where you meet old friends from London or New York or Paris, but you cannot say much to them there and then for the Dunnett home is humming with chatter and laughter.

It becomes quieter somewhere around midnight when the guests troop upstairs to sit in the large drawing-room and listen to Dorothy's newly-discovered young pianist, or a nervous but talented new singer, or a Scottish group of folk-singers whom she wants to help on their way. There are people present who can carry her effort a step further.

In the small hours of the morning she seems to be as fresh and eager as she was at the beginning, hours before. And Alastair, sometimes in the kilt, is performing his farewell ceremony of speeding the parting guest with a toddy.

III

1

In the early spring, about two months later, I was back. I wanted to continue my leisurely look at Scotland; to be beguiled by the new, to remember the old, and to come close again to the unchanging. I hoped to use the spring and the early summer, before the holiday visitors in their thousands blurred the picture out of focus, and then go on travelling in all the seasons of the year.

I wanted also to have another look at young Kenneth Roy and his fellow enthusiasts who, in spite of all the difficulties, had gone ahead with their venture and were in the very act of producing the first issue of *Scottish Theatre*. Kenneth was coinciding publication with the first birthday of his baby boy, Stephen, and planned a small gathering at his home to wish both of them well. 'I haven't forgotten your command to celebrate,' he wrote to me, 'so please come and join us at the double event.'

This time I came back by road. I wanted to have a car by me to wander wherever my inclination leaned. Sheila, for almost the first time in two years, was able to sit in comfort again; was even able and with pleasure to take over some of the driving. We made it in easy stages to the Borders, dawdling through the typical grey-stone towns of Otterburn and Jedburgh and Melrose and Galashiels, noticing – as one does everywhere in Britain – that people were better dressed, and seemed better fed, than ever before in our history. And that the children were wonderful. This was the casual observation of any traveller; anyone who had lived in another generation couldn't miss it. We swung across country to the west to by-pass Edinburgh and find pastures new. I would wander about this border country again, but mostly on my own, when I was empty and receptive.

It was Hazlitt who said: 'One of the pleasantest things in the world is going on a journey; but I like to go by myself. I can enjoy society in a room, but out of doors nature is company enough for me. I am then never less alone than when alone.' And he went on: 'I cannot see the wit of walking and talking at the same time. Give me the clear blue sky over my head, and the green turf beneath my feet, a winding road before me, and then to thinking! Then long-forgotten things burst upon my eager sight and I begin to feel, think, and be myself again.'

The England Hazlitt walked through has changed as radically as the Scotland I was questing, but the sentiment behind his words remains as true today. 'I am then never less alone than when alone.'

The day was incredibly warm, following a previous day when the temperature had steadily mounted, and the barometer was set fair. You can get these brief but gorgeous summer spells in March almost anywhere in Britain, stupefying the natives, astounding the stranger. Overnight it is blazing sunshine and Riviera warmth, and three days later perhaps the ground is white with morning frost. The vagaries of our weather are its greatest delight. In large tracts of Scotland in the winter of 1970–71, I enjoyed an almost unbroken run of wonderful weather, free from snow and frost, with weeks of sunshine and mild weather. In south-east England, and in Devon, there were snow blizzards and intense cold. The frozen north!

It was anything but a frozen north these first days of spring as we rolled through the pleasant green country. We cruised past a farm truck full of brightly-scarved and gaily-shirted field workers. A mile further on an old woman sat on a large stone at the corner of a rough track, her body bent forward, her hands on her lap. I slowed down at once, thinking of a lift, and then realized that she was waiting for the workers' truck coming up just behind us.

She had an old-fashioned sun bonnet on her head (in March!), of a kind I hadn't seen in years, tied round her chin, full at the back of the neck to keep off the sun, almost like a poke bonnet. Her face was old and very brown, and very wrinkled. And patient. Without moving her head, she looked towards us out of faded, still-blue eyes. I raised my hand to her in a wave and she slowly lifted one of the heavily-gloved hands from her lap as high as her shoulder. It was almost like a half-salute. It was her welcome to Scotland.

Less welcome were the empty, deserted farm cottages. They were everywhere: in the Border country, all through the Lothians, dotting the rich Angus landscape. As we carved our way through tracks and lanes, well off the main roads, we could not miss them. Here a single dwelling, here two attached to each other, there a row of half a dozen, derelict and seemingly forgotten. Not all empty. In one row of these low stone houses, two cottages might be occupied, perhaps one, a wisp of smoke coming from a chimney. The others were the ghosts of former happy homes, empty, with the aura of desertion all around their old white walls. And never a soul in sight.

I got out to have a look. This wasn't the Highlands. In the Highlands, on a first visit, you would be shamed by the sight of the many crofters' cottages ravaged by the years, their stone walls tumbled into ruins by the roadside, or shattered, lonely and forgotten in a far field, like the rubble we used to search in after a London blitz.

All over the romantic Highlands they scar the skyline. Once some family eked out a frugal living from the blessed plot around them. In the fulness of time, and man's inhumanity to man, they were evicted, banished to Winnipeg or Wyoming, or some other distant haven where, if they were not too old, they might win a richer life. Behind them the cottages crumbled or collapsed, a sad sight for the visitor, a sadder one for Scots. For the simple reason that their merciful removal would cost money, the country, or the landlords, tolerate them. They are still some owner's 'property'. But someone in the Scottish Tourist Board, projecting the tartan image to the world, must surely shiver.

But this wasn't the Highlands. The deserted cottages in front of me, and the many others I had spotted in this prosperous Lowland country, were in a state of good preservation. True, there had been exceptions along the way. One had a small tree growing up through it, splitting the roof in two. Another, within sight of a flourishing farm,was withering away before our eyes. Less than a couple of years earlier, it could have been saved, could still be saved. Why was it allowed to sink slowly into decay and then oblivion?

But there was nothing like that with these cottages in front of me. They could have been occupied overnight without a penny spent on them. A glance through the dusty windows revealed their worthiness. I'd have been glad to live in one of them myself.

There was a big farm half a mile away through the trees. A sleek Jaguar had purred past us towards it as I got out of my car. Someone was doing all right. But what had happened to the people who had filled these ghostly homes?

'Bloody shame, isn't it?' said a voice behind me.

He was a youngish forty. Bare-headed, sharp-featured, with a warm red face exposed to all weathers. Stocky and hardy. His blue-checked shirt was open at the neck, belted round corduroy trousers tucked into Wellingtons. Over his shoulder I noticed a van down the lane with the words 'Forestry Commission' painted on the side.

'It's going on all over the place,' he said.

'So I've noticed.'

He glanced at the registration initials on our car.

'In England too, I suppose?' he queried.

I certainly hadn't been aware of it. 'Empty cottages like this in England would be snapped up in a minute,' I said. 'I bought one myself a few years ago.'

His laugh had a bit of grit in it.

'These aren't for sale! They've been like this for ages.'

'But they're in good condition.'

'Oh, ay. But they're not for sale.'

He took out a packet of cigarettes, offered me one. I knew he wanted to talk and stayed silent while he lit up, puffed deeply, carefully waved out the lighted match and let it drop at his feet. Even then, he crushed it into the ground under his boot. He'd been out in the open all day, working with nature, probably alone. He'd come on me at the right moment for a chat, and in a situation which he understood and resented.

'All these places used to be full of farm workers,' he said. 'I knew most of them. But mechanization's taken over. Running a farm today's a piece of cake.'

The old-fashioned expression startled me. Then I realized that it wasn't out of date for this man. His ideas were of the time, part of his daily experience and his constant contact with reality. His convictions might be valid but 'piece of cake' was a novelty expression born out of old movies or old television that would stay with him for a long time. Perhaps for ever. I was to notice this tendency all over Scotland with men and women beyond a certain age. Even some of the young people held on to mid-Atlantic phrases that had gone out of current coinage. The glib expressions had taken their fancy, marking them out at one time as men in the swim, and they had never been able to discard them. I don't think this man from the Forestry Commission, in spite of his forthright opinions, knew he had used it. It had slipped out, like the 'OK's' and the 'you're telling me's' that you hear all over Scotland, and all over the world. Only, in Scotland they seem to hang on longer because so much of the living of the people, as young Bob Daw had cautioned me, has been frozen somewhere in time.

But he went on to amplify his phrase in good Scots language. Indeed the cottages were empty because of mechanization. Human labour on the farms was at a discount. It took only three or four men today to handle the field work that used to keep fourteen or fifteen fully on the job. They and their families had all lived in cottages like the ones we were standing by. The cottages were owned by the farmer. You got a cottage to live in if you worked for him, and were glad to get it. It sounded fair dealing, but of course it was a one-sided benefit. When mechanization came along and there was no longer work for you, then there was no longer a cottage for you. No matter how many years of your life you had spent serving your boss and making him prosperous. There must have been exceptional farmers, but the numbers of empty cottages suggested there weren't many.

'The farmer wins hands down,' the man beside me said moodily. 'He just can't lose. The Government gives him a subsidy the minute he turns over a field. He never had it so good. If he grows, say, Brussels sprouts, and the market turns out to be glutted with Brussels sprouts he just ploughs his crop straight back into the soil. I know a chap who always grows the earliest potatoes because they get the best prices. In the old days this would have been a bit of a gamble. No gamble today. He's already subsidized. If the potatoes are OK, he's quids in. If they're not, he couldn't care less.'

He felt deeply about it and wanted to get it off his chest. On his daily round, week after week, right in the heart of the country, he saw it all happening: the brightly-painted labour-saving machines out in the fields; his friends thrown idle; the emptying cottages; the departing families. He was telling me what the villagers no doubt told each other in the local of an evening, but this was a chance to get the steam out of him on a stranger and acquaint someone new to it with a situation which to him was intolerable.

'Look at the subsidy prices for wheat,' he said. 'And barley! They never had it so good! And as soon as they don't need the labour, out they go!'

I turned away to take another look at the stone dwellings, seeing them now as low white tombstones hugging the earth. In memory of the departed. But I didn't understand what he meant when he said they weren't for sale.

'Try and buy one!' he challenged me. 'Man, the farmers aren't selling them. They hold on to everything. No. They'll *rent* you one, if they approve of you and you toe the line. At a price! Try for yourself. But they'll never sell. Surrender their precious bloody land to someone else! No fear! They'll let you do the place up to your heart's content, spending your own money making improvements. And one day they'll wave you good-bye and have a satisfied look round the property you've renovated for them. It's still theirs!'

All perfectly in order of course. Strictly legal; an owner holding on to his precious property. But my Forestry friend was having none of it.

'These cottages belong to the men and women who lived in them,' he declared, 'or ought to! *They* should have them. They've worked their guts out for the land all their lives. There ought to be some scheme by which the local councils make sure they're not turned out like this. If the country subsidizes the farmer so handsomely it should see that it's part of the bargain that the farm workers are safeguarded. It's a bloody shame.'

The early spring day was beginning to draw in, but the sun was still warm and the light was luminous. The earth was about to yield up its riches. The little untended gardens round the cottages were already sprinkled with daffodils, which no hand now would gather for the vase upon the table.

2

It was Robert Burns who wrote:

> From scenes like these old Scotia's grandeur springs,
> That makes her loved at home, revered abroad:
> Princes and lords are but the breath of kings,
> 'An honest man's the noblest work of God.'

And Burns' honest men in *The Cotter's Saturday Night* were the hardy sons of toil, the farm workers he knew, whom he hoped would 'be blest with health, and peace, and sweet content!'

In our silence, each deep with thoughts about the inequalities of life, we had both reached into the past. The poetry of Burns had come instinctively to me; the thought of an age-old injustice was occupying the mind of my Forestry Commission man.

'It's just like the Highland clearances and the evictions all over again,' he said with bitterness. 'When you're not wanted, out you go! It doesn't matter a damn what happens to you.'

I was heartened by the spirit of protest in him, but I did not think these empty cottages resembled in any way the historic evictions of the Highlands in the early nineteenth century. You had to go much further back for the main causes of much of Scotland's misery and poverty, whose marks are still on its people today.

Indeed, there was no point on which you could lay your finger and say 'This is where it all began.' It had been with us from the beginning, a condition of extreme hardship rooted in poverty and the ferocious character of its people, and the avarice and blood feuds first of the Highland chiefs and then of the nobles and lords. There wasn't much to choose between the main culprits. Throw in the religious conflict brought about by the Reformation from the Roman Catholic religion to the Calvinism of John Knox, and the wonder is that Scotland wasn't ruined altogether and that her people had lived to survive, if not completely to emerge from its dark background.

My Scottish boyhood, in class and out of school, was enlivened by heroic tales of the clansmen. There never were such fighters! There could not ever, possibly, be such glamour in any country as was attached to the glens and the hills, the great-hearted chieftains acting as father figures to their clan, the clansmen bound in loyalty to their chief. I nearly said 'undying loyalty', but that would scarcely be accurate; 'dying' is the more appropriate word, for they died in their thousands, locked in clan enmity with their fellow Scots, for causes that seemed sometimes worthy, if vengeance is worthy, but mostly senselessly and savagely. Later that bravery and disregard of self would serve a real cause in the wars of independence against England, but while it was a family matter, Scot against Scot, Scotland itself lay stricken under the blood-letting.

The clan system has much to answer for. It beggared Scotland, depriving the country and its agricultural development of thousands of men. The chieftains held sway over their private armies of clansmen, whose numbers could add up to nearly ten thousand fighting men, ready to launch themselves joyously, recklessly, on rival clans in lunatic, bloody slaughter.

Fighting was continuous. The chiefs were a law unto themselves, although theoretically they owed allegiance to the crown. There did not have to be a reason for a raid on a rival chief, or a wholesale assault for plunder or vengeance on a farmer or even a landlord. Blood-lust was enough.

And added to all this, there were the English! In her illuminating book, *Scotland Under Mary Stuart* (published in 1971 by George Allen & Unwin at £3.50), Madeleine Bingham writes graphically of this uncivilized period and Scotland's wild and treacherous people.

'In the years immediately preceding Mary Stuart's birth, Henry VIII had sacked Edinburgh, and he continued to alternate between policies of seeking a royal marriage between his son and Mary Stuart, the infant Queen, and either waging outright war and devastation, or resorting to threats of war. In this he was helped by the clan system and its factions.

'The fact that the Scottish peers were often in the pay of the English king did not lead to improved relations with clans who were not, or to the general pacification of the country. Bribery was, and continued to be, even in the age of Elizabeth, a plank in England's Scottish policy.'

That makes sad reading for Scots today who pride themselves on a world reputation for honesty, integrity and incorruptibility. Perhaps it is only at certain levels that Scots have no qualms about serving their own interests and filling their pockets. But to take the kick-back in money or land or privilege (or all three) from the auld enemy – ah, that hurts.

'On the Borders between England and Scotland and in the Highlands, a system prevailed which, in many respects, fell little short of anarchy. The clan system led to bloody feuds which continued from generation to generation and it was only when these rose to intolerable, anarchic heights that the sovereign of Scotland intervened and was compelled to lead a punitive expedition against the warring chieftains.

'Officially, the clan chiefs were responsible for the actions of their followers, but when, as was often the case, the chiefs were engaged in the same depradations against the farmers as their followers, there was no material benefit for them to be on the side of the law in general, or on the side of the sovereign in particular. The reavers or plunderers continued to seize cattle or crops as and when the opportunity arose.

'Blood feuds were indeed a major curse. Hundreds of years of internal wars and raids had augmented this evil. One murder by an opposing clansman, a hanging by a sovereign, a killing in a Border raid, was never forgotten either by the surviving members of the immediate family, or the kinsmen in the clan. On a simple basis of arithmetical progression, the numbers of blood feuds must have grown at a terrifying rate with resultant bitterness and disorders.'

Some of them are, alas, not even forgotten, or forgiven, to this day. Incredible as it seems, there are Scotsmen who cannot bear to hear the sound of the name of some clan that once did their forebears an injury. 'Don't mention these Campbells in this house!' I once heard an angry father storm at his son, a schoolboy friend of mine. I stared at the father in astonishment. His son, long since briefed in the story of the ancient Glencoe massacre, understood and fell silent, ashamed at his unforgiveable lapse. His father, a prosperous business man, a graduate of Glasgow University, continued to fume.

All over Scotland men made their own law, followed their own strength and savagery. There was no clan system in the Lowlands but that did not save the borders from a kind of double-death; plundering and murderous raids from their own countrymen, and raids from hostile forces just over the English border in Northumberland.

There wasn't much chance of a country growing up and looking towards its national economy in conditions like these. And the nobles who might, and should, have led, were much too concerned about accumulating more and more personal wealth and power. They were the gainers when the Reformation brought about the Dissolution of the Monasteries, making them the inheritors of the Church's riches in land and treasure.

To quote Madeleine Bingham again: 'In many of the nations of Europe at this time, kings and emperors were increasing their own power by curbing that of the nobles, but in Scotland the progress had not even begun. The Scottish nobility, by their clan system, had actually increased their power over more than two centuries.'

The country was wretchedly poor and backward by almost any reckoning. No one seemed concerned either about its welfare or that of its people. The lords who controlled the law also collected the taxes and dues, a state of affairs that led to all kinds of swindling. 'God have mercy on this afflicted land,' prayed the Marquis of Montrose, who died on the scaffold at the age of thirty-eight.

During the minority of James VI, the young son of Mary Queen of Scots, the country was governed first by the Regent of Moray who was assassinated, then the Earl of Lennox who was killed; then the Earl of Mar who died worn out by the country's troubles; and lastly by the Earl of Morton who was executed for his part in the murder of Darnley.

'Between England and Scotland there is perpetual war,' wrote Sebastian Munster, 'and there is no hope of composing it unless the two kingdoms should be united.' He stipulated 'by royal marriage', but he could just as easily, and as accurately, have put the period where I have. Union of some kind seemed inevitable, unless reform of a drastic nature could carry the people with it.

3

A first step towards bringing order out of the chaos and carnage was made in the early seventeenth century through what is known as the Statutes of Iona. Bishop Knox of the Isles managed to bring about an agreement with the great chiefs which, importantly, reduced the size of their private armies. It was a beginning. A little later, in 1725, came the road- and bridge-building programme of General Wade. And a quarter of a century after that followed the wholesale abolition of the hereditable jurisdiction of the chiefs.

Gradually agriculture improved, responding to these initial attempts at reform, but conditions through the realm remained primitive until well into the nineteenth century. The people were getting up and leaving. The almost compulsive urge to emigrate, which has moved the Scottish people throughout its later history, setting down communities of exiles in the far corners of the earth, was now in full and prolonged swing. It was given further impetus by the 'clearings' and 'evictions' which my Forestry Commission friend, staring tight-lipped at the empty farm cottages, had mentioned.

The immense clearances of crofting areas in the Highlands to make room for sheep runs in the nineteenth century took little account of the crofter's plight, suddenly bereft of his little holding and his home. Old and young, they had to get up and go. You can still find glens with a mere handful of people where once, as local records and remains of dwellings and sheilings show, many families were able to wrest a meagre living from the unyielding soil.

There is a poem by Marion Angus, who died in 1946, which, in three beautiful stanzas, describes the destruction of a family and a home, and the heather slowly taking possession, creeping over the place that had once been the wife's drying green for her family washing. It is called *The Fiddler.*

A fine player was he...
'Twas the heather at my knee,
The Lang Hill o' Fare
An' a reid rose tree,
A bonnie dryin' green,
Wind fae aff the braes,
Liftin' and shiftin'
The clear-bleached claes.

Syne he played again...
'Twas dreep, dreep o' rain,
A bairn at the breist
An' a warm hearth-stane,
Fire o' the peat,
Scones o' barley meal,
An' the whirr, whirr, whirr,
O' a spinnin' wheel.

Bit aye, wae's me!
The hindmaist tune be made...
'Twas juist a dune wife
Greetin' in her plaid,
Winds o' a' the years,
Naked wa's atween,
And heather creep, creepin'
Ower the bonnie dryin' green.

Naked walls between. You can still see the naked walls, the roofless huddles of stones, in many a famed Highland beauty spot. The families live on, in scattered remnants, great-great-grandchildren who may never have seen their homeland but have been brought up on its ballads and its legends.

The stir to get up and go, to leave what people felt to be a dying country, or at least a country that had little to offer them, was moving through the Highlands and the Lowlands. It touched restless families who had nothing to do with clearances or evictions. It touched all Scotland. My own family, and myself, moved across the world where opportunity beckoned. What adventurers and pioneers these Scots are!

say the admiring English, and many another national, not knowing or understanding that most of us were escaping and not, for its own sake, adventuring.

I know a family from Skye who, when their mother died — last prop of a way of life that was gone for ever — went all together to the United States. Two brothers and two sisters who in the early 1920s, moved to North Carolina, where another McLean relative had long preceded them. One brother took his medical degree in America, the other became a dental surgeon. The elder sister went to a wealthy New York family on Fifth Avenue as a companion. The younger, Babs, was sent back to Edinburgh to study medicine.

My best friend to this day, an Edinburgh man called Bobby Williamson, met her and ran about the town with her, both madly in love. When the girl's brother in North Carolina discovered that his sister was doing no studying but having a high old time, he cut off her allowance and recalled her to the safety of North Carolina. Bobby followed her there, married her, and went into business in Oregon. These Scots!

Now the pair are back in Edinburgh; their own attractive daughter has taken *her* medical degree at Edinburgh and is now practising successfully — guess where — in America. She comes home for brief holidays, has given her mother a holiday among the family on the other side of the world. One day, says the daughter, she'll come and settle in Scotland. So too said her two medical uncles. They are still in North Carolina, both in their seventies. It is more likely now that they will die where they have spent their lives, in that far-off corner of a foreign field that is for ever Scotland.

IV

1

I was in Galloway, wandering by the Nith, and idly watching some children down by the river bank. One of the boys had a line out, hoping for a catch. My interest wandered from him to an older girl whose arm was protectively round her little sister's shoulder. Above the white frilly stuff of her sleeve, the child's head gleamed brightly red in the sunlight.

And with a sudden delight I remembered the sandy pows of the chums of my childhood and the auburn hair and ginger curls of their sisters. Instantly the word 'carrots' flashed back to my mind, and I remembered my schooldays, and the struggles in the playground, and the warm red heads bent over the classroom desks. I realized that this little girl was the first redhead I had consciously noticed since crossing the border.

Had I been blind, preoccupied? I had made plenty of notes in my notebook about this and that. Yet I had not until now observed any redheads. Surely they could not have vanished altogether from Scotland?

When I was a boy there were as many redheads, girls and boys, attending my school as all the other shades of hair put together. Every tinge of the colour was there – fire-red, russet red, ginger, brick, auburn, sandy, flaxen, butter-bright, honey-hued. My first chum, with whom I ran Scotch-horses on my way to school, was a fiery-tinted, freckle-nosed boy from Wester Ross.

His sister, a year older, had soft sandy hair falling down over her shoulders. In my earliest dancing class, at least a third of the girls had degrees of red hair, although by then they were brushing it back from their foreheads, and bringing it in a plait around their heads, leaving the back of the neck exposed, fair and fragile like a baby's. There was a fresh light colouring in the complexion that seemed to go with this hair, and the eyes were not so often blue or green as you might expect, but deep brown or amber, sometimes with golden flecks in them. And quite frequently there was a feathering of freckles dusting the high cheek bones.

It may have been that this hair and this colouring, giving its own beauty to many Scottish women, marked itself on the mind because it was more arresting. It may at first notice, by its challenge to the eye, have overshadowed the darker heads with their own particular beauty and appeal. Yet for me this lighter colouring has always been associated with certain elements in the character of Scots women, and I know that early influences must have had something to do with this personal feeling.

My mother was not a redhead. She could never have been called 'carrots' or 'ginger' at school. But her fairness was out of the same family of colouring. And her small build – she was only five feet – went with the general smallness of Scottish women, a smallness that is so deceptive because it conceals a toughness of fibre and character that is a continual astonishment when events reveal it.

She had blue eyes, not the amber or brown, and she had no freckles. But she had the high Scottish cheekbones with their shadowed hollows that artists love. None of my three sisters had this colouring, so I imagine that in addition to the normal closeness of a youngest son to his mother, I was more aware of her, with her fairness, always flitting about the house in the endless work with which Scottish women try to destroy themselves. 'She was like a little doll,' my eldest brother once described her, long afterwards. But a very strong doll, with six children to bring up and a brilliant but erratic husband to fend with.

One of her sisters had the same colouring, and one of my father's sisters, my auntie Bell, who lived with her sister in Linlithgow, near the Palace where Mary Queen of Scots was born. It was in my aunts' care that I spent much of my childhood when I was not in my own home. I was impressed by Bell's fair colouring and the character which, I naturally assumed when I thought about it later, went with it. For this aunt was also tiny, gentle and capable; and indestructible as steel. And sensitive to all a little boy's needs and dreams and hopes.

You grow up with what is all around you. It was only now, long afterwards, in recollection, that I saw that first school, those dancing lessons, the evening classes, the flirtations of adolescence, and remembered the redheads. And the thought came to me that the time in which I lived must have had something to do with this prevalence of warm Scottish colour.

I grew up in another time, a time before radio or television. The first flickering movies had made their debut, to many a curiosity rather than the beginning of a revolution. Talking pictures were a long way in the future. Aeroplanes were still in their infancy. You could not then fly to the ends of the earth in a matter of hours. Even motor cars were a new-fangled thing, strictly for the well-to-do.

There was nothing of all the hurry and change, the endless comings and goings of men and women in every strata of society, the upheavals of today. Life was a static affair. You went on where you were born, and probably died there. At least millions of people did. There were always Scots going away from their country, but there was no influx, to speak of, of any fresh blood.

All this could have affected the numbers of redheads who peopled my childhood. If there is little movement in populations, there are close marriage relationships. Families tend to stay bound together in the villages and small towns, and even in the cities. Girls marry the boys they have always known, from the same town, the same street.

The Great War, changing everything, was only then about to burst on us, splitting communities and families, bringing strangers with their alien ways and manners, and their alien heritage, into neighbourhoods whose stream of life had been uninvaded for generations. Were the many redheads I remembered a natural outcome of that older close existence, of Scot marrying Scot, of kindred families binding together all through the years?

And the movement of peoples begun in the Great War was accelerated in the years that followed, by the new inventions, the speed of transport, the ideas and mass communication that turned humanity into something like one world. The Second World War and its jet-age aftermath uprooted millions of people, throwing all nationalities together. Soon after came the new towns in Scotland and the new industries, attracting men and women from all over Britain. Somewhere in all this the red-headed Scots may have become submerged by their darker-haired brothers and sisters.

Had I made a discovery? It was the kind of discovery that the returned exile might land on. To the native population the thing would happen, if it had happened, almost imperceptibly. I tried to tell myself

I was wrong; my memory had betrayed me; there hadn't been so many redheads, after all, when I was a boy. I had noticed them perhaps because they were the striking rarity. A few there had been; the others existed in my imagination.

I was only fooling myself. They had been there all right. I can remember even now many of their names. I can see them in different places, in different activities. I remember three in my school football team. I could name two redheaded girls with whom I was in love at different times. My Scottish regiment was full of redheads fifty years ago. The emigrant ship on which I sailed to Canada had many. Even in Montreal, accompanying the prevalent Scots accent, was the familiar red hair.

After dinner in my small hotel that evening, I turned to one of the books I was carrying with me on my travels. I might chance on a clue or two within its pages. It was a volume, *Scottish Short Stories,* an anthology, first published in 1932 by Faber and Faber, and then reissued ten years later. I had read all the stories before and knew that although their appeal and their sentiments were enduring, they were set in another age. An age perhaps when there were more redheads. Sufficiently more for them to attract the notice of Scottish writers? If I had been so aware of them, then surely authors would have noticed them also and mentioned them in their work.

I was well rewarded. I turned first to John Buchan's short story, *The Outgoing of the Tide.* Buchan was as alive to the redhaired women of Scotland as some of us others, and as appreciative. I read with pleasure:

'The lads of the parish might cast admiring eyes on her bright cheeks and yellow hair as she sat in her white gown in the kirk, but well they knew she was not for them.'

From Buchan I turned to Lewis Grassic Gibbon, whose Mistress Menzies in his story, *Smeddum* (which means spirit, or 'guts'), has 'reddish hair and a high skeugh nose.'

It seemed a natural then to try Barrie. In *The Courting of T'nowhead's Bell,* he has this revealing bit of dialogue.

'I don't care for her hair either,' continued Jamie, who was very nice in his tastes: 'something mair yallowchy wid be an improvement.'
'A'body kins,' growled Sam'l, ''at black hair's the bonniest.'
The others chuckled.
'Puir Sam'l,' Pete said.

The phrase 'very nice in his tastes', suggest that Barrie too might have had an eye, and a heart, for the warmer tresses.

The Little Tinker is a lovely Scottish story about a wandering tribe of tinkers. Its author is Jane H. Findlater, and her story was important to me because I wanted to see what a woman observed or felt about the redheads. She did not fail me. Her heroine is introduced at once with sympathy and warmth.

'The mother was a tall finely made woman. A faded green tartan shawl fell cornerwise from her shoulders almost to her heels, and on her crisply curled yellow hair she wore a knitted woollen cap.'

There seems to have been a great deal of yellow in the hair in those days, but a little boy in Robert MacLellan's story, *The Mennans,* speaks of women admiring his 'boonie reid hair,' and always wanting to lift him up.

I went happily to bed. From now on I would keep a lookout for redheads on the stretches of road ahead of me. And, a last-moment decision just before I fell asleep, I'd visit the Royal Scottish Academy next time I passed through Edinburgh, and see if the Scottish artists, like the Scottish writers, had had an eye for the redheads of my memory.

They had indeed. It required only two portraits by Allan Ramsay, the son of Allan Ramsay, the poet who wrote *The Gentle Shepherd,* to show me something of the image I had carried inside me all through the years: the image of Scottish childhood and the Scottish womanhood that had been closest to me.

The first, of the child, is *Magdalene Erskine.* It was painted in 1747. There were redheads then, for the canvas shows a bright, button-eyed little girl looking straight at you with what the catalogue rightly describes as 'impudent cheerfulness'. The Scottish independence is already marked in this young, apple-cheeked, rosy-lipped child. Behind the cheerfulness is inherent strength of character. A saucy, witty, determined face; and framing the face her sandy-coloured hair, in ringlets. Little Magdalene Erskine was long before my time, but I knew her like in my early schooldays, and I saw her like playing with other children that day along the Nith.

The other portrait has even more meaning for me. It is *The Painter's wife,* done by Ramsay about the year 1755. The artist's wife was the daughter of Sir Alexander Lindsay. It is a most subtle and delicate work. The sitter has turned away from a posy of flowers to face the artist, her left hand still raised to touch a rose. A light lace shawl is about her shoulders. The young oval-shaped face has an expression of half surprise as it looks outwards at you.

All the fresh colouring (that warmth *under* the skin) that I remember in my mother and in other Scots women is here, and the deep-set wistful eyes, and the long sensitive nose. It is an unsmiling, thoughtful face, but the lips might easily part, and the smile would be gentle and understanding. And above the light eyebrows the sandy-coloured hair is brushed off the forehead and brought in a plait round the back of the head. It is held together with a pale blue ribbon falling forward towards the brow, brilliantly conveying the suggestion that the dark brown eyes might in just such another face, and with such colouring, have been blue.

I sat looking at the face, trying to read the thoughts behind it, and I remembered other faces like this which I had known, or glimpsed in Scottish streets or Scottish homes or Scottish restaurants and theatres. Everywhere in Scotland. It would not have surprised me to turn round and see a visitor in the gallery looking out from such a face, and indeed one of the two girl students closely examining a picture at the far end of the room was a passing fair resemblance.

It is a face suggesting depth of character and feeling, an intensity of inner life. And there came back to me something that John Buchan had once said about Scots women being different because of their 'innerliness'.

V

1

In the end Sheila couldn't make it with me to Kenneth and Margaret Roy's little house at Inverkeithing. Not that first time anyway. She was still aware of her mending spine and prudently decided to play it safe. If we had gone together we'd have motored up from North Berwick where we were camping out in our half-furnished flat, would have lunched in Edinburgh, and in the early evening driven over the Forth Road Bridge.

So I went alone, going by train to Edinburgh. I had checked with Ken that someone of his team would be going out from the city who could give me a lift. I'd also arranged that I would stay at his party only a short time for a drink and a peep at the sleeping baby, and take a train about nine o'clock back to Edinburgh and then North Berwick. I knew it was the right thing to plan. We would all be talking the same language, but they would talk it in the idiom of a generation later than mine, and they would all be more than a generation younger.

It was funny how you had to adjust to life, and how you did it naturally and imperceptibly. I had once upon a time been the youngest editor of a newspaper. For quite a time I was accustomed to the 'youngest this' and 'youngest that' feeling, and to the people around me who accepted it and nobly supported me, even in all the youthful mistakes I made. The changes must have been going on around me all the time, but journalism is an obsessive occupation, and one can grow accustomed to recording social and world change and overlook it in oneself. I was young enough, twenty years later, at forty-six, to choose to switch from newspapers to magazines, seeing in the medium a great opportunity for enormous expansion in the post-war world of 1946.

Yet I must have been an oldish man to the young teams I was again leading, although nothing in the happiness and the hilarity and friendships of our association or, fortunately, in the successful outcome of our operation, ever gave me anything like an inward intimation of this. This was not the blind folly it may sound. I was blessed with a young and contemporary outlook, I was pretty quick on my feet and in my head; and my wide experience and natural aptitude for publishing kept me in stride with the younger generation. I never felt at any time the onset of age.

Yet I was ageing, and I knew that the people at Ken's celebration would be young like himself, young and beginning and with faith in their venture. And in the specialized world of the theatre, which wasn't mine. You have to know when you are odd man out, even if sometimes the young, in their decency and politeness, give no clue that they think so. But there were two things I had learned for myself in a long career. The experience you can pass on is useful and is appreciated, but the young have to learn for themselves; and so you don't bore them unnecessarily with your presence. The other knowledge, which had come gradually in later years, was that starting as a young leader leaves you lonelier in age.

My staffs on newspapers had in the main been older than myself. I could not have foreseen in the clamour of the job and the richness of our friendships, which seemed to promise a contentment unending, that the years would pick them off one by one, and that in the end there would be very few left alive to whom I could say over a drink, 'Do you remember?' and live again with gusto the glorious battlefield that had been our daily life.

I would enjoy meeting Ken Roy again and his wife and baby, and the other young people. But they would belong to one world and I to another. What they were in the process of living, with all its seemingly intolerable and insoluble problems and burdens, and fleeting happiness, I had long since wrung out, like sheets in a wringer, till the drops of water didn't come any more. What they guessed at, I knew. What they were hoping for, I had experienced. There would be no one there to whom I could say 'Do you remember?' They were all in the process of building up their own memories for a future which I would certainly not share.

This drew them to me with a curious intensity. I had sensed this when I had met Ken Roy and seen the almost defiant blaze of life behind his watchful eye, his steady stare when I had mentioned something that had startled him. Celebrate! It was a long road of experience that had taught me to celebrate with my colleagues. These celebrations gave meaning to the immediate past, stimulus to the pressing future. They were a release from effort, the pause before the next jump, the 'getting-to-know-you' of the musical-comedy song of my time.

2

Alastair McNeill was taking me out to Inverkeithing. I had arranged to be standing on the steps of the NB hotel so that he would have no parking problem. My train from North Berwick brought me to the Waverley a bit on the early side. I took the convenient lift which goes right up from one of the station platforms into the hotel. At all times this lift is a convenience, in winter it is a godsend. The Waverley must be one of the coldest stations in the world, perfectly designed for catching pneumonia. It was a mild spring evening, but I took the lift.

It brought me into the lobby of the hotel, and having a few minutes to spare I turned into the golden lounge. There might be someone I knew to pass the time of day. Bill Watson was sitting alone at one of the round tables with a pot of tea. The lounge is a favourite of Bill's also, and is conveniently near *The Scotsman* building on the North Bridge where, as features editor, he produced the lively *Week-End Scotsman.*

He looks young for the job, with a gay look of courage in his eye, and an impish wit. I don't think I know anyone who shows such swift, frank welcome in his glance; and it was there on his face as he looked up and saw me.

He couldn't have been better met. He was the one man in touch with all that went on in the Scottish arts who could fill me in. He was particularly involved with the theatre and was probably even now waiting for his Catherine, who worked with the Perth Rep.

'Welcome home,' he said. 'And I hope you're here for good this time.'

'Not yet, but I'm going to stay quite a while.'

'I saw your name on a poster last night.' He never holds back. He hands out the good news to you generously. A prince, when you know all the ones who knock rather than help.

'A poster?' I hadn't a clue.

'Very dashing,' he laughed. 'For the first issue of *Scottish Theatre*. It was all over the Perth Rep.'

So Ken Roy and his team really knew their stuff.

'There's one at the Traverse too,' he went on. 'I think they've blanketed all the reps, and the Lyceum — the lot. I hear they've got a lot of subscriptions.'

'And the mag,' I said. 'Have you seen it?'

'Yesterday. Just out. And very promising.'

I had hoped to hear more than that.

He understood. 'I mean promising, good. Not promising, mediocre. To be absolutely fair, it's really more than promising.'

That was typical Bill Watson. Editing himself, he would judge the new production professionally.

'Will they get away with it?'

'To tell you the truth, they've got away with it. To everybody's surprise. At least they've produced it. And I think it will go.' He broke off. 'What about some tea?'

His companionship was tempting.

'Thanks, Bill, but I won't even sit down. I'm just waiting to be picked up. They're taking me over to Inverkeithing where we're having a small celebration drink with Ken Roy. Can I add to the occasion by quoting you?'

'You certainly can. I hear they did it on a shoe-string.'

'Slave labour,' I said. 'Voluntarily. In this day and age!'

'Yes,' he reminded me, 'but in this country! And for a cause. What they won't do for a cause! I see it at Perth, where Catherine is working her head off night and day and is gorgeously happy. So are a dozen more of them.'

'Give her my love,' I said. 'I'll get up there to see her some time soon. And now I'm off. Thanks for the glad tidings.'

He said: 'I didn't know until I saw the poster that you'd had a hand in it. Nice to have you with us among the delinquent young.'

It hadn't been much of a hand. The small gesture from a distance. If only I were living in Scotland, I thought.

Alastair McNeill guessed his recognition of me as he pulled up at the entrance. He gave a toot, and I opened the door of his small car and went in beside him. His wife Norma had put herself into the back seat.

Perhaps it was the pebble glasses that made him look a very serious young man. And the large forehead. He was quiet, scholarly, maybe shy in the presence of the monster Ken had oversold to him. But I was glad at once to see he wasn't a bit like Ken Roy. It's the variety of individuals in a publishing team that gives it its balance, not their similarity. Ken was a natural leader, perhaps a born editor; certainly, as I soon discovered, a very good writer. I guessed Alastair to be the mind that would watch over the business problems.

'I've got the job of finding the ads,' he said, as we began a running discussion all the way to Inverkeithing, hardly even breaking off as we slowed down to pay the half-crown Bridge toll.

'I'll bet that keeps you busy.'

He stole a sidelong glance at me but didn't take his attention from his driving.

'We're not doing so bad.'

'Not so bad!' his wife's voice said indignantly in my ear. 'We're doing wonders.'

Touch wood, I thought. Touch wood. It's early days yet. I was remembering Ken's anticipated one thousand readership, and the coolness of the Scottish public to the theatre.

'Plenty of subscribers?' I asked. At two and six a copy they wouldn't need a *Daily Express* circulation to pay for the printing.

'Surprising. They're rolling up.'

'That's a good poster you have in the rep. theatres,' I said.

'You've seen it?'

'No,' I had to be honest with him. But I added the cliché: 'My spies are everywhere.'

Norma laughed. Alastair did not laugh so easily. He was carrying his own burden.

I told them of Bill Watson's enthusiasm.

'And what do *you* think of it?' he asked.

'I haven't seen it yet. I expect my copy's gone to Sussex and I missed it on the way up. But I'll collect a copy from Ken tonight.'

We talked about advertisements and the whole page ad Scottish Television had booked for a year. I wondered if Alastair knew how lucky they had been. STV, which might have considered a theatre magazine to be almost competition, had acted in line with its policy of encouraging all the arts. Under the enlightened leadership of William Brown, its managing-director, STV has been one of the major patrons of the arts in Scotland as well as providing regular employment for a large pool of Scottish actors, producers and dramatists. Even in the hard financial times that followed the Government's imposition of a levy on TV advertising, causing STV a crippling downturn in its revenue, the company continued to set aside money for this purpose and for specific projects which might be called pump-priming. Its support of *Scottish Theatre* by taking advertising space, was courageous and far-sighted.

'But getting the mag off the ground must have been bloody hell?' Nobody in Scotland, I had discovered, swore so casually and socially as the people I was accustomed to in England. 'How did you get the initial capital?'

'That *was* a bit of a nightmare.'

I said, almost unthinkingly: 'How much did the Scottish Arts Council pitch in?'

They answered almost together: 'Nothing!'

'You really mean...'

'Not a sou!'

We went on in silence. It was hard to believe. But I thought I would leave any questioning till I had a chance of speaking to Ken Roy.

I used the short silence to do a bit of reflecting. The Scottish Arts Council was an off-shoot of the Arts Council, that pool of tax-payers' money that subsidized art forms of every description. It kept the National Theatre going in London, and many other theatres up and down the country. I had seen the Scottish end functioning when I helped Tom Fleming with his Edinburgh Royal Lyceum. There had been plenty of Scottish Arts Council money put into that, and the Edinburgh Town Council had added a further generous contribution of ratepayers' money.

If culture was an important part of the British welfare, coming at last in line with pensions and medical aid and unemployment benefits and farmers' subsidies, then the Government would see that taxpayers stumped up all the money required. I had seen at the Lyceum a subsidized theatre playing to quarter-capacity seating, and even less. We were all paying for the bounty that the theatre and its company enjoyed; but few of Edinburgh's citizens were walking up to the box office. At least, though, the actors were eating.

My own attitude to all this compulsory and public generosity was a conflicting one. The liberal sympathies that had been with me since conscience and awareness of privilege and injustice were first awakened always moved me in favour of equality of opportunity, if not exactly of the lavish hand-out. At the same time my puritanical Scottish upbringing, believing in salvation through suffering, success after struggle, made me watch the general subsidizing of creative workers with suspicion. Perhaps even with envy! My thoughts might have been out of step with what was going on. So much has changed. I belonged to that other day when writers worked at their own expense, often went hungry to do what they believed in; when artists were lucky if they could pay for their paints; when actors were still a bunch of rogues and vagabonds, living on hope and not much else.

Did I really in my heart want to put the clock back? I don't think so. But neither do I believe that the best work comes from a full belly and a mind free of care. I still believe that a man should have to fight his way to recognition, success and fame, and not have it handed to him. How dated I am. But I thought of some who had won it that way.

Would D.H. Lawrence have been a better writer if there had been money in the kitty and his early life hadn't been an economic and emotional hell? H.G. Wells? Was Shaw subsidized? Well, yes, he was in a way; Charlotte was a wealthy wife and that must have stood for something. But a lot of Shaw's work had been done before his marriage, with only his belief in himself as his umbrella. Robert Burns? A few pounds, from almost anywhere, might have saved his life; they would certainly have taken some of the carking care out of his days and nights. But they might also have taken him away from his plough that turned up the frightened mouse, and the world would have been deprived of its 'wee, sleekit cow'rin', tim'rous beastie'; and his epic poem *The Cotter's Saturday Night;* and all the haunting songs that have enriched our lives.

In the year that Kenneth Roy started his *Scottish Theatre* out of his own pocket and a few other half-empty ones, the Scottish Arts Council handed out quite sizeable sums. Ten of the beneficiaries, a mere handful, were:

Scottish Opera	£125,500
Scottish National Orchestra	£113,320
Citizens' Theatre, Glasgow	£65,073
Edinburgh Festival Society	£50,000
Edinburgh Civil Theatre Trust (Lyceum)	£49,908
Dundee Repertory Theatre	£28,078
Pitlochry Festival Theatre	£23,100
Perth Repertory Theatre	£17,750
Traverse Theatre Club, Edinburgh	£15,310
Richard Demarco Gallery, Edinburgh	£4,700

I had no way of knowing whether Richard Demarco's art gallery was a more deserving cause than a magazine designed to keep interest in the Scottish theatre alive and kicking, and a later visit to the gallery has left me unconvinced that it was. But in any case there was plenty of room for both to benefit. The bounties all added up to a tidy sum doled out in generous dollops, but there was much more to play with where all that had come from, and many individual creators and small groups of estimable entertainers had good reason for remembering the Scottish Arts Council in their nightly prayers.

A sum like £250 to Sean O'Casey at one time would have meant the difference between hunger and nourishment. It might have stopped *Juno and the Paycock* in its tracks or pushed O'Casey on to even greater achievements. But he contrived to write his masterpiece without any help from any Arts Council.

3

'I hear the Scottish Arts Council gave you no money,' I said bluntly to Ken.

We were standing in his living room, a drink in our hands.

He laughed. He could afford to. A small mountain of his magazines was piled up on a table waiting to be posted.

'Who told you that?'

'Well, you didn't. But is it true?'

'True.'

He wasn't laughing now. I had known from his first letter to me, from our first meeting, that here was a young man with a dream, wanting to produce something for the theatre he loved. And determined to do it.

'But surely you asked them for help. With a theatre venture like yours?'

'Of course I did. I needed the money.'

'What happened?'

I think Ken Roy was still too near it then to talk about it, or that wasn't the place or time to job backwards into the details of his difficulties. In any case, he had surmounted them in his own way.

But it was too important a matter to let pass, and much later, when I was winding up in Scotland and writing this book, I asked Ronald

Mavor, the Director of the Scottish Arts Council, by letter, why the Council had not helped Kenneth Roy when he had asked for help.

To my surprise he replied that 'the sole reason was that we were not asked'. He went on to say that he would be interested to know the source of my story, 'which has been related to me before'.

When I showed this letter to Ken, he produced a copy of his first dated letter to the Arts Council, the opening paragraph of which read: 'I am writing to you to seek the support of the Scottish Arts Council in producing a new monthly magazine of the stage, to be named *Scottish Theatre*'; and he went on fully to describe his aims – in much the same manner that he had first addressed them to me before we met.

I relayed this information to Ronald Mavor. He then discovered Roy's letter in his own Arts Council files. And his own dated reply to it. This expressed his interest in the venture, but added that he thought it 'very unlikely that the Council would be able to find the money with which to offer you financial assistance for the magazine in the coming financial year'. And he confessed 'to some doubts as to the practicability of establishing such a magazine in the present climate'.

He invited Kenneth Roy to give the Council some fuller information and to arrange a meeting with Mr Alisdair Skinner.

It was the 'present financial year' that mattered to Ken Roy. Not this year, next year, sometime, never. Playing it the right way, he might well have received help – sometime. Ronald Mavor had held the door open. But the real clincher as far as Ken was concerned was the Director's confession of 'some doubts' about the project. It wasn't the best augury for having another go and risking a rebuff. In his place, certainly at his age, I should probably have done what he did. He sent a brief reply to the Scottish Arts Council saying 'we do not feel that it is necessary to take the matter any further at this stage'.

He said also that he would send a copy of the first issue of the magazine to Mr Mavor and be glad to have his views on it. A whole year later, with the magazine on its feet, surprising all theatre people in Scotland with its excellence, Ronald Mavor wrote to Roy 'congratulating you on *Scottish Theatre* which I have read with great pleasure over the year'.

But all this came to light later; not that night standing drinking in Ken's little home. And ultimately the Scottish Arts Council found its way to give Kenneth Roy a helping hand.

I looked round the room. It was small, but Margaret, like all these clever young wives today, had made the most of it. Attractively uncluttered. A minimum of furniture. Modern colours and themes in the curtains and carpets to give space. Modern lighting, helping to make the room half as big again. A small table against the far window with a few bottles on it. Three to be exact. No soda syphon, but a glass jug of water. It was a celebration carefully within the means of the hosts. I had taken a very small whisky and a lot of water with it. It would last me for the time I was staying.

I had noticed the untidy garden, the uncut grass against the tiny house as I came in. No garage. First things first in a new house, with a new baby. The minute hall. The tight stairway going up to the two bedrooms and the bathroom. I had gone up to see Stephen as soon as I came in. Fast asleep, his right thumb in his mouth, the fingers of his left hand spread open against his head when sleep had caught him. It was the same sleep ritual that my own grand-daughter Anna moved into as drowsiness gradually overtook her.

I had brought for Stephen's birthday a small, gaily-painted carousel which the slightest touch of a finger spun into motion.

'He'll love it,' said Margaret, leaving it by the baby's bedside for his awakening.

I looked down at the sleeping boy for a moment longer and touched his cheek gently with the side of my forefinger. He had his part in the drive and ambition that was pushing his father on. As had Margaret. And also the house, trim and neat, and £1,000 cheaper than Ken could have bought in Edinburgh.

I glanced out of the window before going down the stairs with her to join the others. The view was high, wide and handsome. The small estate of houses on this elevation overlooked the Forth. In the distance, the lights of Edinburgh glowed in the evening sky. Westward lay Stirling, gateway to the wilder country of the north. The Roys had chosen well. The situation probably had its disadvantages, a far remove from station or bus, a climb up the hill after shopping. But it was all part of a Scottish family at its beginning. There obviously wasn't a penny to spare. Income was earmarked for necessities even before it came in.

They were in the full flood of their young beginning, enjoying every minute of it, but aware of the modern pressures and the nag of anxiety that haunts all young husbands in this situation. The other mouth to feed, the other new life for which you have to carry the responsibility for so many years; a hostage to your own progress. 'Are you married?' asks the prospective employer. 'Any children?' The boss can pretend that he is looking for a man with a sense of responsibility, but he knows that in nine cases out of ten he will take on one who has dropped out of the completely independent class and who, in any conflict of opinion or interest, will have to think twice before spitting in his eye.

I remembered my own inner doubt when I was first faced with the prospect of fatherhood. How could I possibly afford to be a father in my precarious business of journalism? In that death-knell year of 1931 which heralded the country's grimmest depression? With three million unemployed and not a hope in hell of a job for many of them for years to come.

With the approach of a first-born the world is always dropping away from under the feet of a man who has not much money or security and who now realizes he is going to have less. Father-pregnancy pains have as much to do with this as with associative-sympathy towards the wife. This is the time for the incipient ulcer, the onset of hypertension and the long wakeful nights, wondering how we are going to manage. The unknown future is full of dread. It is another small death in the long trail of deaths. And in the event, mostly, we pass through this one and fear is stilled in the determination to fight for one's precious own and a place in the sun.

In my own life, I know now from hindsight, I never took on a new responsibility (children included) which did not subsequently reward me, through its incentive, with riches or happiness. I am not saying the recipe is infallible. And sometimes the reward is scarcely worth the effort. But the acceptance of responsibility is a condition of the full life.

The Roys would look back on these first anxious years and remember them with happiness. The happiness was already there when we reached the living room. It was a simple matter of a drink in one hand and a copy of their magazine in the other. And a gabble of talk about only one thing.

They had included me in what was obviously a purely personal party, the half dozen young men and women who had seen the thing through from its speculative start. I now already knew Alastair and Norma, Ken and Margaret. I noticed that she was listed on the contents page as Margaret Campbell, Production. The deputy editor was Colin

Liddell: the associate editor James Aitchison and there was a student editor, Sheena Mackay (who later would become Colin Liddell's wife).

We stood together in the small room; there were no separate conversations. The drinking was frugal; the talk bubbled over. We all spoke at once. Yet they were critical of themselves and their product to the point of a mocking sadism; and they could laugh now at the hurdles they had vaulted, at the gaffes they had made on the way to this moment, at the friendly gibes of the people who hadn't believed they could do it. They had done it.

This was the atmosphere in which my life had been lived: the enthusiasm of young people. I had shared it in large cities all over the world; to be a small part of it now, here in Scotland, was really home-coming. Scotland had got its *Scottish Theatre,* and the voice of Scotland was stronger for it. I did not know how good the magazine was; I would study it in the train on my way home, and be happy to find it very good indeed, with writing of a high quality and a fine fighting mettle running through its pages.

None of us knew that evening that twelve months and twelve issues later, Kenneth Roy would be one of the best-known names in the theatre in Scotland, and that he would be celebrating his first anniversary issue with an editorial beginning:

> 'The magazine has survived the year, thanks to the support of its readers and advertisers, without any form of public subsidy; it has done so in the belief that total independence is one of its strongest assets. Public subsidy has, however, indirectly played a major part in making the magazine possible, for without subsidy, all of Scotland's professional repertory companies – with the exception, perhaps, of the Byre at St Andrews – would collapse overnight. And in that event, the fodder of these pages would also collapse.'

And on that occasion he would be sending me a note saying: 'It is now a year since you became the first person in Britain to say they were interested in a magazine called *Scottish Theatre,* and that is something that I don't forget.'

But that future was still unborn. The present, with its young people and the raised voices and the laughter was satisfaction enough. I had been at rich and riotous parties in my time, with champagne flowing and bright established people doing their stuff. Half the fun had been in knowing that so many of the famous had had their beginnings much like this.

My new friends decently protested when I said I had to leave them. But Ken understood. The 9.10 train from Inverkeithing was the only possible one for me to connect at Edinburgh with the last train down to North Berwick. Alastair drove me round to the station, made to wait with me, but I waved him away to go back to the festivities. Besides, I like being alone to turn things over in my mind.

I got my ticket and went over the bridge to the opposite platform. I had five minutes in hand before the train came in. It was only then that I realized I was alone in the station. It was deserted and silent. The platform echoed my solitary footsteps, like the beginning of a Simenon story, full of atmosphere. I was almost ominously alone under the yellow lamplight. Who else on a Saturday night at that time would be going in to Edinburgh from Inverkeithing?

Inverkeithing. I had not forgotten it, but its full significance had dimmed with time; and if I had been travelling back by car, this station would have been by-passed, and I should have missed the next precious minutes whose memories were inextricably mixed up with my whole life.

I had stood on this platform before. Many times. But it was fifty years since I had last been in Inverkeithing station waiting for a train to take me to Edinburgh.

VI

1

In those fifty years since I was a young infantry soldier going home from camp for the afternoon, totally unaware of what my future would be — if indeed I had a future at all when the Western Front was finished with me — my whole life had shaped itself back to this reunion. Then, on the threshold of manhood, what lay in front of me had been a dark mystery, no part of it predictable. Now the whole trail of my life lay mapped behind me. The unknown had been breached, the mysteries had all been solved, or at least encountered. For me there could not be many more guesses. Between that long-ago eager impatience for the incoming train and this indifferent waiting on the same station platform, my life had spanned fifty years of fruitful activity, and whatever it stood for.

In the silence and emptiness of the station it was difficult to believe that I had been part of that long-ago bustling occasion with half a hundred fresh-faced Scottish soldiers of my own age jostling each other through the gate on the other side of the bridge, hell-bent for their Saturday midday-to-midnight leave. Their boots clattered against the metal as they thundered across the bridge, headed for the Edinburgh train, with or without official passes.

The lucky ones with Passes could travel straight through to the Waverley station without a qualm. The others, and I had often been one of them, faced the hazard of watchful Military Policemen prowling around. You could try to dodge them in one of two ways. The train always stopped at Haymarket station, a mile before its final destination at the Waverley. It was a platform, rather than a station, and poor waters for MPs to fish in. There was seldom one there. So you could take this chance and get off at Haymarket, and if you were undetected or unquestioned get a tram in from there to your home. It was risky, because one MP on that platform could swoop in a handful of Absents Without Leave.

The other way was to go the whole hog and leave the train at the Waverley in a surging mass, all running for the stairs, your own special friends with Passes all bunched around you. My own close protectors were a six-foot-two rebel called Jim Mortimer, who practically wrapped himself round me and ran, and a burly lad from Glasgow called Williams. You could not afford, if you had no Pass, to saunter isolated along any Waverley platform. But the frontal surge, startling many unfortunate civilians, left any MPs little chance of stepping in to stop it.

We usually got away with it. How often, I wonder now, not really because the MPs were as sadistic and bloodthirsty as we imagined, but because they were human and understanding, and one look at us was enough. Lambs about to be led to the slaughter.

I never knew what happened to Jim Mortimer, but my last sight of Williams was of him sitting on the shattered railway line to Arras, leaning forward as if to adjust his puttees, with German shells churning the earth into a heaving sea as we tried to go forward. Williams was already out of the storm. Apparently unhurt, the whole of his flesh was the ghastly grey-blue hue of shell blast, and he sat there rigid as a piece of sculpture.

But nothing of that future was in our thoughts as we all charged into Inverkeithing station, no older than boys still studying at public schools. In the gay excitement of escaping from camp we were a roistering, happy-go-lucky bunch, as bound together in our common Saturday afternoon purpose as, on the parade ground, we were stamped with the *esprit de corps* of the regiment.

2

I was stationed for the first part of my training in a condemned lodging house on a hill above Inverkeithing. My home was only twelve miles away, but separated by a river, a guarded railway bridge, and Army Regulations. I was a private in the infantry, the Royal Scots Fusiliers. I had few privileges that seemed likely to get me over to the other side and so home to Edinburgh as often as I'd have liked.

But you never know; the army has some strange tricks. One day, after barrack square drill, my platoon sergeant came round asking for someone who could work a typewriter. You never volunteer for any job in the army, short of going out on a dangerous mission to be shot at. I was too young and inexperienced to know that. I could type, and said so. My sergeant loathed me as I loathed him. He was one of the old type, pre-war regular sergeants, an illiterate bully. With the fiendish smile of an H.M. Bateman character, he sent me off packing to the Orderly Room, up on the hill towards North Queensferry.

I had a glorious, tantalizing view of the Bridge. I took the place of someone who had gone off sick, typing Battalion Orders and other rubbish, and so missed my parades and all the fun of the platoon. When I returned to the regiment several weeks later I was soft, out of training, and a ready target for my sergeant's wit.

It was a 'cushy' job indoors, if that was what you wanted. To me it seemed like prison. Actually it provided me with a means of escape. The vital Forth Bridge had armed sentries at both ends. Every morning a password for the Bridge was concocted; it stood good for twenty-four hours. If you knew the password you could get on to the Bridge. While I was in the Orderly Room I knew the password.

I did not need to make use of it going to Edinburgh on Saturday afternoons when I could get away. There were then several trains which took on passengers at Inverkeithing. But it was another matter getting back late at night. There were no late returning trains stopping at Inverkeithing. The few very late trains went right on through the station and through the night into the dark north.

But there was a late bus from Edinburgh going as far as South Queensferry. I'd leave Edinburgh late, get off the bus at South Queensferry, in the darkness climb the hill to Dalmeny Station, and walk along the railway line to the viaduct. Challenged by the sentry, with a rifle aimed at my stomach, I'd call out to him 'Edinburgh Castle', or 'Wee Wullie Winkie', or 'Highland Fling', or whatever the password happened to be, and be told in return to 'Pass Friend!' Idiotic language. But the language of freedom.

I was alone on that beautiful and massive bridge. Alone in an incredible world of isolation in the black of midnight. With nearly two miles to go. I can't remember that I felt then anything but open satisfaction at beating the system and being where I was; but when I think now of that lonely and hazardous trek beside the rails to the far north shore, I surprise myself.

There were some wild nights of wind and storm. I had never made the journey in daylight, so I was always feeling my way. But I was eighteen, and at that age experience is everything. You can do anything. I was lucky to be there. I had a small haversack with me containing scones and cakes baked by my mother. A small bit of home was going back with me for comfort.

Sometimes trains came out of the north, crashing past with a drawn-out shriek, quivering my solitary world, while I clung to the rail. When they had gone, clattering into the darkness, I seemed more alone than ever. Far below me, in the impenetrable blackout of the west, lay the naval base of Rosyth, sheltered in a wide bay beyond the bridge; the Rosyth to which the battered British Fleet had limped back after the Battle of Jutland just a year before. Directly below me, but unseen, were the small fortified islands of Inchgarvie and Inchcolm, and farther away down the Firth, the larger Inchkeith. Beyond was the North Sea; the North Sea or German Ocean as we had named it in our geography lessons at school.

Inchgarvie! That strikes a chord. Some years ago I wrote for a magazine a brief account of my Forth Bridge experiences. It prompted a reader Arthur Logan, of Balerno, to write to the magazine:

'Mr Drawbell's description of how, when only eighteen he often walked across the Forth Bridge from South Queensferry to Inverkeithing reminds me that during the First World War, when I was a member of the Forth Royal Garrison Artillery company manning the battery on the island of Inchgarvie, upon which rests one of the pedestals supporting the bridge, I was occasionally detailed to carry the outgoing mail bag from Garvie northwards across the bridge for delivery to the post office at Inverkeithing.

'This entailed the climbing of the long flight of steps (my memory says 139 steps) from the stone pedestal at Inchgarvie before emerging through the man-hole in the cat-walk on to the actual bridge. Normally one walked alongside the railings bordering the foot-track but there were occasions on dark nights of howling, gale-force winds and driving rain or snow when one had recourse to walking on the lower level between the actual railway lines, all the time listening intently and keeping a wary eye open for the possible approach of an engine or train from the north. I was then a good few years older than Mr Drawbell's eighteen and, although not scared in any way, it wasn't altogether a pleasant journey but quite an experience.

'I have heard men tell of the sight of British warships limping up the Firth of Forth, battered and broken, on their return from the Battle of Jutland; and of the disastrous occasion on the bridge when a detachment of the Inchgarvie garrison, carrying rifles and proceeding along the cat-walk, was mown down – some being killed and others seriously maimed – by a rifle becoming inadvertently jammed in the wheel of a moving train or engine and dealing out this terrible damage to life and limb.'

You see what I mean.

At the end of the bridge, I had still another two miles to walk to get to camp, but it was along a main coast road, reached after I had somehow slithered down from the high railway track. I could not remember just where that happened, but I know that it was before I got as far as North Queensferry station.

Crossing the bridge now after Ken Roy's party, I peered out of the window of the smooth modern diesel, trying to piece together something of my memories. It was all so different with lights on the north shore and the south; lights up the river towards Grangemouth; lights directly below from ships on the water; and in the east Inchkeith sprouting a lighthouse. Its beam came on while I gazed towards it. I had a personal identity with this bridge.

3

I wanted now, in the daylight of a lifetime afterwards, to walk again that Forth Bridge which I had half-stumbled across in the blackness of my Saturday nights, never knowing or seeing where my feet were treading. A closer acquaintance with it could at the least be regarded as a kind of recompense for past inconvenience. How pleasant to stroll over it in the bright sunshine and come face-to-face with it.

But getting on to the bridge proved to be as great a problem as when I required a password. Then, the bridge had belonged to the army; now it was the jealously-guarded property of British Railways.

'Ye canna jist walk on to the bridge,' said the man who came out of the little wooden house on the approach from Dalmeny Station to question me. I should have known better. Anyone can walk across the new Forth Road Bridge. There is a spacious pavement on each side flanking the road traffic that streams past for north or south.

When I mentioned this to my questioner, his head seemed to rise a little with a kind of derision and pride.

'Oh ay; that's for cars and lorries and anybody that wants to walk it. But this is still the railway bridge, the real Forth Bridge.' The strong noble old-fashioned reddish one with the three spans on it.

I could tell him a thing or two. He listened with polite interest. He could have known little if anything of that First War that was to end all wars. He'd never walked the bridge as I had; had probably never been on it in the dark. If so, I thought scornfully, he'd have flash lights, torches or even searchlights to make it easy for him.

'Ay, that must have been something,' he conceded; 'but how did you come by the password? I mean, you were only a private, you said.'

Full marks.

'I won it,' I told him, laughing at the memory.

He guessed what I meant and laughed with me.

He returned to reality. 'Ay, well, you'll have to win yerself an official pass afore ye get on this bridge, son.'

I had forgotten the old-fashioned way Scotsmen can say 'son' to each other, even though the man addressed is often older than the speaker. It's an affectionate term, putting men together in the same category as brothers. As this man used it, he meant it protectively, like giving advice to a young lad. He was accepting me as one of his kind. The 'son' softened the disappointment he was passing on. This man's wife, and other Scotswomen like her, might use the word 'hen' when talking guidingly to a girl or woman. 'Oh, ye don't go doon that street, hen; ye turn to the right and keep straight on.'

A diesel slid slowly past us from the north and stopped at Dalmeny Station; another passed swiftly through headed for the north, with people at the windows getting ready to enjoy the view from the train. My companion's attention was now on his job, and I left him with a wave. I would have little difficulty about getting a pass. From the station, I phoned Max McAuslane. As editor of the *Edinburgh Evening News* he could fix it for me with British Railways.

'Leave it to me,' he said at once. 'Any particular day you'd like to choose?'

I mentioned a day a week or two ahead.

'What about lunch?' he asked. 'Are you coming in to Edinburgh now?'

But as I had my car parked at Dalmeny station, I had already made my decision to push into the blue. I did not quite know where, but I had a few golf clubs in the boot and St Andrews was not so far away.

'Lucky you!' said Max.

It was luck indeed to be able to go off where and when I liked.

I drove down the hill to South Queensferry, parked my car facing the sea between the two bridges, sat for a few minutes admiring distant Fife and the Lomonds. I got out to look around. There were only a few cars parked along the sea front, but behind me I had noticed a couple of touring coaches, there were lots of people in the little town, and the café and souvenir shop seemed to be doing brisk business. I was glad to see that. Things were bucking up. I went round to the landing stage which, for hundred of years, was used by the ferries crossing to and from North Queensferry.

Shortly after the new Road Bridge was opened by the Queen in September 1964, I had motored up to Aberdeen. The thought came to me then to drop down off the main motorway, which now by-passed South Queensferry, to see how this favourite little town of mine was faring. It wasn't faring at all well. In fact it had an appearance that reminded me of Goldsmith's deserted village. The ferries had all gone. A ghostly board on the old landing stage still said FERRY; all that was left of busy other days. The village was empty. I pulled up at the garage for petrol and a chat.

'Pretty dull,' I said to the nice girl who supplied me.

'It's the new bridge.'

'Nobody coming here any more?'

She shrugged. 'We're only doing about a quarter of the business.'

'The same with everybody else?'

'We're all in the same boat.' And then realizing that that was the wrong word to use, laughed for the first time. 'I mean, we're sunk. Or it looks like it.'

I looked along the lonely front towards the little town tapering into a bottle-neck. There was no traffic in that bottle-neck. A train rumbled overhead on the railway bridge. The purr of a passing car could not kill the sound. You could hear the gulls skirling.

I had spent many happy hours in this little place in my youth, waiting for the ferry. Sometimes it was a nuisance and a waste of precious time to have to take your place in the car queue on the special occasions when it stretched right along the street. St Andrews and the

Open Golf Championship were somewhere ahead, waiting for us all, and we were dependent on the boats to get us across the water. But what fun it was to be able to enjoy the leisurely crossing, to stretch legs standing in the wind, to be part of the beauty of the river and the banks on either side. And if you were going even further north and had to cross the Tay, the prospect of two main water crossings on a day's journey was an adventure and a poetic experience as well.

It had been a personally pleasant experience that first time when I came back to pull out of the brand new bridge road and slip down to South Queensferry, park my car facing the sea, buy a hot pie from the café and spend ten minutes of sheer delight, remembering the past, enjoying the present loveliness. But it was far from pleasant to face the reality of the idle town. Was this how a proud little town that had played its part in history died?

Some people didn't intend to let it die. Ernest Wells, who ran the popular café, and some of his friends, banded themselves together to change things. One was Gerry McTeague, owner of the Hawes garage; another was Bobby Mackinnon, mine host at Seals Craig Hotel. Alan Harrower lent a hand. So too did Andrew Todd, then a Town Councillor in charge of roads.

They went to the Secretary of State for Scotland. If anyone could get something done, he surely could. All they wanted was that their town should not be by-passed or forgotten. They asked that a large notice board should be placed on the wide new Bridge motorway, just before the lead-off lane marking their own South Queensferry. The town meant little to the thousands who were now speeding past it, many unaware of its history. Before, their route north would automatically have dipped down into the town to board the ferry. They might have to wait. They might *prefer* to wait, and catch a later ferry. They might have lunch at the famous Hawes Inn, mentioned in Sir Walter Scott's novel *Antiquary* and Stevenson's *Kidnapped.* They could wander through the town, picnic on one of the seats looking across the Forth, see the famous old church.

All that Ernest Wells and his friends requested was that their large notice on the main road should tell the speeding motorist that South Queensferry existed! A few words only to show the traveller what he was missing. A modest and natural request you might think.

But you have to understand how things are conducted in Scotland, over-lorded for over two and a half centuries by England. There is no Scottish Parliament; there are few requirements that can be met by a sensible and swift decision in Edinburgh. Down to London go the causes and claims, the pleadings, the reasons. How many of them are ignored or forgotten only the Scots know. And probably they don't even know the half of it. In my sojourns in Edinburgh I was gradually becoming aware of many things. I had had no yardstick with which to measure the land I loved and left as a young man. It never entered my head that Scotland had faults or that the Scots were not the salt of the earth.

I had been more than forty years out of it. All the years I had been knocking about the world, forming tenuous love affairs with different countries and cities, making contacts with so many people, periodically pulling myself up and setting out once more for the mirage on the horizon, and making a mish-mash of my life and habits and emotions, life had been going on where I had left off in Scotland.

I returned with the same beliefs about it that I had taken away with me. I foolishly expected Edinburgh not only to be its incredibly lovely and unique self, but to be something of a London and a New York as well. I ought not to have been disappointed at the discovery that it wasn't; I should have been highly pleased. And to find that it was a small town, with a small town's ways, ought not to have dismayed but delighted me. But surprise was my real reaction.

I was surprised, too, where I had expected the keenness and zest with which I had always associated Scots, to encounter instead what seemed to me to be apathy and indifference. A kind of inertia, almost a lack of ambition, a cautious if not actually a suspicious approach to innovation or enterprise. This was the real shock. I had always thought of my people as men and women who were afraid of nothing. I could see little of the fighting defiant spirit and the rugged individualism I had expected. I had mostly in my own life made the mistake of leading with my chin. I had seen other Scots do the same. We were brought up to say what we thought, to stand up for what we believed. The one thing you could stake your life on was that a Scot was never a yes-man.

One of the most brilliant young men of my generation, A.G. Macdonnell, had set it down squarely in his book, *My Scotland*:

'The Lowlander is direct in thought and speech and deed, and this is often mistaken for bad manners. In a sense of course it is bad manners. But in another sense it is a perfection of manners, for it cuts out all the fripperies and exposes at once a complete sincerity. The shattering bluntness of the Lowlander means that you are not being deceived. Without the waste of a moment he shows you what is in his mind. You may not like his method but you must admire his unflinching integrity of thought. He values his own sincerity more than he values your praise. His manners bring him enemies, but enemies have never been so repugnant to him as frippery.'

But that was written nearly forty years ago. Maybe they were still like that, but I was noticing evidence of change. Had a slow erosion of character been going on throughout the years? I could see little indication of a people 'direct in thought and speech and deed'. Sometimes they struck me more like people in a railway carriage that had been shunted into a siding. Not indignant people, thrusting their heads out of windows to know what the hell was the matter, and who was doing what about it? They were accepting the situation. That was it. Their attitude was one of passive acceptance. The train might have been waiting there for ages. They did not in fact seem to expect it to move. They were submissively getting on with their reading or knitting, filling in their football pools, and puffing at cigarettes or pipes. Nobody it seemed was going to put his foot through a window in anger. Why bother?

Now and again I had the oddest feeling that Scotland didn't seem to belong anywhere, even to itself. I was quite sure it hadn't always been like this, but the coming back and living with it for a while made it noticeable, the contrast with the outside world so marked.

We were like someone's poor relations; and I suppose that when you have little say in your own affairs you do become like a poor relation. When you see Great Britain always referred to as England, as though Scotland and Wales and Ulster were no part of it, that must have some psychological effect, however small. When you know that your country's business gets a few hours' time in a year at Westminster, you are bitter at first and then indifferent. I felt as if some malignant growth of an inferiority complex, once only a fear but now a reality, had been slowly growing within the body since the Union with England in 1707.

I tried some of these thoughts on David Hastie, half expecting him to be provoked and annoyed. David is the one-hundred-per-cent Scot. He is nearer to it all than I. He is one of the most down-to-earth Feature Editors in the newspaper game. He was a features editor at twenty-eight. And he is a Glasgow man.

The people of Glasgow are something special. They pull no phoney stuff on you, but give it to you straight. They have a long-standing contempt and derision for Edinburgh people, whom they see as stuck-up and pretentious, nearer the English concept of living than the folk of any other town in Scotland. David wasn't angry; he didn't lash out at me in rebuttal of my vaguely-defined impressions.

'Why?' he repeated my last word. 'Because they feel down-trodden. Imposed upon. If you like, "conned" by centuries of having to submit to the people of the south. *They* get all the pickings. It makes people here feel insecure and resentful. One of the results, all that Scottish push and bragging, is only a form of asserting themselves. They're basically insecure. Like kids lashing out without knowing why they do it.'

I began to understand why some diehards, still vocal and virile, were sounding off with battle cries. Up the Scots! Few Scots want a revolution, and nobody wants bloodshed. Only a minority want Home Rule, and most are quite glad to go along with England. But *all* want a Scottish Parliament that can represent their own people and further their business, understand their aspirations, cherish and encourage their hopes, and respect their traditions. The humiliating position into which the Scots have been forced, with shameful acquiescence on their own part, has never been understood by the English.

5

Why shouldn't Ernest Wells and the good citizens of South Queensferry be able to get a decision about their request without reference to London? What the hell had it to do with London? Wasn't there a Secretary of State for Scotland looking after his peoples' interests from an office in Edinburgh?

But the Secretary of State for Scotland had indeed to refer to London. About a notice board on the motorway to the Forth Bridge! And London in due course turned down the suggestion, adding that if every hamlet in the British Isles wanted a board on a main highway, etcetera, etcetera.

Then the stalwarts in South Queensferry really went wild. A hamlet indeed! Did London know nothing of the history of this royal and municipal burgh, which indeed had been a burgh since 1363? Did they know nothing of its associations with the kings of Scotland, and Scotland's Church, that dated back to Malcolm Canmore and his Queen Margaret, after whom the ferry is named? Didn't they know that the ferry was the principal passage for the Scottish kings when they resided at Dunfermline in the kingdom of Fife, where Malcolm Canmore founded the Benedictine Abbey in 1072, which was the burial place of Scottish kings until the fourteenth century? That James VI of Scotland gave the ferry as a wedding present to his bride, Anne of Denmark? Three of his children were Henry, Prince of Wales, Charles I, and Elizabeth, from whom our present Royal Family is descended.

So much history was ferried over this waterway, which is the very heart of Scotland. A hamlet indeed!

As the years went by Queensferry came under the thumb of the Kirk. In 1635 it was decreed that 'whatsoever persons shall break the Sabbath by sailing their great or small boats to ply this Ferry from the rising of the sun to the 12th hour of the day, these persons shall be fined for the first fault in 12s Scots, and if they shall fail in the same fault again they shall stand at our Kirk door in sackcloth and make confession of their fault before the congregation.'

No wonder the people of South Queensferry fought to save their historic and picturesque township. They wanted people to share in its pride, its beautiful Norman church at Dalmeny, the memorial hall built by Lord Roseberry in memory of his wife, and Hopetoun House, the seat of the Marquess of Linlithgow close by.

This hamlet! Forty-eight hours after Queen Elizabeth opened the new Road Bridge in 1964, the last ferry – the *Queen Margaret* – left North Queensferry for the south bank, and in mid-stream between the two great bridges 500 people took part in a service of worship to mark the closure of the centuries-old ferry.

Ernest Wells and his friends had to fight. There was still plenty of official resistance and bloody-mindedness. But now everybody in the town knew what was at stake. Of course they won the day, and the right to erect their large notice. But permission was given grudgingly, and with conditions attached. They had to pay for their notice. £280 of blood money. You have to beat English officialdom or die. Lord

Roseberry pitched in, as did Lord Primrose, and several local contractors, until the price came down to about £20 from each contributor.

It was pleasant to me that day, only a few years after the bloodshed and the fighting, to see that South Queensferry was becoming restored to its old respectable self, head up in the air, belligerence justified. And as I write these words Mr Goodwillie, the town's Postmaster, tells me that out of the ashes of despair there has emerged a larger and more thriving community than before the new bridge was opened. The new commercial importance of South Queensferry, with its two bridges and near-by airport (and its closeness to Edinburgh), has brought in factories, offices, new houses, and a Forth Bridges Motel. The population has jumped from 2,400 in 1963 (when he took up his appointment) to over 5,000.

And somehow it isn't completely irrelevant that a story told me by my doctor friend, Tom Wilkie-Millar, should flash across my mind at this moment.

Tom was in Edinburgh, at the top of Leith Street, which has always been a tough quarter. I can remember fights there among sailors and drunks, and their molls, from my school days, with tempers flaring and fists flying.

A small scattering of a crowd was gathering. Tom, always the doctor at the ready, joined it. He could not quite push through, but he saw enough. One man was on the ground, another astride him, belting with both fists. The people around were making no move to intercede.

At that moment a motor bicycle with a young mechanic on it turned out of Princes Street into Leith Street. The mechanic saw the commotion, pulled up sharply, jumped off his bike, went right through the crowd like a bull-dozer, pulled the aggressor off the fallen man, bashed him with one terrific right hook, turned scornfully on the crowd saying, 'A fine lot of brave buggers you are!', mounted his throbbing bike and drove off. 'The timing,' said Wilkie-Millar, 'was like a film. We all stood flabbergasted.'

VII

1

I know you should never give them a lift. They'll knife you, or mug you, or take over your car. Especially when they're in pairs; and that part of the advice I listen to and occasionally observe. I am no hero, but I found it easy to slow down and stop very often on my journeys, and to share the company of young people on the Scottish roads.

This young man was on his own, a smallish bare-headed figure, in a neat dark-blue pullover and blue jeans, with a slim rucksack on his back. No sleeping bag; no guitar. He was about a hundred yards ahead when I rounded a corner on the way to Kinross, trudging along the green verge. I didn't give it a thought. I slowed down.

He didn't even turn round and make the violent gestures. Just his right thumb making an almost imperceptible movement in the direction we were both going as he continued walking. He wasn't going to plead with anybody.

I braked and he turned round. He had the faint reddish tinge in his hair, and a freckle or two under the light blue-grey eyes. Twenty-one or two, I thought; his shirt was clean and he had certainly washed that morning. No beard, no moustaches, no sideburns. Ten-to-one no flick knife. I leaned over.

'How far you going?'

'Lossiemouth.'

Even in the single, three-syllable word there was the Glasgow lilt.

He grinned broadly. Lossiemouth was nearly 150 miles further on.

I didn't know where I was going, but I wasn't going that far. Not this day anyway.

'I'll drop you where I feel like turning off the main road,' I said. 'OK?'

'Fine. Anything's a bonus.'

He settled himself comfortably. In a few minutes he said, 'You really done 61,000 miles in this?'

I had to look at my own mileage to check the young detective.

'So it says.'

'She runs like new.'

'I bought her new.'

'Ah!' The wisdom of all his years in the word. 'That's why. Know them from the beginning, treat them right. It's the only way.'

I watched the road ahead and asked: 'You a mechanic or something?'

'Nope.'

There it was again. They all have an American expression somewhere in their make-up. Nope, or yep, or certainly-is.

But he volunteered no further information about himself. He was a seeker of facts.

'How many miles you get to the gallon?'

'Varies. Average about thirty.'

'Ve-r-r-y good. Certainly is smooth.'

I gave him a side-long glance, and guessed: a student. I should have got it first time. But he ought to have been headed for the University of St Andrews, thirty miles ahead.

'Why Lossiemouth?' I asked.

'Uh?'

'Why Lossiemouth?'

'Ramsay Mac.,' he said.

That one surprised me.

'Ramsay Mac.?' I repeated.

'Ramsay MacDonald.'

One of us was nuts. I began to wonder if they were right after all about pick-ups on the road.

'You won't find Ramsay MacDonald in Lossiemouth,' I said cautiously. 'He's been dead quite a long time. Since 1937 in fact.'

'Oh, you know something about him?'

The nerve of these kids. Life began for them around 1948. I should have been the one surprised that one of his generation had even heard of Ramsay MacDonald.

'Not only heard about him,' I said smugly. 'I happened to know him.

I met him several times.'

He swung right round and stared at me.

'No kidding?' He really said it. 'You wouldn't kid me?'

'Why should I?'

'But it's all so long ago.'

The poignancy of the words. Everything is all so long ago.

'Well, I must admit I was a bit younger than Ramsay Mac. But I did know him.'

'How?'

'I was a newspaper editor in London. I knew quite a few people.' Justifying myself to this brat!

'Boy, oh boy.' More to himself than me. 'My horoscope said I'd meet a helpful stranger.'

I laughed aloud with pleasure. He was no goon, but a native son with the native type of humour.

2

I pulled the car into a lay-by. He took a packet of cigarettes out of his pocket and offered me one. I held out my lighter to him.

'What's your interest in MacDonald?' I asked. 'I didn't think anybody remembered him any more.'

'Or Karl Marx?'

'I didn't know him!'

'Oh, but they're both part of the story.'

It began to dawn.

'You're writing a book?'

Freckled people are inclined to blush. The tiniest show of pink came into his young face.

'Not quite,' he said. 'Or rather not yet. A thesis.'

'On what?'

'The economic development of Britain.'

Boy, you should *always* give them a lift!

'For my degree. I'm reading economics and economic history at Glasgow University. I want to do a *real* thesis. Not only the facts and the analyses and the figures, but the principal people and what made them what they were. That's the basis of everything. What motivates people.'

A sprinkle of traffic passed us. Motoring in Scotland is still a pleasure. The cars aren't packed together bumper to bumper. We could hear ourselves talk. It was quiet around us. The Perthshire hills lay ahead.

'Why economics?' I asked.

His mouth tightened.

'My father was a miner,' he said. 'I heard plenty from him.'

I understood. I'd listened to the same from Welsh boys.

'He made me swear on the Bible that I'd never go down a mine. He didn't need to worry. I'd made up my own mind.'

We sat in silence for a few minutes. This thing in Britain is almost pathological; it'll take generations to wipe it out.

'Did you know that mothers and their daughters used to have to work in the mines in Scotland?' he asked.

Before I could answer he had fished out a notebook from his pocket. 'Listen to this from the Royal Commission on the Mines in 1842,' he said, and read his notes: 'The mother descends the pit with her older daughters, when each sets down her basket and into it the large coals are rolled: such is the weight that it frequently takes two men to lift the burden upon their backs: the girls are loaded according to their strength.

'The mother sets out first, carrying a lighted candle in her teeth; the girls follow, and in this manner they proceed to the pit bottom and with weary steps ascend the stairs to the top, where the coals are laid down for sale.'

He raised his eyes to look at me.

'In Scotland!' he said. 'It makes you think.'

I told him that I knew the Report he was reading; that it all happened over a hundred years ago. He bent his head and read aloud: 'They go on like this for eight or ten hours almost without resting. It is no uncommon thing to see them when ascending the pit weeping most bitterly from the excessive severity of the labour.'

I could have added to his condemnation. The conditions in the East of Scotland, where girls as well as boys worked underground, were appalling. These children began when they were only six or seven years of age to face a day of fourteen hours and even more.

But I only asked: 'How much do you know about Ramsay Mac.?

'Not much; I'm only beginning on his human side, but I want to delve plenty. There's something about the man that fascinates me. He seems to have been more of an evangelist than what we know now as a socialist.'

I looked thoughtfully at the young man. Out of the mouths of babes and sucklings. I had always thought of MacDonald as the complete evangelist, a dreamer and inspirer; never a man haggling over wage demands. MacDonald would work to bring about Utopia; other men in another day would reap the rewards and revenge themselves on Capital by wringing its withers. Did this boy know how far the pendulum had swung? In his father's day it wasn't a case of strikes but of lock-outs and starvation. For every job ten men were available. On that summer day of 1970 when we sat by the Perth road, Britain was a country of practically full employment.

'He was a poor boy, wasn't he?' said the young man who, before we went much further, I was calling Sandy.

'He was also illegitimate.'

I wanted to see how he took it.

'I didn't know that.' And then: 'Does it matter?'

'Not so much today. And it shouldn't matter at all. But can you imagine what it was like a hundred years ago? You know your history.'

'I see,' he said slowly. 'You're getting round to motivation.'

'You mentioned the word. Man,' I said almost angrily, 'a girl in this country hadn't a chance if she was with bairn. In Cronin's *Hatter's Castle,* Meg was thrown out of the house by her father. That was fiction. It happened all the time in real life. So you can guess what it was like for the child. Unwanted. It was a pretty bloody beginning.'

He picked up the haversack and opened it. I saw a couple of books, a note book, a clean shirt, a spare pair of socks, a toothbrush, a razor. Not much else. He took out the note-book.

'Hold it,' I said. 'Not here. I've got a better idea.'

A truck had pulled in behind us. The driver was opening a tin of sandwiches. It was time to eat.

3

I started up the car. We were on the outskirts of Kinross and I remembered the Green Hotel at the far end of the little town. A good hotel, standing in a large garden with a huge lawn. I drew up outside.

The boy was taken aback.

'Hey..!' he began, 'I can't possibly ....'

'You wouldn't be a student if you could,' I said. 'Hop out and I'll tell you a story as we go for a drink before lunch.'

He had a bitter lemon; I had a Cinzano bianco. It always gives me the feeling that I'm in the south of France. Kidding myself that I'm lying on the hot sand after a swim. As we raised glasses I told him of a week I once spent in the Mediterranean with George Bernard Shaw. I was in my mid-thirties, Shaw was in his mid-seventies. He was sailing with his wife, Charlotte, as far as South Africa, I was getting off the ship at Genoa. But we touched port at several places, and Shaw and I went ashore. Whenever we needed refreshment, and I reached for my money to pay, Shaw chided me gently: 'This is an old man's privilege.'

'So,' I told Sandy, 'I'm in the position of the older man now; it's my privilege.'

We made a leisurely lunch of it. I had all the time in the world; Sandy was living his horoscope. He had his notebook on the table, and I was glad to see that he also had had the sense to acquire shorthand. He made his own kind of notes. He would know what he wanted to research for himself from the story I told him, which began on a January evening in 1924, when I was one of a vast audience in the Albert Hall in London.

I was then twenty-four, living in a boarding-house in Cromwell Road in South Kensington and trying, like all the young ones then, to make my way upward in the great city.

I had walked the short distance to the Albert Hall, because walking was about the only exercise I got in those days, and walking and saving were synonymous. But I also wanted the time to think of the occasion. I was a journalist, and aware that history that evening was being made, and I wanted to savour something of it.

The fact that the central figure in the drama in the Albert Hall was also a Scot had naturally something to do with my thoughts. There were few Scots who were left unmoved by what was happening. Whatever the nature of their politics, their hearts must have been stirred by the rise to the top of one of their countrymen.

I wasn't much of a political person; my sympathies were mostly with the under-dog and in those days of 1924 there were plenty of underprivileged.

That was what that far-off evening was all about. It was the dream come true of men who had struggled for what, only a few years before, had seemed impossible. That great excited mass of men and women, their faces flushed, their hearts high with triumph, had met together to

100

hold a Victory Demonstration celebrating the remarkable Labour gains in the recent General Election.

The gains had not been enough to give the party a clear majority over the other parties, but they were in second place. The Conservatives were closely ahead, the Liberals closely behind. All depended on a working arrangement in Parliament. Anything could happen; there might be, for the first time in the history of this country, a Labour Government.

If so, it would be led by James Ramsay MacDonald. The hero of that evening, he stood up to a frenzy of applause, of admiration, even of worship. Handsome, distinguished, with a head of greying hair, glowing dark eyes, and a voice that thrilled and moved, he had been — only six years before — the most hated man in Britain. His attitude to the war of 1914–18, misrepresented and misunderstood, had lost him his seat in Parliament.

His party had been in the wilderness, yet by his leadership and personality he had brought them to this evening of victory. To them, then, he was a god. They listened to him expressing their dearest wishes.

> 'We are a party of idealists. We are a party that away in the dreamland of imagination dwells in the social organization fairer and more perfect than any organization that mankind has ever known. We are upon a pilgrimage, we are on a journey. One step enough for me. One step. Yes, on one condition — that it leads to a next step.'

One step enough for me. The old hymn. Someone has said that for every Socialist created by *Das Kapital* a thousand have been created by the Bible. Ramsay MacDonald had in him the true evangelical spirit. His voice, his faith, his words, were all in a spiritual rather than a political key.

Today, when it is all economics, it is difficult to remember that there was a time when Labour was a spiritual crusade, leading men out of darkness into light. It was this that Ramsay MacDonald understood; it was this that he had lived. From his earliest days in Lossiemouth, brought up in poverty, it was the hunger of the human heart that he knew, as well as the hunger of the body. At fifty-eight, after a lifetime of hard work, and on the way to becoming Prime Minister, the spirit was still with him that evening as he ended his speech.

'Nineteen twenty-four is not the last in God's programme of creation. The shield of love and the spear of justice will still be in the hands of good and upright men and women, and the ideal of a great future will still be in front of our people. I see no end, thank God, to those things. That is my faith, and in that faith I go on and my colleagues go on, to contribute something substantial to the well-being, the happiness and the holiness of human life.'

A few days later King George V asked him to form a Government. Although the General Election had gone against Stanley Baldwin, the Conservative Premier had decided to stay in office and await defeat in the House of Commons. He presented his King's Speech. Labour and Liberals joined forces in the debate that followed and the Government was defeated. Baldwin resigned. Ramsay MacDonald, in spite of divisions of opinion in his party, took on the job of running a minority Government.

'Why will we take office? Because we are to shirk no responsibility that comes to us in the course of the evolution of our Movement. There are risks, certainly.' He could say that again. They descended upon him thick and fast. Holding the fort against the Conservatives only with the uneasy support of the Liberal Party was a job in itself. He must, in the difficult days that followed, have been a man always looking over his shoulder.

Yet, if he looked further back, what was there for him to fear? The road since his birth in Lossiemouth in 1866 had been rough enough. His first home was his grandmother's cottage, a two-roomed 'but-and-ben' close to the railway. From the beginning he was deprived of the love and protection of a father, a loss that would affect him all his life.

His mother, Annie Ramsay, was a young servant girl in a farm-house near Lossiemouth. She lost her heart to a ploughman named MacDonald working in its fields. They became engaged, their banns were about to be published in the local kirk, and then they had a quarrel. Annie told her lover that it was all off. She would not become his wife.

He protested that she was going to have his child.

It made no difference to Annie Ramsay. She never changed her mind and went to live with her widowed mother in a cottage near Lossiemouth. When MacDonald was born he was christened James. He was brought up by his mother, and her mother. For many years afterwards their friends called him simply Jimmy Ramsay. Later he adopted his father's surname. His attractive mother received many proposals of marriage but she refused them all.

Two women and a bairn. And poverty. It was not an unusual situation in those days, or even today. But it was not the most promising beginning for the man who, overcoming all his disadvantages, would become Prime Minister.

On a day in 1966 some newspapers mentioned the centenary of his birth in a small paragraph. The larger news was all about the wages freeze, the flight from the pound, our terrible economic plight, and the falling exports. We have been here before. Ramsay MacDonald had seen the future differently: 'I see my horizon, I see my own skyline, but I am convinced that when my children or children's children get there, there will be another skyline, another horizon, another dawning.'

4

A lot of horizons have been reached and crossed since Ramsay MacDonald was born in Lossiemouth. A lot were passed in his own lifetime. He overcame the early burden of poverty. He avoided, by his own bright spirit and readiness to learn, the fate of leaving school early. Indeed, he left school and 'howked tatties' for his first few shillings, but his dominie, the Rev. John MacDonald, had quickly recognized that here was an exceptional boy, and brought him back into the school as a pupil teacher.

He was avid for learning, reading everything he could lay his hands on, from Samuel Smiles to High Miller's *My Schools and Schoolmasters.* A copy of Henry George's *Progress and Poverty* came his way, and MacDonald knew then the road he had to travel.

London was his goal, the huge friendless city where he did not know a soul. Lonely, almost excessively shy, carrying his own private family tragedy within him, he went through the drill of so many other young men before him – and since – trudging the streets looking for work. Any work. He addressed envelopes; he became an invoice clerk at twelve shillings and sixpence a week; in the evenings he studied at the Birkbeck Institute. His appetite for scientific books was insatiable.

What happened to his other appetite? He has himself described how he bought his food around the slums of King's Cross, but his staple food, oatmeal, was sent to him from his home in Scotland, as it was to so many young Scots (students and workers) away from home. Tea and coffee were out of the question, so he made do with hot water. His midday meal was in a restaurant, usually a beefsteak pudding. His total cost for food each day was sevenpence.

Yet he managed to save enough money to take a holiday in Scotland, and all the time he was paying fees at the Birkbeck Institute, the City of London College, and the Highbury Institute. His health broke down, his little store of capital vanished; but at this critical stage in his fortunes he had the good luck to meet Thomas Lough, the Liberal candidate for West Islington. He became Tommy Lough's private secretary, at a salary of £75 per annum, rising to £100, and a new life of opportunity opened up for him.

Tommy Lough got the services of an intelligent young man interested in economics and politics; MacDonald, for four years, saw politics from the inside, mingled with men and women prominent in the political and social world, contributed articles to various publications. He was twenty-eight when he wrote to Keir Hardie applying for membership of the newly-formed Independent Labour Party, and six years later, in 1900, when the Labour Party was born, he was elected its first secretary.

'He was a godsend to us,' declared one Trade Union official. That could be well understood. Here, at the very beginning of the Movement, was the guiding hand of an able and driving young man of remarkable personality and appearance, cultured, experienced in behind-the-scenes politics, eloquent, dedicted to improving the social and spiritual condition of mankind. It was a fortuitous marriage.

Another marriage was in the offing, one that would at last give solace to the inner loneliness of MacDonald and bring him the help of a woman of sympathy and understanding. Margaret Gladstone was the daughter of a distinguished chemist and Professor of the Royal Institution, and a niece of Lord Kelvin, the famous chemist. She shared Ramsay Mac.'s hopes and enthusiasms. Indeed, their first meeting was brought about by a letter he received when he was the ILP candidate for Southampton. The letter was signed 'M.E. Gladstone,' and with it came a subscription for his election fund.

They were married when he was thirty; their union was blessed in every way. Fifteen years later, when he was rising high in his career, tragedy struck at him. In February, his little son David died of diphtheria. Eight days later, his mother died in Lossiemouth. In July, his wife was taken seriously ill and passed away within a few months. She was forty-one.

After that it was only work, and work, and work. Time heals; work helps. MacDonald continued on his way, his passion winning millions to his faith. Criticized, ridiculed, lampooned, adored; the target for innuendo and enmity and bitter opposition; the rallying point for a multitude of hopeful believing men and women. On and on till that evening in the Albert Hall, that victory, and the first minority Labour Government.

Had it ever a chance? How could it have, when the combined vote of Liberals and Conservatives could sweep it out of office? Should it ever have been formed? Should Ramsay MacDonald have accepted office at that stage and in those circumstances? That question will be debated in the Labour Party for a long time.

Soon enough the trouble-makers were at work. Someone discovered that Mr Alexander Grant, head of the famous biscuit manufacturers, McVitie & Price, of Edinburgh, had made a gift to Mr Ramsay MacDonald of a Daimler motor car and 30,000 shares in the business. Some newspapers at once drew attention to the fact that MacDonald, a Socialist Prime Minister who condemned capitalism, was himself a capitalist.

Alexander Grant and Ramsay MacDonald had played together as boys. Grant's father and MacDonald's uncle had been guards on the Highland Railway. Young Grant became an apprentice baker, and in time built up his very successful business. His gift to his boyhood friend was anything but an isolated act of charity. He was a generous giver to good causes.

I remember Lord Macmillan, the distinguished lawyer and Lord Advocate, telling me how Grant had donated £100,000 towards the founding of a Scottish National Library. When Grant's banker handed Lord Macmillan the signed cheque, the amount was left blank. Macmillan was told he could fill it in himself. It was he who wrote the figure £100,000. Then Grant gave another £100,000 towards the cost of a building to house the library.

When Mr Grant was subsequently created a Baronet, MacDonald was accused of trafficking in honours. His own defence in the House was a very lame affair. A note in my diary says, 'When the gift was discovered the Prime Minister's critics and enemies naturally made much of it. MacDonald was foolishly reticent in dealing with the question in the House of Commons.'

105

He was beset by criticism and hostility in whatever policy he pursued. Russia, that red rag to a bull, was down on his agenda. The Labour Government recognized the Soviet Government and arranged a general Treaty on Commerce and Navigation. More howls. But the cause of the collapse of the first Labour Government was what came to be known as the Campbell case.

The *Workers' Weekly* had addressed an open letter to the fighting forces 'calculated', said an Opposition MP, 'to undermine discipline and to create disaffection.' What was the Government going to do about it? In due course the Attorney-General (Sir Patrick Hastings) announced that an arrest had been made.

There was a fury of indignation among Labour members themselves. James Maxton asked the Prime Minister if he had read the article, which was merely a call to troops not to allow themselves to be used in industrial disputes. In the meantime, Sir Patrick Hastings had discovered other facts. He found it difficult to put in the dock, as a dangerous Communist, a man who had had both his feet almost blown off in the war, who had fought in the war from beginning to end, and who had been decorated for exceptional gallantry.

The Attorney-General decided to withdraw the case in the higher interests of the State. Immediately a debate was launched, the Opposition maintaining that the Prime Minister had interfered with the course of justice and had been compelled by pressure from the extremists in his Party to drop the case. At the end of the day the first Labour Government had fallen.

'It is the end,' declared MacDonald with courage and defiance, 'of what has been a high adventure which has contributed to the honour of the country and social stability, and which, when the country has had an opportunity of passing a verdict upon us, will come again.'

It was to come five years later, in 1929, when Labour swept back into office with greatly increased figures, but − once more − without a clear majority. In this situation lay the drama that followed, the tragedy of Ramsay MacDonald and his decline into the shadows.

Already the first rumbles of the economic blizzard that was to strike every country in the world were in the air. In July, at the opening of Parliament, the King's Speech looked forward hopefully to a long series of proposals which would affect agriculture, slum clearances, the coal and steel industries, factory legislation, National Insurance and Pensions, and a host of other much-needed reforms.

In October, Wall Street crashed and the financial structures everywhere caved in. The Great Depression, not immediately recognized as such, which would drag down economy after economy for the next five years, had entered like iron into mens' souls. In Great Britain it was the time of the dole, millions of unemployed, the hated Means Test for measuring a man's right to financial assistance. It was misery and deprivation and suffering unimaginable to anyone in this country who is under forty years of age.

5

In this atmosphere there began to be bruited around the idea of a National Government, a gathering together of all parties to face our common trials. The idea naturally first came from the Opposition. But there is evidence that Ramsay MacDonald was not averse to seeing himself still Prime Minister, leading a kind of State Council of the best in the nation.

There were secret parleys between the parties, private arrangements of details, worried Labour Ministers and members trying to get at the truth of all the comings and goings, the whispers, the rumours. In the end, the National Government was formed in 1931. Ramsay MacDonald was to be Prime Minister, aided and abetted by the Conservative and Liberal leaders. Inevitably, some of MacDonald's ministers would be dropped, but equally inevitably many of them would not care to take part in such an arrangement. The Labour Party was split right down the middle. Old friends and comrades of many years became enemies overnight, and remained so until the end.

The programme of national retrenchment called for by the new Government had its own results. People in receipt of poor relief in England and Wales went up by thirty per cent, and for Scotland by ninety per cent. There was a ten per cent cut in unemployment benefit.

MacDonald, surrounded by Conservative and Liberal Colleagues, was gradually manoeuvred out of office. In 1935 he resigned the Premiership but continued as Lord President of the Council. But his political life was finished. He sat aloof on a back bench, lonely and ignored. Old friends were now his enemies, his new allies in the Tory party slighted him. His health broke down under the strain and the ignominy. He was dead within two years.

I could talk about the tragedy of Ramsay MacDonald to young

Sandy, enlivening the dismal calamity with personal stories of him, but it was more difficult for me to put my finger on the truth behind the tragedy. Where did he fail? It is not necessarily failure to turn former friends into bitter enemies. That happens all the time. Almost all leaders are the targets of extreme admiration and detestation.

But in a movement like the Labour Party in those days, moved by deep spiritual as well as economic impulses, any defections such as MacDonald's, any compromise with the sworn enemy, must have seemed the meanest betrayal of everything they had fought for. At this greatest moment of their struggle, MacDonald's was the hand that turned victory to waste.

It was in the nature of things to overlook his previous services. By his own efforts he had become an organizer, a leader, a man of such cultural and intellectual ability that in his handling of world affairs he surprised and often bested the many foreign diplomats he met. He was high above his colleagues, and gave the party a character which made it acceptable to many people who had previously been suspicious. At the right time he was the right man. Indeed he was the only man.

Perhaps he was too clever, a victim of his own early deprivations and his Scottish ambition to rise above them. There was the initial insecurity in him, a haunting sense of loss, an inner conflict which at times of crisis might bend him towards a not impersonal bias and blur his judgment.

In his last years he was woolly, verbose and vague, clouding the real issues with words, words, words. Perhaps, without meaning to, he not only betrayed his followers but deceived himself.

6

About a week later I had a postcard from Lossiemouth, forwarded from the Scottish Liberal Club in Edinburgh. It read: 'Great; but you didn't tell me that Ramsay Mac. was sustained by his frequent revisits here, sometimes by single-seater plane and pilot, to seek the rejuvenating air of Lossiemouth. Important! Sandy.'

I *had* forgotten to mention that; and, yes, it was important. I remembered the newspaper photographs of Ramsay Mac., his grey hair tossed about his impressive head, stepping into – or getting out of – the open cockpit of the small plane that used to take him north, if only for a couple of days at a time.

But it was more than just the breezes of the Moray Firth he was seeking. It was contact with his native Scotland, the contact we all seem to need. The peace and quiet of it; the company of ordinary people who spoke the language he had learned in the lap of his mother and his mother's mother. It was Scotland that, perhaps, remained the only reality to him; and he had to return there often to gather up his strength to face the political jungle in London again.

VIII

1

Sometimes, stopping at a village or a small town, I could not get away from the idea that I was not in Scotland, but in a French village. Nobody was in a hurry. I thought once of the word, *mañana*, but that did not fit. Almost anything, it seemed, could be put off till tomorrow, but the atmosphere was French not Spanish.

In the shops, particularly the fruit shops which I often visited, I might have been in a French market. Everyone gossips with the shopkeeper. There is no such thing as time. You wait, listening. Sometimes the dialect is so broad, the words coming thick and slow or, in puzzling contradiction, quick and very highly pitched – half an octave higher than in England – that one could be in a foreign land. You feel almost like a tourist.

You have already passed through places with alien signposts and seen on shops names that quite obviously have some connection with our Auld Alliance with France. All Scotland has something of a lingering trace of the friendly country that shared our resistance to our common enemy England; but some places have it so marked that it is startling. And comfortingly pleasant.

The small fruit and vegetable shop is one of them. There the native character is exposed, naked and anything but ashamed. The reticence and reserve are not thrown to the winds. Each customer holds on to his own dignity or her own right to a private life outside the shop door. But within the shop, what a place to have a blether! And a blether, while shopping, is the spice of life.

You don't just buy an orange or a tomato or a banana. The

shopkeeper moves round to the bin with you to guide your purchase for your own benefit. Coming from England, where you have always been warned that the best is the most expensive, it is strange at first to hear the middle-aged woman who owns the shop knocking down her own profit.

'These cheaper ones have more juice in them,' she says, pressing an orange into my hand so that I might appreciate its softness and the thin skin. 'And much sweeter! I had one after lunch and it was awfu' good.'

She leans towards another box. 'Feel the thickness of these. They're bigger, ay! But not nearly as juicy. And a penny more each.'

The important penny to the Scot. How few people outside the country really understand our attitude towards money, born of the frugal nature of our country. The oldest of all the fables is the one about our being mean, and even grasping. One can laugh at the jokes: the postcards of the deserted town – 'Aberdeen on a Flag Day'; the after-dinner speeches with the jibe at the canny Scot looking after his money bags. But the Scots attitude towards money can be simply stated. In contrast to England where money is 'easy come, easy go', the Scots value with realism what has to be won the hard way and often with much sacrifice.

My shopkeeper's concern for my penny was the concern she would have felt for her own. A better article at a cheaper price. The sense of family in the Scottish people expressed in the phrase 'we're a' Jock Thomson's bairns', made her completely one with her customers. And it was this mutual understanding and trust that gave the flavour to the shop's gossip.

While waiting I had already heard the saga of one lady's husband who had hurt his knee badly while trying to land a trout.

'Was it a rainbow trout?' asked the knowing little shopkeeper. She had a shrewd, kindly face, wizened like an apple, that looked as if it knew all the town's secrets.

'However did you know?' asked the customer. 'Has someone else told you about it?'

'No, no. I just guessed it might be at that part of the river. Alec was saying the other night he'd seen rainbow trout there.'

All the while she was carefully emptying a brass scale-pan of potatoes into a brown paper wrapper for her customer before putting it in her shopping bag. I watched this with interest, having seen in other shops the same careful packaging of goods. Potatoes went into a brown paper bag which was tightly closed at the top and then sealed with cellotape. Bundles of rhubarb were never thrust bare at the customer, but were rolled into clean pages of newspaper and also sealed with cellotape. The shopkeepers have an acceptable mania for keeping the dirt of their merchandise from soiling customers' clothes or shopping bags. And a mania for cellotape. A cellotape dispenser is on most counters in almost every shop. It was in a small grocer's shop near Fort William that I first saw such an article, and at once procured one for myself.

'The rocks there are kinda slippery,' the shopkeeper said now, looking up from the potatoes, successfully wrapped.

'Ay, that's what happened.' And then, with all the time in the world, and the attentive sympathy of the little audience in the shop, came the full details: 'He'd just got the trout on the line and out of the water. A beauty, he says. Then it was away, but he held on and moved down the rock, his eye on the fish. And that did it. Before he knew where he was he slipped and caught his knee on a right jagged piece. It went through his trouser leg and into his knee. But you know what he is. He held on, in awfu' pain, jinking up and down the rocks.'

'That wouldn't do him any good,' said one of the enthralled ladies.

'No, it didn't. And in the end, the trout got away anyway. My, was he wild!'

'And what about his knee?' asked the shopkeeper, putting her finger on the really important part of the narrative.

'Terrible! He had to drive back fifteen miles with it. And when he got home it was a real mess. He could hardly move it. I got the doctor right away.'

I thought how lucky she was to get a doctor 'right away', but in these little communities, I was to learn, the doctor or a partner always seems to be available and willing. Their patients are personal friends with an almost religious trust in the doctors' readiness to be on hand, and their ability to heal.

'He did what he could, but just the same he took Tom off to the hospital to have an X-ray.'

They waited expectantly. The story would be recounted round a dozen tea tables, over gardens walls, at the coffee-mornings. The details were all-important, enlarged with the narrator's imagination, or her knowledge of medicine, gleaned usually from personal experience or the *Reader's Digest,* usefully ever-present in the dentist's or doctor's waiting room. Or quite often from a son or daughter studying medicine at one of the Scottish universities.

112

'Nothing broken,' she now reported gratefully; and then, in case the anti-climax minimized the accident; 'but an awful lot of fluid on the knee. They wanted to drain it off there and then; but you know what men are.' Evidently they did, for there was a low murmur. 'Tom asked if it wouldn't be all right to see how it was in a day or two. So he's going back to the hospital the day after tomorrow.'

I listened to see how right or wrong Tom had been. One of the ladies asked the question direct.

'Well, he has to keep his leg up, resting it,' she was told. 'And it seems to be awful sore and awful puffed.'

There was a silence while each of us turned the accident over in our minds, deciding that Tom had made a mistake to delay, or that he was heroically patient and wise. Or just that Tom was Tom.

'Of course,' the wife added, 'it only happened yesterday so it's early days yet.'

Her words could have meant that a miracle would happen overnight, amputation was a possibility, or that her own tender nursing, plus the doctor's infallible expertise, would solve the problem.

All the time, the little shopkeeper, whom I had grown to respect as she went about her quiet business of satisfying her customer's requirements, and almost to love when she came to me and advised me about my oranges and tomatoes, was putting in a wise and cautionary word here and there, and never missing a trick in the business of keeping both the gossip and the marketing flowing. It was a quiet performance I was to watch with other middle-aged and elderly ladies, satisfying their clientele in a way that could have taught many a sales manager the essentials of fair and friendly — and no doubt profitable — trading.

'So, he's off work today, is he?' The whole affair had to be known to its latest development.

'Oh, ay, and likely to be for a day or two, the doctor says.'

'And what are they doing at the gardens?'

I had to wait a second or two to discover that the injured Tom with his passion for rainbow trout, wasn't a gardener attending to one or several house owners, but was employed by the Council at the public park gardens and putting greens available to all ratepayers. An important man.

Smugly: 'They'll just have to do without him for a bit. Or use Peter in the meantime.'

There was a bit of a sniff. Peter, it turned out, was the local handy-man, joiner, window-cleaner, garden-tidier — good enough in his way but obviously not a Tom.

2

The milk-bar was on a corner of the Brechin-Forfar crossroads. Well back from the road, with plenty of space for the cars to pull in, and a background of trees. It was obviously a popular spot, a place for the family to drive out to on a Saturday or Sunday afternoon, and always a stopping place for the far-travelling business man.

On this summer afternoon it was doing a busy trade. It was not long before I discovered that its speciality was chicken sandwiches, and as it was owned by a farmer called Crichton, whose Balnabreich Farm was somewhere unseen in the offing, I guessed that these might be pretty good. There were plenty of people standing in the sunshine with chicken sandwiches in their hands, and I thought the locals would certainly know what was what. They were luscious.

The atmosphere of the place was relaxed, and I remembered again roadside meals in the sunshine of France. But the girl who served me could only have been a Scot. She had all the native colouring; sandy hair, large blue eyes, and the fair skin with a cluster of freckles. And a wide and friendly smile.

She had also, like her companion server at the counter, a little badge over the left breast of her blue overalls. It said 'Valerie'. I could have done without the badge which, in the heart of Scotland reminded me of London cafés. What on earth was Mr Crichton thinking about? 'Valerie'! 'Maureen'! Did it matter which was which? In this Elysian spot only anonymity was important, I fooled myself. You stopped, enjoyed the moment and the sandwich, passed on.

Actually, it was a blessing of identity, providing me now with the memory of a few enchanting minutes. The name Valerie was completely descriptive of the girl who smiled so frankly across the counter and who, in serving me with such utter involvement in the needs of her customer, gifted me with something of her own young and glowing happiness. I was glad to know her name, and so record it.

Trade had slackened at her end and she was able to spend a little time talking to me. I had noticed an amusing 'distance' board tacked up against the counter: LONDON, 443 miles; EDINBURGH, 84; PERTH,

114

40; HONG KONG, 8,630¼; CASABLANCA, 1,274; JOHN O'GROATS, 271; and some others equally far-fetched and no doubt accurate.

It gave me the opportunity to ask why.

She laughed. She laughed easily. There was laughter in her all the time.

'Oh,' she said. 'Mr Crichton and his friends have travelled about a bit, and he thought the board would be fun.'

'Especially away up here. It must remind lots of people of places they've been to.'

'You've been to some of them,' she said knowingly.

'All of them. Except Hong Kong.'

'Lucky you!' she laughed.

But there wasn't the least bit of envy in her. She had been well blessed by nature, and all the wordly things like travel would come to her in her own time. It was just pleasant to stand there in the sunshine talking to her. She was surprised by my interest in her and in the milk bar and the people round about us; where did they come from, where were they going? What did they do for a living? Did she know any of them personally, like regulars, or were they all ships passing in the night?

'You're awfully curious,' she laughed, her eyes wide and mocking.

She was open and forthright in her replies with that fearlessness that comes from utter innocence. Now and again she would turn away from me to serve a boy or a girl with an ice cream or a bottle of Coca Cola, or an older person with a chicken sandwich. But she would glance in my direction, standing at the end of the counter watching the animated scene, and smile across at me.

By the time she came back to my corner I felt certain that she and Maureen were doing this job only in their summer holidays.

'Yes, how did you guess?' she asked in pleased surprise.

'Are you at Aberdeen University?'

She laughed outright, with a young engaging bubble of laughter and leaned towards Maureen who had drifted our way. In the manner that many young girls have, she half-covered her mouth with her out-stretched fingers and whispered to the other girl. Maureen was dark, slim, attractive. I judged that she was more restrained and reticent than Valerie, the elder friend to whom one confided. But I was right about their doing the job as a holiday stint.

Valerie said: 'I'm still at Brechin school. In my sixth year.' And giggled this time — at herself, at me, at life.

115

Still at school. You can never tell their age nowadays. They all look like young women, involved in a career or marriage. What an extraordinary generation of attractive young women this is, in almost every country in the world.

When I asked, she told me she was going in for languages – French and German especially – and that she wanted to be a secretary, or a personal assistant to someone. She was completely open and friendly, without guile.

'Don't forget shorthand and typing,' I said. 'They're the way in to the best jobs sometimes. You may never use them, but they'll get you in. Which is all important. After that it's up to you.'

We were a trio now, the trade having slackened off, and Maureen available to turn to for the amused giggle and the whispered confidence. Maureen said little, but listened with interest. In my own way I was passing on some good advice to this young and appealing girl. I had forgotten how fresh and unworldly young Scots can be, boys as well as girls, and I lingered, wanted to delay my departure, laughing with them, talking nonsense, and now and again a word of common sense.

'Will you want to work abroad?' I asked Valerie.

Her eyes wide with surprise: 'And leave Scotland? Oh, no!'

'But there are so many good jobs abroad nowadays,' I pressed. 'We've all grown so much nearer each other.'

'Oh, I'll travel, of course. For holidays. But never to stay. I love it here. There's no place like it.'

She had given me my answer.

'What's your other name?' I asked.

Her amused eyes mocked my presumption and yet forgave it. She would have told me.

'Officer,' answered Maureen for her.

'Officer?' I repeated. I had never heard the name before. 'Truly?'

'Truly,' said Valerie.

Valerie Officer. If only it had been Officier, the French way, it would have been in keeping with the many other indications along my journey of the old alliance. Perhaps it had been once. But even Officer was surely unusual?

'No,' said Maureen, 'round about here it's not all that unusual. I know two other people with the same name.'

And later I would discover half a dozen in a local telephone directory.

'Why do you want to know?' Valerie asked innocently.

Why would any man in his senses not want to know the name of a girl like this, who had illumined a corner of Scotland for a few minutes with her youth, her honest friendliness?

I was turning away to go to my car. Always make your exits effective.

'Because I'm putting you in a book,' I said.

When I half-turned back to wave to them, Valerie was clinging, unbelieving, to Maureen. The eyes of both the girls were on me, startled. Then as I waved, they both made up their minds. It could only be a joke.

The bright smile came back to the fair face with the freckles. The blue eyes sparkled. She raised her arm and waved. The sun was on her honey-coloured hair.

3

A grey day in mid-October; the splendours of East Lothian dimmed by the prevailing sunlessness. The countryside was seemingly deserted, yet most of the fields were being quietly worked. We were on our way to Stenton.

The roads were empty, until at the crossroad, a quarter of a mile away, a mobile butcher's van appeared and stopped to let a woman get out. The van went on its way; the woman came towards us. She was carrying a small bag, a sort of shopping bag.

We stopped. Could we give her a lift.

'It's awfully good of you,' she said, 'but I've had my lift already. Two miles in the van. That only leaves me four miles to go.'

She was walking to East Linton, a few miles behind us. We had all the time in the world and could have gone back on our tracks and dropped her in East Linton in a few minutes.

She wouldn't hear of it.

'Oh, no,' she said. 'I'm ahead of my time already. And I like the walk. It's only four miles from here. I do this every Thursday. My cousin's garage closes on Thursday afternoons and it's his only chance of having a break. So I go over to keep his mother company while he's away.'

'It's still a long walk.'

She smiled.

'Oh, it's all right on a nice day like this. But thank you for the offer. I'm awful grateful.'

And off she set into the grey afternoon, which looked as if it might rain at any moment, sprightly, upright, the carrier bag in her hand. Looking after her, I noticed she was walking with a slight limp.

IX

1

The American poet Walt Whitman wrote:

> The shapes arise!
> Shapes of factories, arsenals, foundries, markets,
> Shapes of two-threaded tracks of railroads,
> Shapes of the sleepers of bridges, vast frame-works,
>   girders, arches....

He was thinking of Brooklyn Bridge, designed in 1867, whose tall towers were the inspiration of modern New York. But 'Whitman would have been equally delighted with the Forth Bridge, and so am I,' said Kenneth Clark in the brilliant book based on his TV series, *Civilization.* 'Although it is an anachronism, a sort of prehistoric monster – a brontosaurus of technology. Because by the time it was built in 1890, the new shapes had gone in the other direction, the way of lightness and economy, the characteristics of the suspension bridge. The new Forth Bridge is our own style, which expresses our own age, and it is the result of a hundred years of engineering.'

But there was only the brontosaurus when I was young, and it was the most beautiful sight in the world, not only aesthetically, but because it was my swift way home to Edinburgh from the army camp at Inverkeithing. Only in the darkness of night when I stumbled back across it on foot could it have had for me any resemblance to a prehistoric monster. And not even then. I had only gratitude for its existence and for my opportunity to be on it.

In the bright light of day, fifty years later, it was as beautiful as ever, in spite of its new slender rival a mile further up the river. The old rail bridge would always be nearest my heart.

It was obviously a very personal thing too to the man who was to be my guide in crossing it. I had hoped for a solitary, nostalgic trek across the old railway bridge ('Conrad in Quest of his Youth'), but that was out. Max McAuslane had got me official permission to make the crossing, and Gilbert Ogilvie from British Railways Divisional Engineer's Drawing Office in Edinburgh was coming specially to be at my side. When I heard that, I cursed Mr Ogilvie. When we met I liked him at once. Gilbert Ogilvie is a Bachelor of Science, a sturdily-built man with friendly, enquiring eyes, a readiness to smile dryly, a quiet, cultured voice, and a weather-beaten face that showed he sought every opportunity to be out on his beloved bridge, or that he was a walker, a climber, or an angler. Certainly he was a man for the open spaces and the countryside.

He was marked too by that subtle quality which independent men carry with them: he was his own man's man. I can think of no other way of describing it; it means that a man is beholden to nobody; he is himself, modestly confident of where he stands with life and people. The kind of man you want to have by you in a tight spot. I remember their like on the battlefield, in newspaper offices, in the tight corners of physical affront that not infrequently lie in wait for you when you move about the world. He was younger than I and could obviously walk me into the ground. He looked wiry and fit.

We met in the Forth Bridge Office in Dalmeny Station, on the south side of the bridge. I had come out from Edinburgh by train and got there just after a heavy canting and lining machine had jumped the line. (Always be where the action is.) The trains from Edinburgh were coming into the station on a loop line, two or three officials were busy in the little office, and the phone was ringing.

I stood away from it all, but watched the men at their work. This was their job and they tackled it efficiently and without fuss, as policemen tackle a crime. Through a door I could see the engineers at work on the line. Everything was under control. And Gilbert Ogilvie was at my side introducing himself.

'Just my luck to watch this,' I said.

'It can happen'; and he went into a quiet swift technical explanation of the arrangement of gravel and sleepers and rails, which passed right over my head. To him it was only an incident.

While the men around us were tidying it all up, I told Gilbert Ogilvie why I wanted to go on my mission. He understood. Having a real purpose in visiting his bridge suited his own ideas of proper behaviour. He would give any visitor his whole attention, but a special one was a special one, as I thought myself to be. A bit daft, maybe, but at least I had crossed the bridge before, after my fashion.

'I don't think I can give you a repetition of your previous experiences,' he regretted with a smile, 'but if you want to see the whole works, I can promise you something even better than your midnight strolls.'

This was my man.

'You bet,' I said, not knowing what I was taking on.

The office had settled down to its quiet routine. Trains were a few minutes late. The time lag would be made up in a routine way.

'This first,' Gilbert Ogilvie said, pushing a slip of paper and a pen across the table to me.

It was an undertaking that I was crossing the bridge at my own request and absolved British Railways from any responsibility in the event of anything unpleasant happening. We were off to a good start! Even in my war-time days there hadn't been this precaution.

I signed.

'Everybody who crosses the bridge, except officially of course, does it on his own responsibility,' the station master told me.

I had thought I was a unique specimen. But other people are as curious and as venturesome as I. Schoolteachers, science students, engineers. But no women. No woman is allowed to cross the Forth Bridge – a taboo from the time when women's fashions made it unsafe for them to be in close proximity to trains.

'This next.'

It was a brilliant day-glow orange blouse, the type worn by workmen on roads and railways. Sleeveless. I pulled it over my head while Ogilvie donned his.

'And this is Sandy,' he said.

Sandy, already wearing his orange blouse, was our look-out man. I shook his hand, and noticed the whistle looped round his neck on a cord. We were like a patrol going out in the midnight dark of no-man's-land in that first World War.

'What about the Very lights?' I asked.

They laughed; but the bridge would get its own back on me for that crack.

Ogilvie was hatless. I had had the sense to match this by wearing a tight-fitting cap. I knew what the wind could be like up there on the bridge.

'It's not bad this morning,' Ogilvie said, reading my thoughts, and looking up at the sky. 'In fact it's the perfect day. You're in luck.'

2

It is almost a two-mile walk from Dalmeny Station, along the approach to the Bridge, across the bridge itself, and then over the run-off at the other end to North Queensferry station. A nice walk. In fact, it was nothing in the nature of a walk. In my far-off war-time nights there had been few trains but they had caused me plenty of deft foot-work and shadow boxing. I had not bargained now for the traffic that crosses the bridge — 200 trains every twenty-four hours.

Almost before we were over the approach, Sandy was using his warning whistle. It was a slow-moving passenger diesel, just leaving Dalmeny Station. It hadn't even picked up speed as it passed us, standing still on the right foot-path away from it. There was nothing in its passage to indicate the slip-stream, wind blast, and roar and rattle that would be on us in minutes with the fast-moving (sometimes fifty miles an hour) trains coming down from the north, or the non-stoppers at Dalmeny approaching the bridge at speed behind us.

A few passengers leaned out of the windows to watch us, and two children waved.

'Look out for the pennies,' Gilbert Ogilvie cautioned me.

'The pennies?'

He said happily; 'They throw them from the windows for luck!'

'You're kidding!'

'No. Fact!'

I thought of that old song, *Three Coins in a Fountain,* and remembered some of the pools around the world into which I, and so many others, had thrown pennies for luck. I had never before thought of the Forth Bridge and the river 160 feet below in this way.

'Of course half the coins never reach the water,' said Ogilvie. 'They fall short or strike the girders.'

And lie on the footpath, or in the steel gully that carries the rails, which you have to leap over to cross from side to side as you go along. We did this because my guide wanted to show me everything. And because he knew it was wiser, and less windy, moving over to the opposite side away from an approaching or passing train. But this is an arduous exercise.

'You mean a lot of money lies here on the bridge?' I asked incredulously.

'Not for long!' Ogilvie smiled.

He saw my astonishment.

'They're not all Scots passengers in the trains, you know. Some of them don't mind chucking their money about.'

We chuckled, knowing our spurious reputation. He picked up a penny from the path, tossed me for it, won, and threw it over the rail. We leaned over and watched it spin and whirl till, like a tern changing course, it became one with its hazy background and vanished.

Much later on there was a chance for another gibe at our Scottish selves when we came to the North Central Girder where a small plaque commemorated the last rivet put into the bridge. It was driven in by HRH The Prince of Wales on 4 March 1890, when he formally opened the bridge.

'It's said to be a gold rivet,' Ogilvie grinned. 'But painted over — to avoid the rush! They didn't want the bridge to collapse.'

Strangely, a year later while I was still questing around Scotland, a discussion broke out in the Scottish *Sunday Post* about that same gold rivet, and two women went on record with this evidence: 'A gold rivet *was* used in the Forth Bridge. My grandfather was the silversmith who made it. He took it home to show his children (among them my mother) what he'd made for the new bridge. I'm surprised records don't show what became of it' (Mrs R. Crawford, Gourock).

And Mrs Annie Crockett, of Edinburgh, wrote with confident assurance: 'My father made the special case which held the gold rivet for the opening ceremony.'

That Prince of Wales would later become King Edward VII, creator of the *entente-cordiale* with France, husband of the lovely Queen Alexandra. I looked at the plaque again, trying in my mind's eye to recreate the bustle and splendour of that long-ago occasion. I turned back to our business, saw a penny on the line, picked it up.

'Look at this,' I said to Ogilvie.

The head on the penny was that of King Edward VII, facing right. I turned it over. The date was 1910 — the year of his death, when as a boy I was impressed by all the thick mourning-black column rules in the newspapers.

123

'I'm not tossing you for this,' I said. 'It's too good an omen.'

'Your luck's in.'

A minute later I picked up a tiny white shoe, an inch long, slipped from a child's doll. I found it infinitely pathetic, conjuring up a picture of a little girl holding up her doll at the window of the train to see the sea. Or had she been given a penny throw out for luck, and the pressure of the wind had done its own dirty work? I thought of the moment of anguish when the discovery was made; the vain and agitated searching of the carriage; the inconsolable little girl; the despair; the tears. It had not happened long ago; perhaps that same day. The shoe was still white and unbegrimed. The little girl was probably by now at home with her mother and granny in Aberdeen and rewardingly comforted. I wrapped the tiny white shoe in my handkerchief. I knew another little girl who would like to hear the story, and understand.

But this interlude in the middle of the bridge came only after Gilbert Ogilvie had put me through my paces. When I had walked the bridge alone in the night, I had stuck resolutely to one side of it. The trains that passed me on that side seemed very close, and the blast of wind accompanying them quite considerable. It was too risky to cross in the dark to the other side. I did not know what lay in wait for me there, or on the way over. Now I was on the move all the time.

Straight away I rediscovered that slip stream. The first two trains had me holding tightly on to the rail. You can't just hold on with your hands; you have to put your arm right round the top rail of the bridge and cling to it. So there was much good reason for Ogilvie's tactics in crossing from side to side as Sandy's whistle blew and trains approached.

Sandy's whistle was going frequently. I hadn't realized how difficult it is to see a train coming at you on a rail when you are on eye level with it. Only the small distant yellow front of the diesel was in our vision on this long straight stretch of rail. There was no curve to reveal a whole train, no trail of smoke as in the old days. You had to be very quick on the eye.

Sandy was all that. Spotting an engine that I certainly couldn't at first see, whether from the Dalmeny end or North Queensferry, his shrill blast would sound its warning. At once we went to the rail and curled our arm right round it. I know now that Ogilvie was weighing me up. He had spotted that I could jump quite nippily across the track, was fairly sure-footed, and was obviously enjoying myself. I had taken off my cap which, tight-fitting though it was, was still a nuisance, and tossed it down into the sea. Better there than sticking out from a pocket. I had caught his eye on me and saw his approval.

He loved his bridge, and wanted others to share his love. And I think he was glad to find me agile and sharing his enthusiasm. He understood too, my special lust to come to grips with this thing that had stood for so much in my young life.

'Shall we go the whole hog?' he shouted to me.

I hadn't the least idea what he was talking about.

'In for a penny etcetera,' I called back.

3

I was in for it all right. At various distances along the bridge there are hatches. Making sure that the rails were clear, Ogilvie gave a signal to Sandy, who came and stood near the first hatch. Ogilvie raised it. Through the small opening I could see a narrow iron stairway going downward, and somewhere – a hundred miles beneath – the blue sea.

'Go down this way,' said Ogilvie, leading the way, 'and duck your head as I do.'

He was half way through the hatch before I realized he meant it. As he went through, his head bent down into his chest, his body swivelled and he was going down backwards, his hands firmly on the rails. Sandy waited. He could only be waiting to stand guard alone. I followed Ogilvie through the hatch, managed not to crack my head or fall, and we were both in another world.

It was another world that would be repeated at intervals along the bridge. We descended to platforms leaning out from the bridge, blind to what was going on above. From time to time Sandy would yell 'train'. I had expected that, being below the rails, the vibration would be terrific, and prepared myself for the shock. But strangely the passing overhead of the train was muted in some mysterious way, and not nearly as noisy as being alongside it near the rails.

We climbed stone spiral stairways inside granite towers. It was like climbing up the dark steep steps of an old castle. There were no electric lights. Oglivie carried a torch. The steps were covered with pigeon's droppings, and in the flash of the torch I spied a pigeon's nest with one egg in it.

Near the centre of each cantilever, below track level, was a large

125

bothy for the workmen, a surprising discovery. These bothies rest on the cross girder joining the east and west vertical columns, below the level of the railway track. They are roomy and comfortable, with benches and table, a Calor gas cooker, and an Ascot heater for hot water and cold. As the dinner break draws near, one of the gang separates himself from the others and prepares and heats up in the bothy for his pals.

It seemed to me the longest journey I had ever made. I had never expected that I should have to hop around from rail to rail like a goat, bend my head between my shoulders in order to go through hatches and then down stairways into seeming nothingness, and end up looking at the granite-faced masonry of massive piers. Or to climb upwards over the interminable steps within the tower to a kind of crow's nest at the top. It was sheer physical exertion but in surroundings of such beauty that to lift the eyes for a darting moment from iron rail to blue sky, or downwards to sparkling sea, or towards Fife and the distant hills, or backwards to Edinburgh, was an exhilaration and an enchantment.

The bridge was being painted while I was there, painted with Tuscan red oxide of iron that gives it that warm hue, and it was interesting to see at close quarters the extraordinary engineering devices that allow men to clamber like flies all over the bridge in perfect safety. Safety? Far below, nearly 400 feet from the top of the main cantilever to the sea, a stand-by rescue launch rolls gently at its moorings, close to the bridge, when workmen are on the job.

Ogilvie 'lowped' over his bridge like a shepherd lowps over the hills. He was alive with information which he eagerly flung at me in the wind, technical stuff that meant nothing to me. I was much more thrilled by the word Inchgarvie and the sight of the small fortified island of the First World War lying far below us. I remembered the letter of the reader who had written to me about his long climb up the stairway from the island to the bridge. The stairway was still there, but the island had been abandoned and looked desolate, with empty skeleton windows in the stonework of its buildings.

The real surprise about the bridge is that the railway track doesn't actually run along the bridge but is laid on longitudinal oak timbers fixed inside steel troughs – the 'steel gully' I mentioned when I made my first jump across it.

As Gilbert Ogilvie was telling me with his own brand of quiet enthusiasm about the great granite bases, the mighty cantilevers, the 5000 men who worked to build the bridge, the thousands of tons of steel and cement, his eyes watching with pride, almost as if he were thinking aloud, I said to him:

'Is it possible it's almost too strong — that all this material wasn't really needed. Was used to make assurance doubly sure?'

He looked at me shrewdly. He knew what I meant.

'You're almost on target,' he said.

'The Forth Bridge was built after the Tay Bridge disaster, wasn't it?'

'It was completed twelve years after the opening of the Tay Bridge.'

'And *that* was a shoddy bit of building!'

He said sadly, 'Poor old Bouch.'

I knew the name. Thomas Bouch. *Sir* Thomas Bouch, knighted for building the Tay Bridge, doomed to disaster before the first train travelled it in 1878. Eighteen months later, with the 5.20 train from Burntisland to Dundee racing across it in a howling December gale, the thirteen centre spans of girders collapsed, the train plunged into the Tay, taking a thousand yards of the bridge with it, and seventy-five men, women and children. And no one lived to tell the tale.

But enough was known of its building, and more would be discovered at the subsequent inquiry, to mark the Tay Bridge as a mistake from the beginning. British engineering achievements in the nineteenth century were among the wonders of the world, but the Tay Bridge wasn't one of them, and Scottish grief for the dead was shared with Scottish guilt for shockingly faulty workmanship.

The chief culprit was Thomas Bouch. He misjudged the pressure of the wind which, channelled down the Tay between the hills, was known to have caused widespread damage in the Dundee area in the past. He seems not to have known that the bed of the river at that particular point is old red sandstone. It was covered beneath a deep layer of mud and stones and sand, and when the first borings were made it was assumed erroneously that this strata of gravel was in fact bedrock. The slender bridge he designed against these grave errors of judgment, the longest bridge in the world, never looked as if it could take the strain, and many locals predicted that it wouldn't.

The story of the workmanship revealed by the official inquiry is staggering. There were 'grave irregularities' at the Wormit foundry where the iron castings of the bridge had been manufactured. A substance known as 'Beaumont's Egg' played a leading and disastrous part in the construction. It was used to plug the 'blown holes', the faults in the iron castings, melted in and left there to harden. It was indistinguishable from the iron about it, but consisted simply of beeswax, fiddler's rosin, the finest iron borings melted up, and a little lamp black! It was kept 'in a wee box that lay between the turning-shop and the moulding-shop on a brick wall'. Many workmen testified to patching up defects on the iron castings with this stuff. One man had seen hundreds of holes in the cast iron filled by 'Egg'. Another man said they had been told 'to throw tarpaulin pokes over some iron columns which had been filled in this way – 'to hide them from the contractors or the engineers'. The best book describing the Tay Bridge disaster is John Prebble's *The High Girders,* published by Secker and Warburg.

'The downfall of the Tay Bridge,' said the report, 'was due to inherent defects in the structure which must sooner or later have brought it down. Sir Thomas Bouch is, in our opinion, mainly to blame.'

Yes; poor old Bouch. He never left his house in Moffat after the verdict, and died within four months.

No wonder the builders of Gilbert Ogilvie's Forth Bridge erred, if they erred at all, on the side of too much strength. Its strength met you at every point, reached out and smote you. Its strength and its beauty, the combination that, in spite of my fatigue – or because of my exhilaration – I found irresistible.

I had hoped that Ogilvie would be able to join me for a drink (which I badly needed) and lunch, at the end of our adventure; but he is a non-alcoholic man, and he was hurrying back to his office in Edinburgh. We would meet again.

But he had a final treat for me. At the end of the bridge he led me up the steps to the North Queensferry signal cabin, which must be one of the most beautifully situated in Britain. From one window of his cabin George Benzie looks out across the Forth towards Edinburgh; from the important one, he sees the whole bridge; and from a third window he can look over at his home and garden in North Queensferry less than half a mile away. Just above eye-level, and over his levers, is a large diagram of the stretch of the bridgeline and its approaches, with electric lights flickering to indicate the positions of trains.

George has been in this signal box for twenty-five years, sitting on his leather-cushioned seat in front of that diagram when he is not moving around his little cabin, performing his duties. And he has been in the service of the railway for forty-eight years, just on the point of retiring when I met him. Gilbert Ogilvie has served his railway employers forty-three years. All the other men I met had long service records. Railway life must be very healthy, and railwaymen very loyal.

Then Gilbert Ogilvie led me to the almost hidden path, which I had forgotten, under the bridge and leading down to sea level and North Queensferry. In the darkness of the old nights so long ago I would then turn right and tramp back to camp. Now I went straight across the road, my legs a bit groggy.

The bridge loomed vast above me. I looked up at it with a special affection. I had crossed it again after all these years. It hadn't been a bit like what I had expected. Fifty years ago, I had been eighteen, taking it in my stride, treating it almost as a laugh, a happily convenient way for me to get back to camp with my special privilege of the vital password to make all things possible. I had a lot more respect for it now.

5

North Queensferry isn't the most inviting little place in the world. It doesn't figure in the glossy travel brochures or the packaged trips to sunlands. Part of it – the old part, now quieter since the ending of the water ferries – runs round the rim of the sea: little houses, a post office, a few shops, a couple of hotels. The other part is up the hill, residential in the posher meaning of the words, with the larger gardens and the better views; although from almost any part of the little town the views are lovely.

It was the nearest spot at that moment to ease the burden of my fatigue, and the Albert Hotel was the nearest hostelry. There was a bar on one side of the passage and on the other a room for eating in. There was no one in the bar and only two young men sitting at a table in the restaurant. They looked like travelling salesmen, finished with their morning round, stoking up, comparing notes, and then off on the afternoon jaunt. I was glad I was no longer a chain-gang worker of the world.

I ordered a large whisky and the roast pork that seemed to be the dish of the day. Then I leaned heavily back in my chair. I was glad I had done it. It had turned out to be not just a return to a previous experience, but a new experience. Gilbert Ogilvie had provided me with the new experience and in doing so had tested me. I was grateful to him for both gifts.

My daughter would probably have asked me what I was trying to prove to myself. She had startled me nearly ten years before, in 1960, when I had flown to New York to watch the election figures coming in that would make John Kennedy President of the United States, and flown back to London the next day. 'What are you trying to prove to yourself, Daddy?' she had asked, and I was floored.

I hadn't been trying to prove anything to myself as far as I knew. I was in the international mass media business, and knowing about things was my job. I had lots of good friends in New York and two of them had separately phoned me and invited me to join their all-night parties to watch the results come in. It was a momentous election. One of the parties was given by *Time-Life* magazines, the other was more private and intimate. I thought it would be fun to take in both. And I did.

What was so challenging to the human psyche or the human physique to be driven in a private car to Heathrow, to sit comfortably in a jet air-liner, relaxing, eating, drinking and probably drowsing for seven or eight hours? Of course, the New York part was a jamboree. It always is.

But whatever I took out of myself in those hectic and historic twelve hours, I easily made up by sleeping most of the way home the following day. I would have stayed over longer in New York if I could, but the whole thing had come suddenly as an interruption in work, and I wanted to get back to something as important in my own immediate world as the events of the previous twenty-four hours in New York. The fatigue of modern air travel? My foot.

So now with the Forth Bridge. It had been far more exhausting than that other 'challenge', and I was now ten years older. But I had gone to find out, not to prove anything to myself. So I raised my glass to my daughter, distant in London, with three adorable little girls to look after, and drank with deep satisfaction. The whisky was good, the pork was adequate, and one of the young men had got up and put a coin in the juke box.

Naturally there was a juke box. Where today isn't there one? My favourite Supremes were doing *Gonna make you love me* and *A place in the sun,* and it was fine to sit there, relaxed, with the whisky beginning to do its stuff, and the music rolling over me. No one in the whole world who knew me knew where I was at that particular time. The ultimate bliss. To be completely anonymous and non-existent. What greater joy?

It was presented to me next minute when the two young men got up and went away. Like the village itself, the hotel was now deserted. This is when you really enjoy yourself, especially when you're tired and aware of the full, sensual flush of utter solitariness. And not a soul knows where you are.

Presently, I got up and looked at the juke box. Its titles certainly needed updating, but there were one or two good things. I put on Peter Sarstedt's *Where do you go to?* and *Morning Mountain.* I quickly flipped past Petula Clark and Val Doonican and turned on Stevie Wonder's *For once in my life.*

What the hell! How often do you get an experience like that? From dropping out from the top of the sky, up there among the gulls and the clouds and the wind, right down to this deserted outpost which normally wouldn't even scrape the surface of my life and for half an hour or so was now the centre of my whole being? Even juke box music always brings everything back.

6

I went out and climbed into a bus. It was going through Inverkeithing on to Dunfermline. There were only a few people aboard – a woman going to Inverkeithing with a basket for shopping, a young man and young woman going back to work. There was an older man sitting in the back seat and I flopped down beside him.

'Things have changed,' I murmured.

'Oh, ay.' He looked at me sideways.

'I remember going back along this way to Seggsburn.'

'To the camp, eh?'

'Yes.'

'You were in the RSF then?'

'Yes. What happened to the road that led up to the camp?'

'What's happened to anything?' he asked.

We were travelling over a modern motorway that could have been anywhere.

'It's funny you should mention that road,' he said. 'When they started working on it to make it a motorway there was practically nothing underneath. Trunks of trees, ditches. It was like a swamp.'

On the surface of the road above that swamp I had marched endless miles, up and down, up and down, doing arms drill. Arms drill! My fiendish sergeant revelled in it. Slope arms, present arms, order arms. God only knows what arms! All in preparation for machine gun attacks by the Germans in France.

And yet, in its way, it was iron discipline, teaching us that invaluable thing for a soldier – the readiness to obey an immediate command without thinking. It may have saved many lives. Or lost them.

X

1

In Dundee there are three churches, grafted together like Siamese triplets, which form a composite and imposing stone mass in the very heart of the city. I haven't seen their like anywhere before. The churches are old, but the city centre is new, gouged out of countless acres of ancient and condemned property.

It has taken years to create and is one of the most imaginative and beautiful city centres in Scotland, built with great foresight and sensitive understanding of the city's needs. It has an enclosed shopping centre and a handsome new hotel, and weaving around these are wide paths, green lawns (with no 'forbidden' notices) decorated with masses of flowers. The gleaming new Tay Bridge reaches across the river straight into the heart of it, and the view from the bridge as you come up from the south is breath-catching. There are also seats, comfortable wooden seats, which most cities unforgivably forget to provide.

'Build beautifully' had obviously been the guiding directive for the planners, and 'provide plenty of comfortable seats for the citizens and the visitors' to be able to rest and admire. And on fine days, like the one I was enjoying, this meeting place is gay and colourful. In the centre of a city which historically was called Bonnie Dundee and distorted more accurately into Dirty Dundee, a welcome touch of continental light-heartedness has been introduced. And it is all the more striking against the background of the three-in-one churches. The old Scotland and the new.

On one of the wooden seats, I sat contentedly enjoying the scene. My single companion was a typical, cloth-capped, working man, on retirement pension I guessed, grey-haired, pipe-smoking, thinking his own thoughts, a left-over from the dirtier days when men really worked — if they could get the work. He would be a difficult one to know. The Scottish regiments had been made up of his kind, and a lot of his mates hadn't been lucky enough to reach this stage in life and sit in the sun, weighing up the younger generation.

He didn't look towards me, but he knew I was there. We were on a seat which backed against the churches.

'We've got the right thing behind us,' I said, visitor to local lad.

Silently he glanced over his shoulder at the solid stone church walls. Then: 'Ay.'

That would have been the end of it.

'Do many people go nowadays?'

'Oh, ay,' giving me a small glance and seemingly accepting me. 'They're quite well attended.'

'It used to be morning and evening when I was a boy.'

'Oh, if you go yince on a Sunday now you're no' doing so bad.'

Still trying: 'Well, it brought up a good race in the past.'

'Ay, no' sae bad.'

If only they would elaborate, open up, express something of their feelings, even to a stranger. Particularly to a stranger.

A small group lay on the lawn directly in front of us. Three girls and a boy, all in their teens, and a young collie.

'And there's the future,' I said.

My companion nodded his head slowly, his eyes hooding his thoughts. Then he said slowly, 'Nae respect for onything.'

Was he voicing a thought or only repeating a cliché? I just couldn't tell.

One of the girls, in a bright red shirt with a sun-tanned thigh showing beneath her white mini, pushed a cigarette into her mouth in the modern manner.

'Students,' my companion commented; and then in fairness, 'At least these yin's are a wee bit cleaner than some.'

They were much more than that. They were clean and attractive, colourfully dressed, seemingly happy and contented. The sunlight and the shadows playing around them grouped them into an almost perfect composition on the green lawn. They lay close together, their faces to the grass, leaning on their elbows, in casual intimacy.

We sat in silence watching them. I was hoping that my companion would make some further comment, about this generation or about his.

A comparison, praise, criticism, something. I waited in vain, comfirming something I had begun to discover. In Scotland real communication is easier with the young than the old. The old merely gossip.

At last the boy and one of the girls rose, reluctantly, to leave. The girl in the red shirt got up also. The boy held out a long blue coat to her and, standing straight up and rather tall, she made a few spontaneous mannequin poses to the others, completely unselfconscious.

I did not hear what she said, but they laughed at her affectionately. With a large soft straw basket on her arm, her yellow hair lying long and loose down her back, she was part of a painting by Renoir or Degas, all sunshine and green grass and dark trees behind her, and the blurred city colours out of focus. A stir of happiness moved me. She was so much more natural and womanly than the magazine models who did this sort of thing for a living.

Even my reticent friend on the seat approved. 'Ay,' he said again. 'They're no sae bad.'

If his contemporaries had heard him!

2

I walked back the few yards to the Angus Hotel. Sheila was waiting for me, half-way through *The Scotsman* crossword.

We were going out from Dundee to have lunch at Carmyllie where two close friends of ours, Arthur and Barbara Daw, had taken possession of a new home close to a farm. The intention was to spend all the day and evening with them, and then on the Sunday we would set out on further travels.

But in the foyer of the hotel, slipped into a slot on the notice board, I noticed the single announcement: 'Wedding at 5.30. Graham Suite.'

'Do you see what I see?' I demanded.

'So what?' asked Sheila. 'Most wedding receptions are held in hotels.'

'Wedding,' I said pityingly, and repeated, 'wedding!'

'It means reception. Wedding reception.'

But I remembered my boyhood and the customs of my country.

'It means *Wedding*. There's going to be a wedding here this afternoon at 5.30. A Scottish wedding!'

She smiled.

'Want another bet?' she asked.

We have an absurd habit of making fantastic bets on sometimes very minor issues.

I was sure I was right.

'Yes. I'll bet you £100,000 to a penny that it means there's a wedding – *and* a reception – here this afternoon.'

'Easy money,' Sheila said, and we moved with one accord to the reception desk.

'Oh, yes,' said the girl, 'it's the first one we've had in the hotel. We're all excited about it.'

The Angus was a new hotel, built to be part of the lovely centre of the city. But there had been plenty of time to have wedding receptions.

She read my thoughts.

'The first *wedding*,' she explained. 'We've had lots of receptions, but this is going to be the first wedding. I'm looking forward to it.'

So was I.

'So young couples still get married in hotels?' I asked.

'Oh, yes,' the girl said. 'Not so much as they used to. It seems to be dying out. I think more people go to church and registrars' offices. More like the English.'

But in my day, puritanical and church-attending as we all were, there were still innumerable marriages performed in hotels and other places. I had never thought until this moment why this should be so. But the habit, apart from any religious considerations, had many advantages. With the wedding and the reception in the same place, you moved naturally from one room to another, still under the same roof. There was no breaking-up either of the spirit of the occasion or the assembly of people. It was a convenient arrangement, an economy of time and effort and money.

I asked the girl how many guests were coming.

'Seventy-five.'

'And the Graham suite. Is it on this ground floor?'

'Yes. Just along the passage. At the end, on the right. They'll come in at the front door and walk straight forward to it.'

'Would it be all right for me to have a look at it?'

'Of course,' she agreed at once. 'There's nobody there now, but you can certainly have a look.' She laughed gaily. 'You sound as interested in it as I am myself!'

'I am.'

'And what?' asked Sheila, as we turned away and she opened her

136

purse to find the penny she owed me, 'is the big idea?'

'Only,' I murmured, 'that we've got a date with a wedding this afternoon. We're gate-crashing.'

She was silently and properly shocked.

'And don't tell me that you've nothing to wear.'

I knew she hadn't. On the kind of sorties we were making around Scotland, we were travelling light. The order of the day was tweed skirts and jumpers and walking shoes, and for me a rough jacket and slacks. But I had taken the precaution on certain journeys to include a dark suit for occasions, and this was one of the occasions. It was one-up-manship on poor Sheila – that is if she had wanted to go to this wedding as I did. But as she knew the limitations of her wardrobe, and having a much more developed social sense of the proprieties than I have, she set her face against my escapade from the start.

'Count me out,' she said.

'Pity,' I murmured. 'It would be so nice to go to the wedding as a couple. I shall feel lonely on my own.'

'You're not really serious?'

'It should be something to see. A Scottish wedding. The first in the Angus Hotel. You've no idea how nice it will be.'

And it was. When we reconnoitred the Graham Suite, quite empty at that hour, we found there were exactly seventy-five green leather chairs. They were in rows in two sections, separated by a centre aisle which led from the back of the room down to the table at which the ceremony would be performed. The table was covered with a white cloth, and had vases of gladioli and dahlias and michaelmas daises. The empty seventy-five chairs faced the table in an attractive plain panelled and glass room. High up on the back wall, and reaching to the ceiling, was a relief plan of Dundee.

Through a wide door in this back wall was a larger room with tables already laid, a place card for each guest, and wonderful sprays of flowers in abundance. It was satisfying to stand in this back doorway, with no one else present, and imagine the scene, the action, and the characters who would soon fill the stage. We were like a theatre producer making a final check-up before the audience and the players arrived and the curtain went up. The bride and her maids would probably come through this door separating the two rooms, behind the guests, and walk down the centre aisle to the waiting groom, the minister, and the inviting table. In my mind's eye I could see the heads turning as she came in, hear the rustle of guests rising to their feet, imagine the faces and the clothes. I thought of the many women who had had hair-dos in Dundee, the anxious happiness of the principals.

We were, by privilege, free of it all, and yet by standing there we had already become a part of it. It was obvious that the dining arrangements would avoid one of these noisy, stand-up drinking receptions. The married couple would presumably walk out through the door we had just entered, straight from the ceremony, and past the Hammond organ; and somewhere in a room or wide corridor between the Graham Suite and the waiting dining room there would be the quiet, friendly reception, the handshaking and the kissing. Then the guests would almost immediately move on to the large dining room and find their places at the table.

How sensible, how civilized. But how unfortunate for any outsider who had crudely contemplated being a witness to the happy event!

It was the ceremony itself I had wanted to see, a Scottish wedding at 5.30 on a Saturday afternoon in a Dundee hotel; but I had hoped also that I might be able to drift into the usual kind of wedding reception, confess my act to the bridegroom (who I am sure would have understood) and congratulate him, perhaps drinking to his and his wife's happiness.

'Too bad,' murmured Sheila with mock sympathy.

All the arrangements, and rightly, made it impossible. The exact number of chairs; the frontal entrance to the room, straight into the gaze of the early-arrival guests; probably a couple of ushers at the door; the lack of that larger type of after-wedding reception which usually includes other guests not present at the wedding itself; the impossible exit route through the back-wall door into a dining room, with place names on the tables, and the guests eyeing any intruders.

I wouldn't have another chance like this. The day was made for it, golden and happy. This particular hotel was absolutely right for it. The Graham Suite was ready for it. I hadn't ever before wanted so much to be at a wedding.

'There's only one hope,' I said. 'All the guests won't turn up.'

Sheila put me right.

'It never happens. Not at weddings. They'll all be here. All seventy-five of them.'

'But someone's bound to be ill, or running a temperature. Or something.'

'Not today they aren't!' And then with womanly patience: 'And even if they are, you won't know until all the other guests have arrived. And it's too late then.'

3

It must have been obvious to Arthur Daw.

'You've something on your mind,' he said quite soon after lunch.

We were in his garden. The Angus country stretched temptingly away from us, the Sidlaw hills rose in a haze of heat. This was a place to forget the world. My mind was elsewhere. I told him about the wedding.

Arthur and Barbara are permanently in Scotland. Except for holidays and service during the war, they had never lived or worked away from their homeland, and they never wanted to. They had been accustomed to weddings in churches and weddings in hotels throughout their married life, and before that. The habits and customs of their country and their people were something they lived with and understood. They had never had to come back to remember things and learn anew, and sometimes to learn for the first time. They did not have to look twice, as I had sometimes, to make sure; or to tune their ears for the inflection in a Scottish voice that might mean anything. They did not have to wander through Scotland to discover it; they knew it.

'I know how you feel,' Arthur said.

'I haven't seen a wedding like this for so many years,' I said.

And suddenly the thought came to me that it isn't the people who leave and go out into the world who give their country its character. It's the people who stay at home. They get on quietly with the business of doing their job without fuss, and without the ballyhoo that accompanies the successful wanderer. There must be something complete and whole about a man who has lived his life continuously and progressively, in however modest a way, in his homeland, with his own people. This is an act of creative fulfilment.

When I think of my own life, and other lives like it, I realise how much I have experienced, but how much also I have missed. The many who stayed at home in Scotland were part of a closely-knit fabric of continuous living, an uninterrupted stream of *being* against the familiar background of friends, in itself a bulwark against the inevitable disappointments and setbacks of life. Some left their country through the drive of necessity; the many others stayed put out of a sense of duty and family loyalty. Few Scots forget to repay the debts that begin at home; the many sons who take care of their mothers in their old age or infirmity, the daughters who sacrifice self-interest and even wedlock to ensure that lonely and fragile parents are protected and made comfortable. The ambitions of self are set aside, obligations are accepted without question or fuss. There is no soul-searing emotional drama about it; in the quiet of oneself a man or a woman, whatever the longing to escape to the 'glamour' and opportunity of the world, faces up to what he knows he must do for the benefit of his own folk and shapes his life accordingly.

We are a strange mixture of a people; on the one hand, an adventurous, intrepid company of world wanderers, rising frequently through sheer guts and ability and compulsion to the top; on the other, a people of quiet, undemonstrative and deep family feeling, going about its business at home, accepting its responsibilities.

Those of us who have gone out into the world will always, naturally, make the most of it. But our brothers at home will take care of our pretensions. They may make no public demur when the outside world praises our achievements, but privately they make their own evaluation of us. They will accept that one Scot's success is a feather in the cap of all Scots, but they can cut us down to size with a terse judgment: 'Oh, him!' they say, of us, 'I kent his faither!'

Arthur Daw looked into my face as so many Scotsmen do: from a slightly lowered head, with the eyes peering upward, and slightly veiled by the overhanging eyebrow. It is always a searching look, even in laughter, and even when he is a close friend.

So now Arthur said, with a twinkle in his eye:

'I'm thinking you'll really want to be back at the Angus by about five o'clock, won't you?'

I looked at him gratefully. Dundee was less than twenty miles away. We could stay here all afternoon, and still be back at the hotel to see, at least, the guests arriving for the wedding.

To make it the most normal departure, he added: 'And tomorrow we can take up where we've left off!'

Sheila had still her own views about my absurd keenness, but she kept them to herself until later when we were in the car on the way back.

'Idiot!' she said.

I stepped on the accelerator.

There was a canopy out over the entrance of the Angus, a few police

140

cones at the kerb keeping away cars, two or three women sightseers loitering with intent. It was just on five o'clock, half an hour to go. That gave us a chance to sit in the foyer near the door and see the first arrivals. If it was a swell wedding on Moss Bros lines, the small hope in my breast would be snuffed out. *That* we could never be part of in our everyday clothes. But my instinct told me it wouldn't be. And the arrival of the first four early guests, and three others almost immediately in their wake, confirmed my belief that it was a dress-up wedding only in the sense that everyone wore nice clothes, the nice clothes of our affluent times (near-minis which soon, as fashion dictated, would become real minis), trouser-suits, flowered dresses. The men might have been dressed by Hardie Amies or Burtons. I'd get by in this happy company.

4

I got up.

'See you!' I said in farewell to Sheila and waved my hand, *The Scotsman* in her lap, folded at the crossword. She shook her head at me, but I thought indulgently.

I collected my key and went up in the lift. I was glad now that I had a dark blue suit in the wardrobe. I was into it, and a fresh white shirt, in minutes.

Down to the hall again, to see the backs of three people on their way to the Graham Suite. I followed them slowly along the corridor. At the door of the suite they were greeted by a youngish minister in a long black gown. A pleasant attractive crinkly smile of welcome was on his face. The young man standing by his side smiled too.

We shook hands. An order of the service was handed to me. I did not go into the room. There was no one immediately behind me, although another man and woman were approaching along the corridor. I stood admiring the room and the people who had already assembled.

'What a nice day for it,' I said over my shoulder to the two men at the door.

They were immediately involved with the new arrivals. I went further into the room. Two young men were moving about taking photographs. One came over to where I was standing in order to get a long shot. We smiled to each other. His camera looked like a Pentax.

141

'You've got a good camera there', I said.

He smiled appreciatively.

I asked him: 'Are you both guests as well as photographers?'

'Oh, yes. Guests *more* than photographers.'

'Are you together?'

He took another shot bending down on his knees.

'Yes.'

He hardly looked at me as he worked his camera. 'We're going to stand at the back during the service.'

It couldn't be true.

'But you have seats?'

'Oh, yes.' He searched my face with the look of a knowledgeable young man of the world.

'Could my wife and I use them? Only for the service? We're dying to see it.'

He said, 'I knew you were a stranger.' That hurt. 'Of course you can. The seats aren't numbered or anything. And Richard won't mind. He'd ask you himself.'

'Richard?'

He looked me straight in the eye.

'Richard ·Howland. The bridegroom. Your old friend, Richard Howland!'

I said apologetically, 'I hadn't looked at this programme yet.'

We laughed together. People were beginning to come thick and fast around us. I'd better get to Sheila quickly.

'Thanks a lot,' I said heartfully.

I pushed gently through, past the minister and his companion, and ran along the corridor to Sheila. As I got to her I noticed her dark green Braemar jumper, her skirt with the soft blues and greens of her family tartan. She was a natural.

'Come on,' I said, pulling her to her feet.

As she came up, she still had *The Scotsman* in her hand. Automatically she tucked it under her arm.

'Where are we going?' she asked.

'To the wedding!' And before she could protest. 'We've been invited!'

It was almost true. It was true enough because these people were willing and welcoming, and because the nice minister now smiled again at me and shook our hands. Another service sheet was pressed into my hand, and because there were two seats waiting for us we went in and a sea of faces turned towards us. Of course the faces were watching every arrival, not just ours.

The back row inevitably had fewer seats occupied. We made for it, going to the far section across the aisle. We chose the most inconspicuous seats in the room, those at the end of the row, farthest from the room's entrance. We were snuggled cosily in the angle of the back and side walls. Really, we could almost convince ourselves that we were formally part of the assembly. Every head in the room would have to turn now to be aware of us, and every head wasn't doing that.

A young man at the Hammond organ was playing the *Voluntary,* and playing extremely well. I looked at my programme but he wasn't named. I noticed, though, that the date was the 13th, confirming impressions that were beginning to shape themselves in my mind about the people gathered there, and particularly about the two to be married.

They were already wedded in their convictions. They were pretty sure of themselves. They weren't afraid of getting married on the 13th, or of any other superstition. In the people who were their friends there was the same independence of character. It showed in the faces, in their clothes. They were the backbone of any society, conforming to the accepted pattern, but individual in their preferences. There wasn't a long-haired young man amongst us, or an outlandish character from dreamland. Yet the hair in many cases wasn't all that short, and the choice of clothes, as everywhere today, showed personal decision; they were modern, of the time they lived in.

Their Scottish roots went far back, and some of their ancestors would have been stunned by a peep at this well-dressed, comfortably-off, contented group of their ain folk that had emerged from the dark glen of Scottish conflict. I did not see a kilt, but that could be because of our position in the room. But I did see an awfully attractive young woman in long white bell-bottom trousers, and many, as young, wearing modern colourful garments and looking very happy. Happy, in fact, was the word that applied to the atmosphere in the room: the soft music from the organ, the rustle of people settling themselves, the older women in two-piece suits or flower dresses, and the gay flower hats everywhere.

'Glad we came?' I whispered.

'Of course. But I'm worried about the two people who'll be wanting our seats.'

I hadn't had time to tell her about the nature of our 'invitation', but quickly put her wise.

'Now I can really enjoy it,' she whispered. 'It's so different from a church.'

'It won't be. You'll see.'

It was new and different to her, and seemed very unconventional. She had never seen a wedding ceremony performed outside a church. But the Scots go their own way about most things, particularly about marriage. Marriage laws and customs were always different in Scotland. Long before the Reformation, church ceremonies were not necessary. There was a form of trial marriage in which a man and a woman pledged themselves to live together for a year. It was called 'hand-fasting'. When the year was over, they could either marry or separate. Young people in all walks of life, even royalty, handfasted.

And later people in love and wanting to be married whether they had lived together or not, could do so simply by declaring – in writing if they wanted; but verbally would do – that they wished to marry. It was this simplicity of the Scottish marriage at the time, and its legality, that led to so many runaway couples from England making for Gretna Green and the village blacksmith, whose anvil served as the church altar.

5

We were all here now. The minister had moved away from the door in his long dark gown and stood waiting near the table. We had only seen the back of the groom at first. He was a well-built young man with black curly hair, doing his best to appear at ease. But he glanced nervously over his shoulder now and again as if for reassurance, and what we saw of his face we liked.

When his bride made her entrance through the wide door in the back wall, all the faces turned to stare our way. As she stood at the top of the centre aisle, I could see that she was as nervous as the groom. I shifted my head quickly to see how he was reacting. At sight of her his own jitters had passed and there was a wide smile of complete confidence to welcome her. He made a movement and I thought for a moment he was going to come right up the aisle to welcome her and lead her down, then he stood still, waiting for her.

144

As she reached him his hand came out at once to touch her, and hand in hand they turned to the minister to be married. It was a ceremony almost as simple as that. So many things about it were different, a part of their unity and understanding. There was none of the orthodox wedding music, no *Here Comes the Bride;* the young man at the organ played Bach and Handel.

Catherine Duncan was not in conventional white; she was married to Richard Howland wearing a pale gold silk coat and dress, and on her head was a small arrangement of flowers. It was a flower wedding; there were flowers everywhere; the young matron of honour had a scarlet coat, carried a little bouquet of orchids, and had an orchid in her hair.

It was a brief, friendly service. There was no long pontifical advice to the happy couple, who knew what they were about in any case, the hymns were the good old hymns of my childhood, sung with a fervour and knowledge that showed that somebody was still going to church, and I was glad I was privileged to be part of it all.

The minister had a gentle dignity.

'Do you promise in the sight of God?' he asked, 'and in the presence of this congregation to be a lawful, dutiful, faithful and loving wife?'

That was all. The young couple were not required to go through the ritual of repeating phrases. All they said throughout was, 'I do.'

There were two hymns right at the beginning, numbers 12 and 438 *(The King of Love my Shepherd is)*. Then came a short prayer, followed by the marriage ceremony.

It was over almost too soon. The congregation was singing Hymn 229 (Old Hundredth):

> All people that on earth do dwell,
> Sing to the Lord with cheerful voice;
> Him serve with mirth, His praise forth tell,
> Come ye before Him and rejoice.

They were certainly rejoicing, all seventy-seven of them. I have never heard such singing. Later, when Sheila and I lingered behind while the guests dispersed, chatting brightly, but with perhaps one or two backward glances at the couple of strangers still sitting in seats in the back row, we went slowly down to the organist, who continued to play while the guests went through the corridor to greet the Richard Howlands before going into the dining room.

We congratulated him on his playing. That wasn't only a device to kill time till the company had gone; we were sincere and grateful to him. He had helped to make our experience a real occasion. The Hammond was hired for the occasion, he told us, and he came with it. He had enjoyed his afternoon.

I told him I was surprised at the singing.

'They sang awfully well,' he agreed. 'It was lovely to sit here and listen to it.'

We talked for quite a while and then moved off. It would have been agreeable to have had a drink to the couple's well-being. But that was just not on. The crowd had cleared. We could safely move into the corridor leading to the hotel. The music of the Hammond followed us. In love with his music, the young organist was playing *Solemn Melody* by Walford Davies.

We did not linger in the lounge. As we went out through the front door, Sheila still clutching her crossword, a car was unloading in front of the hotel three slim young men in pale blue tartan jackets and dark trousers. They had their musical instruments with them. I guessed that they were the 'Trio', mentioned on the programme, who would be playing for the wedding dinner and the dancing afterwards.

Much, much later that evening, we were going up in the hotel lift. A young man, full of high spirits, just made it before the gate closed. I knew the face.

'Hey,' I said, 'you're the bridegroom!'

'That's right.'

'Richard Howland!'

He laughed. 'Right again. It wasn't me that changed my name; that was Catherine!'

'We gate-crashed your wedding!'

'Good for you.' He smiled at Sheila, forgetting me. 'I'd have invited you any time. It was lovely, wasn't it?'

'But we're apologizing.'

'Don't spoil it. I'm glad you were there. Why didn't you come and have a drink with us afterwards?'

Our own regret. The lift stopped, the door opened, he held it with his foot.

'But should you be here?' I asked foolishly. 'I mean shouldn't you be half-way to Majorca or somewhere by this time, on your honeymoon?'

He laughed happily.

'And miss our own dinner-and-dance! We're staying here tonight. Tomorrow we'll go off on our own!'

XI

1

Because I had breakfasted in the large Angus dining room once before, I chose to go down early on my own. Normally I like breakfast in bed with my newspaper and letters, but this northern breakfast room has something special to offer and I wanted to savour it again. I sat alone at a round table that could have taken three other people, but there were only a few men scattered about the room, and the sense of space and personal isolation, something that is always acceptable, washed over me luxuriously.

There should have been an almost cathedral-like quiet, broken only by the tinkle of a spoon against cup, or the muted voice of a waitress or guest somewhere in the distance. As it was, there was the sound of piped music, but so turned down as to make the music almost indistinguishable, and the sound itself practically non-existent. Indeed, I had difficulty for a moment in recognizing that the murmur was *One moment and my heart seemed to know,* but no difficulty at all in remembering it and all that its melody, and the sound of other melodies like it, had meant to the generation of its time. And I hummed the words that followed, *that love said hello,* as I sat down.

Almost immediately there came across the room to my table a woman I remembered. She was a woman first and a waitress afterwards, one of the several early-middle-age ladies who serve the Angus only at breakfast time in this room. The thinking behind this arrangement fulfils several purposes: it obviously allows the necessary time-off to waiters who have been working late the night before; it provides spare-time employment for these women, so very carefully chosen; and

147

it gives the guest an opportunity of meeting Scottish women of a very special type. You might be in their homes.

There are only two or three, and they move about the room, quietly efficient, with a mothering interest in you that is as warm and welcome as the breakfast itself. All have apple-red cheeks, clear friendly eyes, usually blue, and that directness of manner that comes from understanding, and an inner independence. They take it for granted that whatever conversation passes between you, you will be as interested in their views or news as they are in yours.

Mine was a nice, homely, farmer's daughter of about forty-five. I do not know for sure that she was, or that that was her age, but that was how she looked to me as she came, smiling, to my table.

'What a morning!' she said.

Indeed it was a morning, raining cats and dogs outside, with rivulets streaming down the windows. It made the atmosphere in the room all the more cosy.

And then: 'It's nice to see you here again.'

Ah, what an art is that of the waiter who knows that service is not the demeaning business some make it, but a relationship between people who have, in their different ways, to work for a living.

'And it's nice to see you again,' I said. 'You're really one of the reasons I came down for breakfast.'

Why not? Why not give out to the men and women who give you pleasure and deserve to know that they do? She smiled, again, not broadly, but in quiet acceptance of the truth and the compliment it offered. At the same time she moved away the sugar bowl from my place and brought the cruet over from the far side of the table. There was no need for me to tell her that I would be one of those who took salt with their porridge. I did not fool myself that she could remember *that* from a previous occasion, but she would know my kind at a glance. I might speak in a voice that had sadly long ceased to have the true cadence of its birth, but all the knocking-about the world had not turned me into a foreigner.

'The kippers are awful good this morning,' she advised me, so I followed my porridge with a kipper. In between the spaced-out comings of my pot of tea, and the porridge, and the kipper, and then the toast and marmalade, she would loiter for a little if I supplied the right word, which I carefully did. I not only wanted to hear what she had to tell me, but how she said it.

As she cleared away each dish I drew from her, simply by my

appreciation of the present Dundee, and her agreement with me, an account of the mess the place used to be. I had already seen many indications that its citizens were proud of what Dundee was doing for itself, but it was good to have it straight from a woman like this.

She loved her Dundee, dirty or bonnie, but it had once been a place to flee, not to stay in, and she had seen many of her girlhood friends take off. One in particular was very close to her thinking while she talked to me, and I was to discover the reason.

During the war this girl had met a Canadian soldier and fallen in love with him. Married, and the war over, they stayed on in Dundee for a while, he found one or two jobs, and their first girl child was born in the city. But anyone who has been used to Canada, its freedom and its opportunities, could not be content with what was going in Dundee and what it had to offer his family. He wanted his daughter to have her chance, and if there were to be other children, then they would be born in Canada.

So her friend pulled up her roots and went off with her husband and baby. In her new country her husband became a Canadian Mountie, the growing family prospered and were happy. Its most jubilant member was its first-born. 'I was born in Scotland,' she could boast to her brothers and sisters, and they had nothing to match the boast with. 'I was born in Scotland,' she chortled triumphantly to her school friends, and they gazed on her in envy.

'I was born in Scotland, too,' thought her mother, and after seventeen years in Canada she had her first holiday away from it, on her own. Her husband treated her to a trip to her old home.

'She came by aeroplane, too,' said my farmer's daughter proudly. 'All by herself. She just had to come back to see the old place, and I was there to meet her when she arrived.'

I could feel the thrill in her. 'You should have seen her face when she saw Dundee. "What a change from the old days," she said to me. She couldn't believe her eyes. "It's all lovely," she said. "There's so much to do too! When I think how we used to call it dirty Dundee!" You should have heard her. She couldn't stop talking about it.'

Perhaps I was hearing of the new Britain that we, so near it, sometimes miss. I was watching the animation in the woman's face as she moved round the table clearing up.

'And that's not all,' she confided in me. 'The whole family's coming on holiday to Scotland as a present for the children when they pass their exams. They've heard so much about it from their mother. And it won't be long before their father is thinking of retiring.'

Conspiratorially, she let the words sink in.

'Do you know,' she said, 'I think they'd like to come and live here.'

2

I had brought an old golf umbrella with me. It was larger than most of the modern ones, and unlike them with their red, yellow and green patterns, mine was red all over. Old-fashioned now, I suppose, but in the thirty-five years since I bought it from Ben Sayers, it has only once been re-covered. There was ample protection under it. The rain was almost sleet now, and although it wasn't heavy, it came down with persistence and with no pity. It would be a dreary forenoon in Dundee.

The streets were empty. You can always tell when it's Sunday. The very feel of the day, as if it were missing or forgotten from existence, marks it as something fugitive, almost something furtive. Especially in a city. Especially in a wet city. Dundee was a misty and moist wasteland, avoided by traffic, empty of people, still sleeping off last night's drunk or last night's love or last night's frustration.

Most people in cities lie late on Sunday. Particularly in the hard-working northern cities. Most of all, I think in Scotland. I remembered how late people slept on Sunday morning, almost until noon. There had been less leisure in those days; men and women worked six or seven days a week, and long hours. The long sleep from Saturday night into late Sunday morning was their rare treat. In a world of few diversions, lying in bed late on Sunday morning was really something. And if you could drowsily wake up, have some kind of breakfast in bed, and then pull the blankets around you again and sink into·deep sleep, this was the high mark of the week. It must have meant something to many, for I remember a music hall song that went something like, *Sweet Saturday night, sweet Saturday night; better than Monday morning.*

The habit obviously lived on. I'd have thought that with the shorter hours, more money, cars for workers and bosses alike, something would have happened to this device of nature to restore lost vitality. Perhaps it had. The centre of a city was perhaps the worst place to come to conclusions about people in their bedrooms.

150

I put up the collar of my coat and went out into the rain. When I turned the corner I saw the shabby figure of a man sheltering in a shop doorway just ahead. A left-over from last night, I thought, and a sure 'touch'. The kind of unkempt bundle that tempts most people to cross over to the other side of the street. I had given up doing that a long time before.

I knew he would stumble out from the door, turn to meet me. He did; and he was a pathetic sight even before I got to him. He was worse close up. He had no hat. The rain had made wet streaky snakes of the thin hair clinging to his head. There were traces of yellow and grey in the hair. He had been a blond young man once, years ago, and perhaps his blue eyes now blurred and watery had once had charm.

The stamp of failure was on him: the too-long coat falling down towards his ankles, the wide-bottomed trousers trailing in the wet street, the stubbled chin, grey and yellow like the hair on his head. His eyes were vacant, neither appeal nor emotion in them. And yet their very emptiness – despair of despair – made its own appeal. There was something here that was more than just an alcoholic hang-over from the night before.

I didn't wait to let him begin his mumble. Don't wait for them to ask, I had told myself years ago; they're humiliated enough already. Spare them any more. You never know what happened. It's all very well to say they're beyond feeling; but you never know. You have to give them the benefit of the doubt.

I handed him half a crown. He half-raised his right arm in an attempt at a salute, and the soft 's' of his 'sir', gave me a clue.

'You're not a Scot,' I said.

'No, sair.'

I had heard the accent recently, and the two words were enough.

'A Pole?'

The watery eyes blinked.

'Yes, sair.'

His arm came up awkwardly in that half salute. I can't convey the strange, moving effect it had on me. I remembered the exiled Polish soldiers who had thronged Scotland after their defeat and escape from Europe. And the ones who had been demobilized in Scotland at the end of the war, unable to go back to their own land. They had settled here, and many of them had made good. This one hadn't.

'How old are you?' I asked.

He had to think. 'Fifty-five years...fifty-six.'

151

His shaking hand held a fragment of unlit cigarette. I pulled out my lighter and steadied his hand. I watched his face while he puffed the butt into a glow. It was still dead, vacant, but something remote was happening behind the battered countenance. He was a long way from home.

The rain had stopped, but some drops of water were trickling down his cheeks, and I realized they were tears. A drunkard's tears, perhaps. Or the communication with another human being, the few exchanged words that had put him in touch with life again?

'Married?' I asked.

'Yes, sair.'

'A Scottish girl?'

I remembered how avid the Polish soldiers were for the Scottish girls.

'Oh, yes.'

The talk was unfuddling him and giving him a little ground to stand on.

'Family?'

'Three sons, and a girl. They live in England.'

Miles and miles away. He was his own drop-out, willingly or not.

'You never see them?'

'Not often, sair.'

'You've no job?'

'No, sair.'

'Haven't you got some kind of trade you could work at?'

'I'm a cabinet maker.' A faint echo of pride came into the slurred speech.

I thought of the excellent Polish tailor in Edinburgh who only a few days before had handed me the three pairs of trousers that he had slimmed down for me from three suits bought years before. A man whom a whole circle of people employed and respected. I doubted if this Pole in front of me would ever do any more cabinet making.

My mind went back to the summer of 1940 and the Polish and Czech soldiers swarming the streets of Scottish cities in their long capes and natty caps. I remembered the campaign our newspapers had waged to get some of the closed entertainment places opened up for them on a Sunday, on wet Sundays like this one. We hadn't had a lot of success.

What would happen to this one when I had passed on out of his life? He had half a crown. What would he do with it?

'I need a cup of tea,' he said, 'and now I can sleep tonight.'

At almost everything I had said or asked, his arm had struggled to make that haunting half-salute. He was a victim of his fighting past.

'What is there for you here?' I asked.

His watery blue eyes peered at me out of his wet face. He said the most unexpected thing.

'It is a beautiful city. I hope to die here.'

3

I shook his hand and went on up the dreary street. The rain had started to fall again. I couldn't get him out of my thoughts, that coat drooping down beneath his knees, his trousers trailing on the wet pavement.

Not so long ago he had stood up against Hitler and fought for the independence of Poland, and so for his own freedom. His country had been conquered and he had escaped from it and its subsequent servitude. But he could never go back, and exile has its own agony. He was in the midst of Scots whose country had lived for centuries with the experience of invasion. But it had never been conquered. The English had won most of the battles but they had failed to conquer.

Walking through the dreary rain, wondering at my attachment to this part of Scotland, stirred by something in the contact with my fellow-man, I remembered that just seventeen miles away from Dundee, on the north-east coast, was the little town of Arbroath. Few English people have ever heard of it, this dot on the map, this small grey Scottish seaport with the ruins of an old Abbey. To be accurate, few had heard of it at that moment when I was exploring Dundee.

But only a short time afterwards, Britain was to be deluged with an issue of pictorial stamps bearing the imprint, 'Declaration of Arbroath', and all over England, Ireland, Wales, and perhaps even Scotland, puzzled Britons were asking what the devil was the Declaration of Arbroath. Friends abroad, receiving mail stamped with the Arbroath issue, wrote back enquiringly to people in Britain, turned up their encyclopaedias or history books, or just shook their heads and bothered no more.

In April 1970, it was an anniversary, the six hundred and fiftieth anniversary of the signing of the Declaration of Arbroath and I imagine that this was the occasion for the not very attractive stamp to mark it. The historic Declaration set down squarely what all Scots felt and thought about their independence. Headed by Duncan, Earl of Fife, many other Earls, 'and the rest of the barons and freeholders and the whole community of the kingdom', Scotland declared at the Monastery of Arbroath, on 6 April 1320 – six years after victory over the English at Bannockburn – its determination to defend its independence from English aggression.

It also appealed to Pope John XXII to understand the Scottish situation ('that he would look with an understanding eye on the troubles and calamities brought upon the Scots by English invasion and savagery') and exhort the King of England – who ought to be content with his vast possessions – 'to allow us to live in peace in Scotland'. It promised that Scotland would cooperate with Edward to bring this peace about.

But the Declaration had plenty of teeth in it. The people had chosen Robert (Robert the Bruce) to be their King, and they would stand by him in defence of their liberties, and if necessary be rid of him if he betrayed them, and make another king. We were determined, even if only a handful of Scots were left alive, never to be dominated by the English. (Can I hear another voice in the future! 'We shall fight on the beaches...'?) 'It isn't glory or riches that we fight for, but liberty, which every Scot will defend with his life.'

And then the final thrust: 'It is to the Pope's interest that he should respond to the plea, but if he doesn't, and believes the English point of view, and allows the English to continue the destruction of the Scots, then God will hold him responsible for what might follow between English and Scots.'

XII

1

The framed paintings on the walls were so striking that I said: 'I don't suppose you would sell one or two of these to me?'

'Of course,' said the headmaster. 'Take your pick. We can replace them with a dozen more.'

I thought he must be exaggerating, with a schoolmaster's natural pride in his pupils. But as we turned into another corridor, it too was lined with paintings of brilliant, vivid colour. And I realized that here was the new world of the young, the world that had certainly never been mine or my chums in Falkirk when we were drilled, belted with the tawse, and pressured into acquiring knowledge of the three Rs.

'And they paint these here in the school?'

'In their class rooms.' And then with real longing, 'I wish you had seen the forty-foot mural they did for the Edinburgh Festival.'

I wish I had. It was painted several years ago, and must have been done by some of the children I met when I first encountered James Forsyth and his enterprising approach to teaching. It was the time when I was lending a hand at the Lyceum Theatre at Edinburgh. The headmaster of Gracemount Primary School had persuaded Tom Fleming and the theatre manager, Charles Tripp, to allow 1,000 of his children to come to the dress rehearsal of the theatre's Christmas entertainment; and the following day I sent this letter to *The Scotsman* and the *Evening News:* 'So many criticisms are made nowadays about the behaviour of the young that I would be grateful if you would allow me to pay a tribute to the children of Gracemount Primary School, their teachers, and headmaster. A thousand pupils attended the dress

155

rehearsal of our Christmas play, *Rumpelstiltskin,* and it was a delight to see how well the chilren behaved amidst all the excitement and hilarity.

'In addition, the teachers brought with them polythene bags to collect litter. As a result, the theatre when the party left was as clean as when they arrived. This, in spite of the fact that 1,000 ices, each in a paper wrapper, were served to the children in their seats during the interval. It was a pleasure to all of us here to serve them.'

James Forsyth then invited me to come and see the children at work in his school but alas it was a long time before I arrived at his door on this cold day, unannounced, and just before lunch. He was not unprepared for me, nor was Mrs Pearson, white-haired and blue-eyed, at that time the boss of a beautiful kitchen. Gracemount is a spacious, modern school where lunch is cooked and served in the school, and not delivered in containers, then reheated and – if I can rely on young friends elsewhere – generally detested and rejected in favour of sandwiches brought from home. Mrs Pearson, an ex-Wren with four full-time and two part-time assistants, told me that they had just cooked the childrens' favourite meal: shepherd's pie, peas, and doughnuts.

'Mine too,' I said hungrily.

So for the first time I sat down with James Forsyth and his teachers and 330 children in one of those comprehensive schools that are a blessing to millions and apparently a pain in the neck to class-conscious parents, not a hundred miles from Edinburgh, who beat their brains out for the privilege of paying large sums of money to have their offspring put through the same old mill at the same old school that daddy went to. I wish some of those advocates of a divisive society could have been with me that day at Gracemount primary school, now recognized throughout the world as a unique educational establishment. 'Perhaps the most interesting visitors we have had,' James Forsyth told me, 'were a party of Japanese, and a group of Soviets who had recently completed a course in linguistics at Edinburgh University. They were due to visit Gracemount the day after Russia invaded Czechoslavakia. The diplomatic wires buzzed with protests, but I insisted that the Soviets should visit us. They came, they saw, and they were conquered!'

The dining room was even newer than the school; it had been added only recently. It was large, looked as clinical as a hospital, as attractive as a studio. When the meal was over and the place cleared, six women with electric cleaners would leave the place spotless for the next day's activities. Mrs Pearson created her menus for a month ahead, with standard staple ingredients that could be varied with imaginative cooking. Mince might appear on the bill of fare one day, the following week the same kind of mince is a hamburger; braised steak can become steak pie or steak casserole.

The shepherd's pie and peas were delicious; I could see why it was the favourite menu. The doughnuts that followed were what doughnuts should be, brownly crisped and generously sugared.

'I arrived at the right time,' I said, well satisfied, to James Forsyth. 'How much do I owe you for all this?'

He laughed. 'You can add it to your cheque for the paintings!'

The boys and girls around me, chattering mischievously but answering my questions with intelligence, were the sons and daughters of parents in all the professions; shopkeepers, lawyers, bus-drivers, university professors, electricians, brick-layers. You name it, their offspring were here, bright, animated and, most important, happy.

James Forsyth doesn't use the word 'happy'. He goes the whole hog, preferring the word 'love'. 'In these first precious years of schooling,' he says, 'the children should be guided to fall in love with what they are doing, and then themselves gradually realize that they have to apply themselves seriously to work.'

James is no egg-head theorist. He came up the hard way and is an inspired realist. He told me he was just on the point of taking a group of boys and girls, fifty in all, off to the Continent.

'But it's term time,' I said. 'Surely they ought to be working.'

'You think they should go in their holiday time? And make a high old holiday of it?'

I had remembered that that was usually the time for taking children abroad.

'Not with us,' he said. 'This isn't a holiday. This is part and parcel of their job of learning, the follow-through to their two years of primary French. We don't let it go rusty on them. We throw them right into the middle of what they've been studying. This is work, and the best kind of learning.'

The year before, he had taken another fifty pupils to Paris. In term time. Three other people accompanied him, two women teachers and a photographer. No amateur photographer. A real professional, whose record of their activities on the Continent was displayed in large blown-up prints on the school's walls, and in folders. You only have to glance at these blow-ups to see how active and alive and enthusiastic the children were on their trip and to understand the psychological effect these have on the other children growing up in the wake of the lucky group. And to know that the photographer knew his job. They were as good as anything I had seen in a newspaper or magazine office.

'Who took these?' I asked, back with James in the corridors of the school, wandering about at random, reaching out to the school's activities on impulse.

'Dougie McCaskill,' he said.

'Isn't he on the *Daily Record?*'

'That's right.'

I thought: Once a headmaster, always a pupil. This man was ready to learn from anyone and ready to use them for the good of his children. I looked at him more closely, not with a new respect, but with a new curiosity. He is a rugged man, not impeccably dressed. Rather haphazardly dressed in fact, as if clothes aren't all that important. An odd contradiction. Indifferent to appearance in himself, you could mistakenly think 'sloppy'; yet like an eagle in unobtrusive vigilance over his flock of the men and women of tomorrow.

His voice is rough, a little hoarse, with a natural Scottish accent. He doesn't bother too much with what is left of his hair. And he stoops forward a little, the posture of a man who has been looking down at desks and books, bending over to share a pupil's preoccupation with a problem. In spite of his incisiveness, he's a tantalizingly evasive person, difficult to fathom. But rouse him on anything and he'll talk your head off, he has so many convictions.

And one of them is that children should learn from experience. That trip to Paris was an instructional eight-day exercise for his group, all the way from Edinburgh to London, from Victoria station to Dover, from Dover to Ostend to Paris; all round Paris, to Versailles, to a dozen other points, the normal and the unexpected.

I only had to look at their eager faces in the photographs, their smiles, the exuberance of them, and to pass their friends now in the school corridors, to see how they would attract attention wherever they went. At one of the hotels where they stayed, an American could not resist coming over to the school party while they were having their evening meal, all of them a little high with excitement. He asked James: 'Where on earth do these lovely children come from?'

The headmaster's heart beat faster with pride, but he let the children answer for themselves.

'Scotland!' they sang out happily.

It must have been a moment for James. He hadn't always been a headmaster. In fact, Gracemount was his first headmaster's post, and James Forsyth was the new Gracemount's first head. And it hasn't always been easy for him. Yet he has always been close to a school, part of a school.

He was born in the Castle Hill of Edinburgh, and his father became janitor of Castle Hill School, at the foot of the esplanade near the Castle. High up over the city and the lights of Princes Street. Was it here that his ambition was born?

Then something else was also born here. So close was he to the Castle that his early memories are of listening at the end of each day to the Argylls playing the Retreat. That was the bugle call of high adventure, firing a Scots boy's dreams. He grew up with the sound, longing to be a soldier and a headmaster. Strange combination? You have to be a fighter and a believer in both professions. The bugle call of the Retreat cast its own spell; the closeness of the school, his father's occupation, and his own dream of what a school should be, did the rest.

He joined the Territorials before Hitler's war. In the war itself, he had such fluent command of the German language that he was used as an interpreter in SOE operations in Sicily and elsewhere. He will go back to revisit Sicily and his other old battlefields one day when he finds the time. At least, he thinks he will, but I believe that a man like this, with so much concern in him about children and learning, will have a lot on his hands for many a day.

He made the other part of his dream come true when in 1952 he became deputy headmaster of the Links School in Leith, worked there for nine years and then took on the overall responsibility of Gracemount like an actor stepping into a part tailored for him. How lucky are the men who know almost from childhood their life's ambition, and then achieve it. They bring to their job a complete absorption and self-abnegation that communicates enthusiasm to those around them. No longer having any personal goal to achieve, they are free to devote their lives to others. I could understand the impact of this man on children the moment I saw them together, but complete realization came much later in the day. Somewhere in the school a bell sounded. I glanced at my watch. It was 3.30.

'Wasn't that the bell for the end of the day?' I asked.

'Yes,' said James. 'But I can't get them to go home. Look at them!'

I had been watching them for the past half hour. We were in the large playroom, a wonderful place with high ceiling, huge glass walls, smooth parquet flooring. Usually a home for gym work, basketball, music, dances and so on, it was today being used for a new purpose. This was certainly my lucky day. I had chanced in on James, fulfilling a five-year-old promise. It happened to be the first time in Scotland that an exciting educational innovation was being introduced to the school.

Back in my old hunting ground, the Lyceum Theatre, a wonderful new adventure had been .launched called 'Theatre in Education'. Administered by Brian Stanyon, a number of actor-teachers from the theatre were visiting Gracemount and using the large room as an arena on which to present a play. The pupils of two classes, 60 youngsters from 10 to 12 years old, were taking part. And, fitting in with James Forsyth's own ideas, the performances were designed to involve them not only in entertainment but in education. Two of the school's teachers sat on the sidelines watching.

No wonder the children didn't hear the sound of the school bell! Here was every child's dream — acting in a play. And a well-conceived play at that, some of it being left to the impromptu creative impulses of the boys and girls themselves. It was called *The Blew Blanket,* and for 'Blew' read 'Blue'. 'The Blue Blanket' in the time of James III was the privileged Standard or the Craftsmen within the Burgh of Edinburgh, restored to them by privy seal in 1482 when they and the Merchants and other loyal subjects had marched on Edinburgh Castle and freed their imprisoned King.

The colourful denouement, full of action, is when the craftsmen and troops march to the castle, the English flee, and King Jamie's life is saved. The final stage direction in the script will show you what a climax the play reached, and what an organized clamour resounded through that lofty playroom: 'The Baillie explains value of charter and significance of Blue Blanket and suggests the townspeople show these gifts to the whole city. Whereupon Jenny, Elizabeth, Minstrel and Baillie organize a civic procession round the hall and back to the classroom.'

The script of the play covered events during the latter half of the fifteenth century, tracing the development of trade, the conflict between merchant guilds and the craft associations, and the growth of the corporation. To this day one of the reputed original Blue Blankets can be seen at the Museum of Antiquities in Edinburgh.

The actor-teachers involved, Gordon Wiseman, Sue Birtwistle, Andrew Dixon and Win Hunter, carried the main burden of the production, but very cleverly infiltrated the children into the action and dialogue, and skilfully used them in the crowd work of craftsmen and merchants. The 'message' of the play came over through the actors but few of the children in the production could have separated themselves from the general theme and action of the story.

For three years previously these actor-teachers had all been at the Belgrade Theatre in Coventry engaged in similar school work. But *The Blew Blanket,* and other plays to follow, would be based on historical happenings in Scotland. Forty-eight primary schools in the capital city would reap the benefit of the undertaking, and a number of secondary schools would have demonstration programmes based on *The Crucible* and other plays.

I had come upon the performance when it was well under way, the playroom full of colour and sound and movement; and for a little while I had to find my way through its meaning and significance. The background screen represented Edinburgh Castle. I realized that twelve ordinary school tables were the High Street Market, displaying the merchants' and craftsmen's wares. A rostrum in the centre of the floor, with a bell on it, presumably was the City Cross. At this point Gordon Wiseman slipped a copy of the script into my hand, and the first words my eyes caught were: *Enter Court Official. Rings bell. Reads proclamation.* And after that: *Fanfare. Exit Court Official.*

The fanfare came from a tape recorder, concealed with other props and sound effects behind a curtain in a backstage space at the 'entrance' end of the room. Then I began to sort out the Craft Signs in the room, the Merchant Insignia, the Scrolls, somebody's Chain of Office, something that could only be a money-bag. The rostrum was the pivotal point, and around it on the spacious bare floor of the room, representing the city streets, the sixty children moved freely, wrangled over merchandise, assembled to hear the occasional dignitaries who mounted the rostrum, formed their procession for the march on the Castle. It must have recreated for them the meaning and the activities and atmosphere of the time. They were indeed learning while playing.

And they had brought a certain amount of home-work to the job. Before their morning class break, they had studied medieval maps and objects as visual aids to the performance to come. They had discussed fifteenth-century Edinburgh, its houses, streets and people; heard about merchants' guilds and crafts associations, traced the growth of trade and rivalry between merchants and craftsmen. They had been well groomed in the most pleasurable and instructive way for the historical incidents that came to life through their active participation in the afternoon.

More than that. The Lyceum Theatre's 'Theatre in Education' had prepared a list of suggestions for class follow-up work when the play was over and the actors had departed. It was highly imaginative, including subjects such as History: the development of the Corporation of Edinburgh; trade routes at the time of James III; trade routes today; a further look into the everyday life of the craftsmen, houses, possessions, etc. When has the Blue Blanket been used? And with what results?

Under the heading Commerce, it suggested: present-day trade; modern markets; what brings money into Edinburgh today? Creative Writing: each craftsman and merchant write out his or her life story; were you born in Edinburgh? If not how did you come to be here? Describe your daily routine. And under the heading of Art: model-making; a medieval market; a modern market; sewing group to embroider a Blue Blanket. And Music: look at the ballads of the time; sing them; write your own ballads. Even Maths was not forgotten: bargaining in merks, pence or equivalent goods. And visits were suggested to the Cowgate, High Street, the Museum of Antiquities.

I had come upon the playroom thinking that life at James Forsyth's school was almost too good to be true. All that colour on the walls, the sparkling faces of the children, the good food. I had watched through a glass door an enthralled class of the smallest boys and girls listening to a story, told by Miss Murray. I could hear nothing, and I saw only the back of her head. But I was facing all the children sitting on the floor, looking up to her. They could have seen my face at the door if they had wanted to. They never took their eyes or their ears from the story-teller.

We moved away at last from the playroom to go back to James Forsyth's office. Janet Arnold, his secretary, brought us a cup of tea. Behind the headmaster's desk there were photographs on the walls.

'Former pupils,' he said, catching my glance. And then, fishing into a drawer; 'Have a look at these.'

He brought forth two thick bound volumes. One had a tartan cover. The other had a 'fashion' motif. Both were beautiful books, the inside pages written and hand printed in colours, and illustrated with drawings

162

and appropriate cut-outs from magazines. They had style and finish. The sense of composition, with its wise use of white space, was excellent. Whatever the text was like, the lay-out of both volumes was good. I read a few pages of the editorial accompanying the illustrations.

'Pretty good,' I said.

'The *History of Tartans*,' explained James, 'was done by one of our girls, Jane Gillespie. The *History of Fashion* was done by another, Melodie Milne.'

It had been a school task in sustained workmanship.

'It took them three months. Working at school and at home. You can't believe the amount of research they had to do for text and pictures.'

But I could. Work like this isn't turned out without personal devotion and application.

'Can I borrow them?' I asked. 'I'd like to mull over them.'

Janet Arnold was already reaching for two large envelopes.

James said 'That's what I hoped you'd ask.'

He was happy. It had been a good day for him, sharing his life's work with someone who wanted to see something of it. In nine years his young flock had grown from 200 to 1,000.

I had realized, hours before, that this was the new world, newer and more important than any other change brought about in social history in this country in the last fifty years. Not only in this country; everywhere. Understanding of what we do with a child, the environment in which he works, how we teach and encourage him, is now almost universal.

The difference between this pleasant but disciplined place with its bright colours, its light and space, its uninhibited atmosphere, its complete separation from anything that savours of cruelty or humiliation or discouragement (its green fields glimpsed through the large windows), and the early schooling of my own generation in Scotland (with its cement playgrounds, its sordid sanitation, its leather tawse of punishment hanging threateningly behind the teacher's head) was the difference, as far as a child's mind is concerned, between heaven and hell.

XIII

1

I took the work of James Forsyth's young artists away with me. Would any of them, from these early paintings I wondered, go on to become a Willie MacTaggart? Would any of his young scholars follow in the footsteps of Walter Scott or Robert Burns or J.M. Barrie? Barrie? Would any of them want to?

While Barrie was writing he lived to know his fame and sometimes to enjoy it. But there were experiences in his early life that must have made complete enjoyment difficult. Now, only forty years after his death, who in Scotland cares about him or his work?

D.H. Lawrence lived a full life of endeavour, of ecstasy and torture, but although his genius was recognized by a few, his name and his voice were unknown to most men and women. Forty years after his death, Lawrence is known to everybody and his genius acknowledged.

Yet both Lawrence and Barrie, contemporaries, and once on the threshold of acquaintance if not of friendship, have achieved one strange and similar fate. Both are without overwhelming honour on their own home ground. In Eastwood, near Nottingham, where Lawrence was frugally and painfully reared, and in Kirriemuir, where Barrie was born in the now famous humble home, few of the natives have more than a casual and disparaging attitude to their native sons, when they are persuaded to discuss them at all.

This astonished me about Eastwood. What could possibly have alienated the locals from their greatest son? His poetry? His haunting descriptions of nature, his sense of atmosphere and places? His novels which are now sold in millions and seen in films by us all? More likely the history of his youth and his love for Margaret Chambers, and his desertion of her. Local gossip where local lads and lasses are concerned can tarnish the reputation of a man for life – and after – however much the rest of an ignorant world wants to acclaim him.

And Barrie who roared away to success, leaving so many of his contemporaries stuck where they belonged? He was the poor Scots boy who made it to London and won success and wealth, and knew all the big yins there, but hadn't too much time to spare for his native Kirriemuir, although he was always at hand in time of family need.

They never put up a monument for him in Kirriemuir. It is a cold corner of Scotland, and they have a tendency not to fall over themselves about their successful sons. You can always find 'the Window in Thrums' if you look for it, and the cricket pavillion that Barrie gave to the town. But his true monument is the house at number nine Brechin Road where he was born. That is in the safe hands of the Scottish Trust, and 6,000 visitors on an average visit it every year from all over the world, grateful for what was brought into their lives by the strangest little man who ever came out of Scotland. So somebody remembers him.

When I stood in the back yard of that house and went into the wash-house, with its tub and boiler and cradle, where the young and tiny Barrie acted out his first childish plays, two voices from the past whispered for my attention. 'Courage is the thing,' said Barrie in his later life. 'All goes if that goes.' And Bernard Shaw's: 'There are two tragedies in life. One is not to get your heart's desire. The other is to get it.'

I never saw *Peter Pan* – 'that dreadful masterpiece' as someone has described it – when I was a boy, and I do not know whether to be grateful for this or regretful. It was, and still is, a childhood experience that stamps itself on the young mind seemingly for life. Caught by Barrie in childhood, you were captured for good. This was the measure of his skill and his own almost pathological relationship to a juvenile realm of impossible dreams.

I was a father when eventually I was confronted with the play, eager to give my young son and daughter the pleasure I had missed. I was full of anticipation myself, young enough in heart to hope that my afternoon with the famous fairies would provide me with some bewitching moments. I should have known better. You have to come to *Peter Pan,* and to Barrie, very young and innocent, with the wide-eyed wonder still in you. You have to come long before life gets you by the throat.

I was more entranced by the little boys and girls around me, caught in the magic of never-never land. Their faces were raised to the stage as to a warming sun, their happy hearts were away on a distant journey.

But I had eyes too for their accompanying grown-ups. I thought it was fairly easy to recognize the ones like myself who had come new to the experience and the others who had brought their childhood adoration with them and were once again reliving old dreams and surrendering to the old wizardry. And, unconsciously, being part of Barrie's own tragic and lifelong struggle to escape from the world of reality.

I had time to think of Barrie and his strange life, and his work that reflected that life, and I wondered whether a new generation of grown-ups coming objectively to Barrie in this day and age, without being brainwashed before, would accept him for the wonder boy he was only the day before yesterday. Or even accept him at all.

Of course I brought to my thinking some knowledge of Barrie and his work, a natural interest in his Scottish beginning in Kirriemuir, the ambition that was born there, and his upward fight for success. I knew too the kind of guts it takes to 'grind' away (the word is Barrie's) in order even to make a beginning. In his first five years in London, Barrie wrote hundreds of articles for newspapers and magazines. Much of it was hack work churned out day after day on any subject under the sun for a few guineas an article.

I lived in the world when Barrie was alive and flourishing, and knew well the sort of world it was, and how its people existed, and what they felt and thought and hoped for. I had seen, like him, the beginning of the end of that world, with the grief and suffering of the Great War; and I had lived on after he died in 1937, to watch the world plunge into another war, and been caught up in the upsurge of a new, questing, rebellious spirit that is constantly challenging the past.

It would be odd indeed if the young men and women of this new age who question almost everything could take a Barrie to their hearts in the way he was acclaimed on an evening in December 1904, when *Peter Pan* was shown for the first time to an audience which must have been, in years at least, entirely grown up.

Barrie was then forty-four, a successful author and playwright, a crazy, mixed-up kid if ever there was one, still working out the grief of his childhood and the ingrown desperate flight from real life. And doing

166

it with masterly professional competence, and the spell-binding quality that could spill over from work into his relations with people. There were few people who could resist him.

Barrie was already famous and wealthy when *Peter Pan* was born. He was friendly with all the great ones of the land, in all the important walks of life. He had set out from Kirriemuir with £12 in his pocket to make his mark on life and he had made it. There would be another thirty years of work and living (one always thinks first of *work* with Barrie, and *living* afterwards), more successes, with a baronetcy as a bonus, before Barrie would die, as lonely as he had lived, with something of despair clutching at him in the last years, and certainly something of defeat.

2

When he made his famous Rectorial address to the students at St Andrew's University in 1922, he chose 'Courage' as his subject. It was not lightly chosen, nor was it lightly prepared. For nearly a year Barrie had been thinking about it, working on it, trying it out in the silence of his flat until he could deliver it without looking at the text, like an actor with a part. Even the first nervousness, when he fumbled with a paper knife on the table in front of him, was calculated and deliberate. What he could never have bargained for was the student who yelled out, 'Put the knife down, Jamie, or you'll cut your throat!' – and so set the ball rolling on one of the best performances Barrie ever gave.

'When you reach the evening of your days,' he said, 'you will, I think, see that we are all failures, at least all the best of us.' And he went on to say that Burns, 'the greatest Scotsman that ever lived', had written himself down a failure. He quoted Burns' words:

> The poor inhabitant below
> Was quick to learn and wise to know,
> And keenly felt the friendly glow
> And softer flame.
> But thoughtless follies laid him low,
> And stained his name.

And eight years later, on being installed as Chancellor of Edinburgh University, he mourned aloud: 'Unions and Hostels, such as, alas, were not in my time, now give Edinburgh students that social atmosphere which seemed in the old days to be the one thing lacking; the absence of them maimed some of us for life.'

It was an odd phrase to use; but all who knew Barrie and were attracted to him, who were dazzled and bewildered and flattered by him, who were warned and chilled by his swiftly changing moods, all knew that somewhere within him his personality was maimed. The demands he made on the love and loyalty of his friends were outrageous; they were also irresistible. The tyranny of his silences and withdrawals would have lost any other man most of his friends. But Barrie's cronies were all his children, to be played with, or chastised, or charmingly ordered to do what he wanted. But he had always to remain his own child; no one was permitted to intrude on the inner sanctuary of his own secret self.

Peter Pan was a milestone in Barrie's life. It was a goal for which he had been striving over many years. It was at last the perfect vehicle for his fairyland of childish dreams. In it he could run riot with every wisp of whimsy, every poignant longing of childhood. Fairies, pirates, beautiful mothers, mermaids, red-skins, crocodiles. And flying! Floating through the air, midway between the ceiling and the floor of your bedroom. The lot.

It's important to remember *Peter Pan,* and that Barrie was forty-four when he put it together. It's important, when *Peter Pan* comes on the scene at this stage in a man's life, to forget for a moment some of the work that has gone before — *Auld Licht Idylls* or *The Little Minister* — or even *Margaret Ogilvy,* that book about his mother which, written while he wept, was still an artist's expression rather than a son's.

Barrie never even partially released himself from his mother or his family. He carried them with him to the grave as he had accepted them, and his total protection of them, when he was a boy. The significance of *Peter Pan* at his age, is the measure of his need, in mid-life, to remain bogged down in childhood. Its glory was that he could translate it into terms that would satisfy his own longings and entrance millions of other children, old or young.

By this time work was everything. Every waking moment was concerned with the work that would eventually screen him like a wall. Always submerged in it; and always tormented by splitting headaches. From the age of seven he had committed himself. He had promised his mother then that one day he would raise her to the stars, the stars that had gone out for her with the death of Barrie's elder brother.

David Barrie was the light of his parents' lives. All their high hopes rested in him. He was to be a minister. He died suddenly when he was fourteen. It was at Bothwell, in the cold bite of winter in 1867, that David took off his skates and gave a friend a turn with them. The boy went spinning away, crashed into David, who fell heavily, head first on to the ice. With a fractured skull, he survived only a few hours.

J.M. Barrie was just seven at the time. At this highly impressionable age, he saw tragedy strike at the mother he adored. He was with her when the news was broken. He never forgot her grief. The terrors of life touched him at that moment, and he fled from them for good and all, evolving his own tortured way of keeping them at bay.

The story of *Margaret Ogilvy* tells how he resolved, at that tender age, to make up some day, somehow, for his mother's terrible loss. His course was set, and he never turned from it.

His mother lay in bed silently holding the christening robe in which all her children had been baptised. He peeped in many times at the door, and then sat on the stair and sobbed. A sister found him, a solitary little figure, not knowing what to do. Death had stamped itself on Jamie Barrie from that moment, and his mother's needs and demands would shape his whole life, helping to ruin his own marriage, and condemning him, in spite of dazzling success, to inner grief and loneliness.

Those of us who were brought up in Scotland in another day, know how close this relationship between mother and son could be. In a day when families were larger, when the economic background was bleak, and when home was the centre of all life, it was easy for many a young son, watching his mother's unending work and worry, to assume the mantle of the future protector. One day he would deliver her from her toil. It was the spur that led to his fame.

Few of us in such a situation saw the larger and more natural relationship of mother and son as did Robert Louis Stevenson in his poem:

> It is not yours, O mother, to complain,
> Not, mother, yours to weep,
> Though nevermore your son again
> Shall to your bosom creep,
> Though nevermore again you watch your baby sleep.

So Stevenson began his poem and after five other stanzas, completed it
with these two verses:

> And as the fervent smith of yore
> Beat out the glowing blade,
> Nor wielded in the front of war
> The weapons that he made,
> But in the tower at home still plied his ringing trade:

> So like a sword the son shall roam
> On nobler missions sent;
> And as the smith remained at home
> In peaceful turret pent,
> So sits the while at home the mother well content.

3

I could understand Barrie's resolve. I made a similar one myself.
Hundreds of Scottish boys have done the same. In my case, I can
remember the day it happened. My father, who drank more than was
good for him (or for us), had 'shamed' us all — my mother and her six
children — on a horse-drawn brake on the way to Bridge of Allan. I was
the youngest.

My hand was in my mother's. I looked up at her, knowing her
shame, knowing my own. It was in that moment that I became bonded
to her, that she saw in me perhaps some hope for the future. In my
young bewilderment over my father I could not accept that this was the
meaning of life. Like Barrie, and those many other boys, I would make
amends for my mother's unhappiness. I would belong to a life that I
was sure would be different from the existence around us.

The pattern is familiar to many whose childhood wasn't a bed of
roses in those days long ago. The determination to repay one day
parental sacrifice, or to make up for parental hardship; and the life-long
struggle to carry out the purpose. It wasn't peculiar to Scotland,
although naturally in an impoverished country like Scotland there were
more families in difficult economic traps.

D.H. Lawrence in his boyhood was bonded by such ties to his
mother, and their relationship was close and lifelong, beautifully
described in *Sons and Lovers*. But unlike Barrie, Lawrence was never

170

afraid to face up to life. He saw it for what it was, and battled with it. The stuff he wrote was the stuff of life, and he suffered in his own way because of it. The people in his pages were recognizable human beings, reflecting life, and saying courageously what they thought about it. Where Barrie made friends, Lawrence made enemies.

Barrie was attracted at once to *Sons and Lovers*. Not only because of the theme, but because of his appreciation of good writing. It was 1914. He was famous and on the crest of his own wave. He tried to get in touch with Lawrence, as he did with most promising writers, but Lawrence rebuffed his approach, and although they met, no friendship followed.

Lawrence was one of the few who resisted the Barrie spell. Around him Jamie gathered all the great literary figures of the day, a circle of mutual admiration, an impregnable barrier of his own kind keeping the everyday locked out. He made them all his children, even persuading many of them to turn out on English village greens to play cricket!

Close family relationships had much to do with Barrie's in-turned thoughts, but an equally disturbing emotional strain was caused by his religious conflicts. It must have been hard for him to break with his Auld Lichts religious background. The Barrie home was a citadel of puritan belief; the brother who had died was to be a minister – the highest hope of his mother and father.

Yet somewhere along the line Barrie must have made the break with his tradition and upbringing. You cannot become a famous London playwright, choosing for company the wordly men and women of the theatre, without in some way weakening the links with the old kirk. The Calvinist must often have been at war with the playwright.

He had to forget or fight down the other family tragedies in his life. While his beloved and adoring sister, Maggie, was preparing for her wedding, her fiancé was thrown from his horse and killed. Once more Barrie accepted the role of protector. He would take care of his sister in her grief. No, more than that – he would look after her for ever! It was all sincerely meant, but what manner of dramatics was really at work here?

He plunged into his self-imposed task, carting her off to a village in England, setting aside his friends, but not his work, to devote himself to his sister in her mourning. It went on for nearly a year when, to his relief and her happiness, she became engaged to the brother of her dead fiancé and married him.

Of course life caught up with Barrie in the end. He was no ordinary man conditioned for marriage and intimate contact with a normal woman. Yet he was incessantly attracted to beautiful women. Mary Ansel, a young actress more than caught his fancy. He hesitated long, making the poor woman wonder what was wrong, but at last — with or without his mother's permission — he married her.

Barrie was impotent. It was a marriage of friendliness, of strain, of bewildering uncertainty for the wife. It lasted — God knows how — for fifteen years, but its end was inevitable when Mary met Gilbert Cannan, a man capable of loving her. Barrie desperately asked her not to seek a divorce. It would ruin him professionally, he pleaded. But Mary had found the real thing at last and nothing would stop her.

4

The divorce deepened his loneliness. The world, whose regard he prized so immoderately, and which he secretly feared, continued to reward him. But he knew himself to be alone. His mother was now dead, buried on the same day as his eldest sister, Jane Ann, who had died three days before her. He had carried out all his promises to be something, to become famous and wealthy, to take away from her the tears that had plundered his young life. Alas, the tears are always there, mingling with his own brand of pawky humour, in everything he wrote. The sentiment at times is so raw that you blush for him. His professional writing friends could not put a finger on the secret of his success; but time after time he pulled it off and confounded them. The Barrie spell prevailed, coming through the pages or over the footlights.

He belonged to the age he lived in. It was another world when Barrie was thrusting upwards in the late 'eighties' and the early years of the present century. Everyone knew his place in it, God was in heaven, and good Queen Victoria, and later King Edward and Alexandra, were on their thrones, and all was very much right with the world.

The theatre was a place for entertainment, It was a social filling-in. The players acted out moonshine to tickle the palate or appeal to the superstitions or sustain the existing myth; seldom to challenge the mind.

Barrie fitted into this life of his time like a hand in a glove. He was the poor Scots boy, with magic words and fantasies floating about in him, and a passionate need to get them off his chest. He wanted to change nothing. The set-up was perfect for a talented writer who sought only to get away from the terrors of life. He was back in the wash-house behind his home in Kirriemuir. It was its own small world, separated from life. It served all his purposes and brought him fame, wealth, and position.

He could go on playing with people, pretending, and satisfying that urge to work. And that other one to meet and surround himself with pleasant people, so that there was never a free moment for loneliness and the inner voice of fear. Until perhaps, the last guest had gone, and he was alone with himself, behind his closed door. Only Barrie knew what happened then. Only Barrie, until the final years of his life, when his personal helplessness had at last to be revealed to the few friends around him on whom he depended.

The years had flown, the Courage address at St Andrew's was a long way behind him, the wife had departed, the old faithful friends were dying off, the flat that sheltered him in Adelphi was going to be pulled down. All the buttresses of his life were disappearing, and Barrie's stock was slowly sinking. A new age was coming in, a new war was looming up on the horizon.

He was wealthy, seemingly secure; but lonely and lost. He badly needed a reaffirmation of his greatness, a restorative, one of the old-time smash-hit theatrical successes. He wanted to be reassured, although he was well over seventy, that he was still the little wonder who had held them all in the hollow of his hand.

For the last few years of his life he was desperately engaged in writing and bringing to the stage his play *The Boy David*. Elizabeth Bergner was secured to play the leading role. Charles Cochran, the great impressario, presented it, first in Edinburgh and then in London. It proved to be Barrie's final curtain. Ill and stricken, he survived its failure by only a few months. The magic, and the master, had gone.

XIV

1

So many fleeting impressions....snatches of talk in hotels and bars
and tea-rooms...glimpses of a way of living from car window or
train...unexpected bits in local papers...contacts with complete
strangers...friends made....

Jimmy Wood. Green-keeper at Kilspindie, one of the loveliest golf
courses in Scotland. Dark, gentle, slow-speaking. He sees me approaching the green he is mowing and stands away from it. I wave to him and
he waves back. My shot is luckily near enough the pin for me to pick up
my ball without bothering to hole out. I join him on the fringe of the
green.

'All alone,' he says, his brown eyes smiling. 'You should have had a
gallery to see that yin!'

'And to see this,' I say.

My eyes are on the view. Jimmy half-turns to share it with me.

'Ay, it takes a bit of beating,' he murmurs.

The sea laps the rocks below our feet. The coast of Fife, dappled
with sunlight, stretches across on the opposite side. The hills rise mistily
beyond. We have stood like this at other greens on other days.
Kilspindie, on the large estate of the Earl of Wemyss, is a natural
promontory in the wide Aberlady Bay, itself a beautiful nature reserve.

A private road leads to the golf course, and at the end of it is peace
and silence unbelievable. We stand in the silence watching the slow
shipping in the Firth; in all that wide stretch only two boats, a timber
vessel coming in like a phantom from Sweden, a smaller and nearer
freighter gliding silently out towards the Bass Rock.

'Ay,' he repeats softly, more to himself.

The one word is enough. This is his life. Day after day he lives and works in this quiet grandeur. It never dims for him. Or for me. The wide bay is alive with birds. The oyster catchers are far across the sands, flying low in a long strung-out line. The sea is a bright blue beyond the bar, and the bar itself is churning blue and white like a water mill, presaging the tide change which will quickly flood the bay. In the shimmering light and against the distant blue, the sand is the colour of milk chocolate. The sky is immense, the colours dazzling.

The estuary waders are everywhere, sandpipers, bar-tailed godwits, oyster catchers. The gulls skirl and wheel, and the terns are there one moment in the sky, tightly packed in flight, and then, banking swiftly, merge into the atmosphere and vanish.

Jimmy Wood and I have this in common. We have another bond that is so different as to be almost laughable. Half a mile across the course at the club-house is the professional's shop. Here Joe Dickson, whose watchful care perfects every green, bunker and fairway of this dream course, also sells to Scottish golfers the kind of gaily-coloured gear that once only Americans wore, and which we soberer folk all then derided.

It needs no confidence trick on Joe's part. We may be years after the Americans, but all Scotland's golf courses are now gay with tammies and trews and windjammers and scarves and shoes of every colour in the spectrum. You could be in Miami or Palm Springs — except for the weather.

When I mentioned this, speculatively, to Jimmy Wood at one of our first meetings, he chuckled happily. 'Ah, the Americans!' he said, 'they're great!' And then, tentatively, 'You must have had a great time in Manhattan.'

I must have shown my surprise, both at his awareness of my activities, and his use of the word Manhattan. For a moment I had to adjust to the fact that New York was really on the island of Manhattan.

'I read your book,' Jimmy explained. 'Manhattan! What a place! There's plenty of life there all right.'

And it only needed a prod for him to spill out his memories — and, strangely, containing the same kind of nostalgia that I often have myself — of Manhattan. Jimmy had been in the RAF in the Second World War, stationed in the Bahamas for two years. Three times in transit he had passed through New York and been caught in its magic.

To the quiet, shy, serious-living young Scot (he was then in his twenties), the gorgeous bedlam of his Manhattan had been a glimpse of another, an impossible world. For a young man at any time New York is the greatest show on earth; for a young man from Britain, in the middle of a war, the lights and glitter of Manhattan must have cast its spell for ever. With Jimmy it did.

Jimmy had spent his life in this quiet corner of Scotland, always on a golf course. Beginning at Gullane, where his father also worked, he had moved on for himself to Kilspindie. Only a couple of miles away. The sights and sounds about him were the same. The plaintive ripple of the curlew, the singing of a lark overhead, the slow shipping through the tricky tide, the greens, tended with the care given to young animals or children, the few far-off golfers silhouetted against the golden light.

Manhattan had burst upon him, brassy with its effervescence, bewildering in it ceaseless gaiety and din. It stood in his life as an experience sudden and different from everything that had gone before.

He was bewitched. I could understand. In my time I had been bewitched by Manhattan too, when I was as young, if not younger, than Jimmy. You had to experience it to know what Manhattan could do to you.

And before he had ever met me, Jimmy had read that I had felt about Manhattan as he had felt, and still did; and that, incredibly, I had gone on living and working there. So we had this thing in common; a bond of experience that held us together for a few moments. Of all things! – the fever and fervour of New York; and its possibilities.

After our first meeting, I wondered about him. It was easy to understand his enthusiasm; what puzzled me was that, so in love with America, and realizing its vast potential, Jimmy hadn't emigrated there after the war. He was still a young man. His pre-war routine had been interrupted. Why not a fresh start in a place to which you had already surrendered a part of yourself?

But Jimmy knew better. Only his routine had been interrupted. He knew what his life was to be and where he belonged. The bright lights and the enormous possibilities of Manhattan, were enjoyed and understood, but his place was in his homeland. His roots were in this corner of heaven. This was where he belonged, doing the work he knew, picking up where he had left off. What greater happiness?

Of course I was intrigued. What was it that Manhattan had done to this likeable man? What had it stood for? To me, the opportunity to have a tilt at the world; for Jimmy, a privileged glimpse of a fabulous lunacy which, although he would never forget it, only confirmed his belief about his own destiny.

Jimmy is the Scot that didn't get away. Manhattan didn't get him, nor Sydney, nor Saskatchewan, nor any other of these outposts that claim so many of us. What could Manhattan possibly have given him in exchange for what he now enjoys?

He came home at the end of the war, and soon he was married at Arbroath by the padre of his regiment. Now he has a son of twenty-one. There's not much chance that he'll ever see Manhattan again, or want to. And it's almost a certainty that he'll never live there. But to be able to talk, if only for a few minutes, with someone who shared his experience and his knowledge of that mythical other world, and so re-create it — ah! that makes the memory the more precious, and the present the more ensured.

Jimmy likes to tell you a humorous story or two when you can get him away from the golf course. The kind of story that begins, 'Have you heard the one about....' So you know straight away that it will be based on complete unreality, and therefore innocent and delightful; not taken from real life and so carrying behind the laugh a hint of violence or sex.

Jimmy's stories reflect the innocence of his way of life. They are more indicative of character and personal preference than a biography would be. This one, almost exactly as he offered it to me, waiting for my chuckle: A golfer died on the golf course and was immediately transported to hell. Corridor after corridor of baking heat. He longed for relief. At last, turning a corner, he came upon a mirage — palm trees, blue sky, the perfect golf course laid out in front of him. He staggered towards it. In a line near the front tee were golf bags stacked with clubs. 'I must get a load of this,' he said. He picked up one of the bags with a match-set of Gary Player clubs, Then he discovered there were no balls in the pocket. He went along to the next bag. No balls there either. To the next, no balls. Right down the line it was the same: not a golf ball in any of the pockets. Plenty of golf clubs, a beautiful course, no balls. There was a chuckle behind him and he turned. There was Old Nick himself, standing grinning. 'What's the big idea?' the golfer asked. Nick nudged him playfully in the ribs. 'Just for the hell of it!' he said.

And this one, also in Jimmy's exact words: Two old ministers were floating up to Heaven, and floating beside them was a lovely blonde girl of about nineteen. When they all got to the pearly gates, St Peter beckoned to the blonde first and admitted her. The two worthy men who had served God all their long lives looked at each other, a bit taken aback. 'Don't worry,' said St Peter. 'That girl got a fast new sports car as a birthday present, and for the last six months she's put the fear of God into more people than either of you ever did.'

2

Joe, the Irish barman from Limerick. A bitterly cold damp night in November. The Golden Lion Hotel in Stirling, trying bravely to keep out the winter cold, with half its front being restored after a recent fire. Stirling, which I remember once with pleasure, arriving there by Motorail on a summer morning to a station warm with flowers.

I am putting up at the hotel for one night, being wanted early next day by James Wilson, the BBC director, with a camera team, doing a documentary; with me getting on to a train and travelling to the town where I was born, talking into the camera on route. A tricky mission; a hell of a night.

Another lone soul is coming out of the bar as I go in, leaving me alone with Joe. The lights are glowing, and their reflection in the gay bottles behind Joe gives the place its own warmth. So does Joe.

'Hell, isn't it?' he says genially. He is one of my own kind. 'A night for the monkeys. What's it to be, sir?'

'A large whisky. And have one yourself.'

I settle myself as comfortably as any bar stool permits.

'Thank you very much. I don't usually, but tonight I'll be very glad to. Anything particular you fancy?'

They are all there, all the well-known blended whiskies with their coloured labels, and a few good malts. Joe looks at them and then at me. He is young, dark, experienced. A man who knows his job, and his customers.

'I leave it to you,' I say, 'You know as well as I do there's nothing to choose between any half dozen of them.'

He laughs delightedly, a real Irish laugh. He eyes me speculatively.

'You're not a Scot, then?'

It's my turn to laugh.

'Actually I am. But not the kind that pretends by a sniff, or a sip, or a label, that he knows immediately the difference between a Grants or a Crawfords. Many of my friends are, but I'm not.'

'Well, well, well! This is a barney.' He lifts a bottle down from the shelf. 'I'm partial to this myself.'

It's Jameson's. Irish whiskey.

'That's nationalism, not preference,' I taunt him.

'No,' he says seriously, 'This is what I drink. It's got something that Scotch hasn't got for me.'

'Irish blood in it — that's what! I can't drink the stuff.'

He is fondling the bottle. 'Why not, sir?'

'It's too rough for me. Too much edge to it.' And then in fairness to Jameson's and Joe: 'Pour a sip into a glass and I'll have another go at it to see if my palate has changed.'

He does so, and I try it. Nothing has changed. I have no Irish blood in me. 'Sorry, Joe. No go. You have your whiskey and I'll have that Chivas Regal.'

'Ah, now you're talking. I thought you said....'

'And I still say it. I like Chivas, that's all. I like other whiskies too. It doesn't change what I said. More than half the Scots who kid themselves, and others, that they know one whisky from another, or the name of the whisky they're drinking, are just adding to a myth.'

In my travels I'd heard, and watched, and drank with them. I'd seen barmen run out of one branded whisky in demand, secretly fill up an empty labelled bottle with whisky from another brand. I'd watched the chaps drink. And they didn't know the difference.

It hardly mattered anyway. Almost all whisky is good. But it might have done something awful to the national ego, if someone — as I am now — had bruited it about. And I might have had many an awkward argument.

We toasted each other and drank in silence for a minute. Then, wanting to find out something, I said, 'Quiet here, isn't it?'

He shrugged. 'Tonight, yes. You can't blame them for staying indoors; and there aren't many people in the hotel.'

'Well, it saves me offering anybody else a drink.'

'There's that about it!'

I had got to where I wanted.

'Tell me, Joe; I'm a bit puzzled. Quite often, coming into a bar, and there's, say, an acquaintance there — not a friend; a friend wouldn't do it on you — or one other solitary drinker, perhaps, I've said to him when ordering my own drink, 'Have one with me.'

I could see the professional interest in Joe's eye.

'And straight away the chap says, 'Thanks, I'll have a double whisky.' I then look down at his glass and find he's been drinking half a pint of bitter. Do they all do this?'

Joe took a sip of his Jameson's.

'Nobody's ever asked me this before,' he said. 'Because I suppose they don't need to: once bitten twice shy. But I've noticed. No, they don't all do it. But there are some greedy drinkers about, and I suppose they feel that if you're mug enough to offer them a drink they've a right to take you for a ride.'

'That's not the way it used to be.'

'In Scotland?'

'Of course.'

He stayed silent, taking another sip from his glass, his eye on me over its rim.

'Well,' he said. 'This is how you cope with it – if you still feel like acting muggins. Don't offer the drink till you've looked at his glass. If it's beer, you just say 'Have another half with me.' That'll do the trick.'

I was enjoying my evening. The cold had gone, and the warmth of companionable understanding had taken its place. Even the morrow didn't seem quite so forbidding. We stayed for a while exchanging views.

What I liked about this young Irishman was his definiteness. It was what I had found in the young Scot, Kenneth Roy, but not in too many others. Joe knew what he wanted to do, where he was going. There was no apathy or inertia or 'what's the use?' in this young man. He was a bachelor, had learned his expertise in London, Edinburgh, and now Stirling. Next stop was to be the South of France.

'That's where I want to learn more about wines,' he said.

'And then what? Your own place?'

'That's it!'

'Where? London? Scotland?'

He laughed his open laugh.

'Stop kidding! The old country. A real pub, with real catering. In tourist Ireland it can't miss.'

I could bet he's right, and I hope it works out for him.

I went out into the dark, damp deserted Stirling streets. A drizzle of rain came on. The few people waiting for buses sheltered in doorways or against bus stops. The usual lighted windows of closed stores – shoes, cosmetics, clothes. Mostly men's – Burton's, Hepworths (with clothes designed by Hardy Amies). Where was the action in a place like this on a winter night? For me, in an un-exploring mood, it was back in my hotel, with a room with a bath, and a meter that had to be fed shillings to give me some extra warmth.

3

Coffee from a flask in the car on a cold clear morning. The lonely corner of the small farm close to the sea. The bleak stone farmhouse. The door opening against the wind and the white-haired woman coming out from the house, still with bedroom slippers on, a cardigan round her shoulders, and a big old sheepdog held tenderly in her arms.

She put him gently down on the ground, and held up his tail and back legs. He was so old and done that he hadn't the strength to relieve himself without this assistance. She stood, holding him, waiting patiently for the process to start functioning, her eyes scanning the lovely countryside, casting an occasional glance in the direction of two younger sheepdogs dashing about like mad. The quick and the almost-dead.

At last, patience rewarded, she picked the old dog up and carried him back into the house.

Next morning about the same time I drove my car into the same corner. I drank my coffee. I had to wait a little time. But the farmhouse door at last opened and the white-haired woman, with a raincoat on this time, came out carrying the old dog.

Again she lifted up his tail and back legs, waited, watched the other dogs running about, looked out at the sea. I got out and sauntered towards her. She smiled a welcome. Her white hair was deceptive; she had a younger face, dark eyes and eyebrows.

'He must be very old,' I said.

'Over fourteen. We just can't let him go.'

'I know what it's like.'

'He's one of the family. The children love him. We just can't think of the day when....' Her voice faltered.

His name was Spot. The whole family went without their summer holidays so that they could still be near him and know that he would be cared for properly. They dreaded the day, especially the little boy and girl, when the inevitable would happen.

Spot sprinkled the grass. The white-haired woman gathered him closely to her, smiled to me, and carried him into the farmhouse. The younger dogs scurried past her legs. The door closed.

D̦electable fare offered by the Scottish Patriots at an evening get-together: 'A Tattie and Herring Supper will be held at HQ on Saturday, 14 March. Tickets are 5/- each and we welcome all who would like a good night with good Scots fare and Scots company. Please send for tickets as soon as possible as accommodation is limited.'

5

TV commentary by Scotland's most vigilant and trenchant newspaper critic, John Gibson: '...it was so short that it seemed austere and it's not the calibre of play I'd care to put up to compete on any terms' (with TV from other than Scottish channels). 'However, I'm all for TV drama hatched in this country, by either channel, that rids us of the small world, parochial, tatties-and-neeps approach they've shown too often for too long; and for Scottish Television this is a break-through.'

6

The hands-across-the-sea spirit that never dies, as demonstrated in small, down-the-page newspaper item: HEATHER APPEAL FOR SCOTS EXILES: An appeal for small sprigs of heather to send to Scottish socities overseas for St Andrew's Day celebrations has been made by the St Andrew Society. Heather should be sent to Mr Ian Barbour, the society's secretary and treasurer, at 45 Queen Street, Edinburgh.

7

Sean Day-Lewis reviewing television in the Daily Telegraph: 'A point of view was the main thing lacking in Christopher Brasher's *Beloved Wilderness* (BBC-1). He was very free with words like faith and soul, so free, in fact, that they seemed to be applied in every possible direction.
    'I wonder what it is about Scotland that makes documentary

manufacturers so stodgy? Do they perhaps eat too much porridge in order to keep out the cold? There is never the smallest hint that life ever has been or ever could be, even for a few isolated moments, fun.

'There were some marvellous pictures of Highland scenery and a great deal of very deliberate common sense from Prof. Sir Robert Grieve, Chairman of the Highlands and Islands Development Board. But even this became a little diffused before the end.

'A Whicker was sorely needed to give direction and to search out some enterprising crofter who had, perhaps, written fifty symphonies, or even drunk fifty pints of beer consecutively while standing on his head. Mr Brasher remained so hopelessly objective that in the end I was as doubtful as ever about whether the Highlands are a good thing.'

8

A drift of conversation from a near-by table in the lounge of the Braemar Arms near Balmoral. An English voice: 'Well, we actually were thinking of buying a house and retiring here. But when I heard about the feu duty – I mean, that although you buy a house it's not freehold like in England, but you've got to go on paying some blighter an annual feu duty for ever, because it's on *his* land – I ask you!'

A mildly protesting Scottish voice: 'Oh, it doesn't amount to so much each year....'

'My dear chap, with the house I wanted it would have been £100 a year. A year! In perpetuity! Although I'd be buying the house and it would be mine! What right has someone to go on raking money out of me for ever?'

Scottish silence.

English voice: 'How can you all possibly put up with such usury? Why do you stand for it?'

An attempt at explanation: 'Well, you see, someone got the land in the old days, from some king or other, and his rights in it, or some feu rights, just continue down the line.'

'Too damn right they do! You must be crackers to put up with it! Nobody's going to give up a good racket like that unless you stop it.'

I'd wondered myself about this 'feu duty' that almost every house owner in Scotland goes on paying to some unseen presence, living comfortably in the background on the useful accumulated annual proceeds of hundreds, perhaps thousands, of houses.

'It's all perfectly legal, you know,' the Scottish voice said. 'It's Scottish law.'

'And you don't want to change it?'

A bit of a guilty laugh. 'Oh, we want to change it all right.'

Insistently: 'But you don't?'

'Well, there's been a move. The Conservatives when in opposition said they'd abolish the feu duty in Scotland, but we've heard no more about that now they're the Government. And even if it was abolished, the house-owners would have to compensate the Feu Superiors.'

The Englishman spluttered his drink.

'Feu Superiors! Who the hell are they?'

'The lucky buggers we pay our feu to.'

'Dear God!' A long pause. 'What century are you living in? Feu comes from feudal obviously?'

'That's right. This is a good old feudal custom.'

'And a good old feudal country, by the sound of it.'

They were middle-class men by all appearances; each had been to a good school. The English voice was very English; the Scottish accent was slightly Anglicized. The Englishman was weighing it all up, sipping at his drink. I judged them to be acquaintances rather than close friends, yet there was the affinity of their social position between them, the common problems of their way of life. And both were well in their cups.

The Englishman said ruminatively: 'I get the picture. Someone was born on the wrong side of the blanket two or three hundred years ago, and his father – or his mother – got paid off with land.'

'Maybe even further back,' said the Scot. 'But they might have got the land through fighting for it, or grabbing it. That was Scotland in the old days.'

'They were all cutting each other up, weren't they?'

'More or less. But a lot of them were fighting for what they believed in.'

Sardonically: 'And were well rewarded.'

'Why not? It was the same in England. In every country.'

'But in Scotland there's the feu duty! If I buy a house or a flat in England, I buy it freehold. It's mine. I pay the rates on it, and the other usual upkeep expenses. But nobody has the right to demand of me a so-called feu duty every year over and above it all. They wouldn't stand for it in England. Why do they stand for it in Scotland?'

He was the kind of Scotsman who doesn't let fly with his fist. It was satisfying just to sit there and hear him quietly express his own troubled views. It was like a monologue, as if he were glad at last to have a listener, even so unreceptive a listener as this fiery Sassenach. And although, in the bustle of the lounge, I missed much, the gist of it was something like this. 'We stand for it because we've got used to standing for it. There's not much we can do about it.' Once more I heard the fateful year 1707 mentioned, the year of the Union of Scotland and England. The Scots were never conquered – this with emphasis – yet the Union, brought about by those who had most to gain, had hit Scotland below the belt. It had been regarded – and was still regarded – as a betrayal, a surrender.

'And you've never got over it!' The English voice said with sarcasm.

And the quite serious reply: 'You know, I don't think we have.' A bit of a laugh: 'We're still in a state of shock you might say.'

9

My old friend, Sir Philip Gibbs, was fond of telling of a time when, covering a royal tour in Scotland for his newspaper, he and several other correspondents occupied a car which followed immediately behind the royal car. One of these correspondents, a big man with a moon face, a rather long nose and a ready smile, sat in the front seat beside the chauffeur. The car in fact contained a rather odd-looking lot, and because it bore no Press label, people naturally wondered just who these chaps were. Somewhere in the countryside the procession paused and a farmer or labourer, leaning on the fence, removed his pipe from his mouth to suggest, 'Ay....they must be the King's bastards.' Gibbs said he laughed all the way up to Balmoral, or wherever they were going, and all the way back again. When asked if the farmer had been serious in his suggestion, he said, 'Dead serious!'

XV

1

'Every time I go back to Glasgow,' says James MacGibbon, 'and stand in the Central Station, the old feeling comes back. I'm home.'

James MacGibbon is a publisher, a famous one, a London one. That means that London has been his milieu, his battlefield, the place where he has had his being most of his adult life — and met his triumphs and despairs. He goes out of his busy office, hatless, at midday, to lunch with other publishers or writers: the hopeful and beginning or the assured and successful. Or flies off to New York or Paris in search of the pot of gold that can be tapped out on certain magic typewriters.

He is large, loosely built, with a sensitive face that shows something of the scars of living, and a watchful eye; and a head of hair that is left more or less to take care of itself. There is nothing in his easy relaxed manner to show that like most men of his calling, he is awake half the night reading manuscripts, most of which are a gamble. There is nothing, either, in his speech or manner to show that he is a Scot who was born in Glasgow and educated at its University.

By now, in his fifty-sixth year he is indistinguishable from the successful educated men around him in London who were born in Leeds or Birmingham or London itself. I know nothing of his youth in his own country (except that he learnt to sail on the Clyde and is now glad, most week-ends, that he did so), or how often or infrequently he returns to it. I have probed him gently on occasion only to find if he carries it with him, as I have done all my life. Most men carry something of their birthplace with them but I have always had the conviction that Scotsmen carry something more than the others.

The Scotland I had known and loved was the Scotland of my childhood (anything but an ecstasy), my adolescence (troubled and precarious), and a brief young manhood (marred or made by experiences in my Scottish regiment). But even so, I knew then that others, my playmates and friends, felt as I did. We *burst* with love of the place we lived in. 'Burst' càn't be quite the right word, for the explosion never came. That would have been very un-Scottish. But inside us we built up quite a head of steam about our native land and what it did to us. Was this a malady or a happiness peculiar to Scotland? What forces in the country, then undefined by us, had made it so very special?

When I mentioned to James MacGibbon, hesitantly, that this was something that I would like to find out, I could feel his mind sail alongside my own. The look came into his eyes of a man remembering.

'What fun,' he said, really meaning, I think, 'I wish I were coming with you.' And then: 'I don't suppose we're all that different from other people, but I know how you feel and why you're going. All my life, I think, I've felt something of a stranger almost anywhere outside Scotland.' And then he repeated himself: 'When I go back to Glasgow, and stand in the Central Station, the old feeling comes back. I'm home.'

2

'Our home port was now Greenock,' writes Nicholas Monsarrat in the second volume of his autobiography, from which he has generously allowed me to quote.

'Greenock — a small unlovely collection of bricks and granite terraces, well-run docks, dirty streets and shops with flyblown cardboard advertisements designed, seemingly, to drive the customer elsewhere at the fastest clip he could manage. For the moment the town had borrowed a certain professional consequence, being dominated by the vast upper-works, the steel elegance, of HMS *Repulse,* which was in dry dock for a refit before setting sail for eastern seas again.

'Further down the coast was another town, Gourock, of the same drab, mean quality, though it had a hotel, the Bay, held in high esteem by rollicking sailors and presided over by a lady whose universal nickname, Two-Ton Tessie, was never a subject of dispute. Such were the nights that waited us ashore.

'Twenty miles away there lay in wait for us the grimy maw of Scotland's pride and joy, the City of Glasgow.

'Perhaps it takes a Scotsman to love Glasgow, or even to put up with it; if so, I remain defiantly proud of owning allegiance to Liverpool, and nowhere else. To me Glasgow seemed uncouth, filthy, and complacent, all at the same time; and on Sundays it added a fourth element, a God-fearing pursed-mouth piety which closed the cinemas and pubs and spread an additional layer of gloom over the whole grim city.

'Though this, at least, gave the pavements outside a breathing-space after Saturday night's vomit, it meant a dreary Sunday indeed for sailors tempted to explore the dark interior of what the natives called, without a trace of sarcasm, Bonnie Scotland.

'Of this mecca they sang: "When I've had a couple of drinks on a Saturday, Glasgow belongs to me", before collapsing in a maudlin heap under the nearest railway arch. Of themselves, they hiccuped "Here's tae us! Wha's like us?" as they ogled themselves in the saloon bar's happily distorting mirror.

'Here, as the rain coursed down the raddled tramlines of Sauchiehall Street, civic patriots roared "Scotland for aye!" and shouldered aside all lesser mortals.

'It has been said that the name Glasgow means "Dear green place", and was so christened by St Ninian (circa AD 40), "the scope and extent of whose work", according to the encyclopaedia, "are the subject of much controversy".

'Between convoys, such was my choice of relaxation ashore; Glasgow's brawling crudity (though to be fair there was one excellent restaurant with the good old Scottish name of *La Malmaison;* Greenock's pubs or cinemas and Gourock's Two-Ton Tessie, all to be prefaced by a bracing trip ashore on the open deck of a herring drifter.'

When I asked Monsarrat to allow me to quote this 'encomium' of Glasgow, he said. 'They won't like either of us if you do.' But I thought I knew better. I did not know Glasgow well, or many Glasgow people, but few Scots are unaware of the great roly-poly mass of Glaswegians, warm-hearted and oozing out friendliness like warm breath in a cold climate. The opposite pole from Edinburgh, and proud of it.

The last time I arrived there, getting off the air-bus in the centre of the city, there were no taxis in sight. Seeing me at a loss, a man half-leaned towards me on the pavement.

'No taxis!' I said, damning his whole beloved city with two words.

He was wearing a cloth cap, and no coat on a nippy day. He might have been waiting to pick up a bob for carrying someone's luggage. But you would be foolish to make such a snap judgment in Glasgow, the most democratic, caste-less city on either side of the border. There was a very expensive pull-over under his jacket. You couldn't place him if you were a stranger in Glasgow.

'Whaur ye gawn?' he asked, with that lilt in the voice that you listen to, fascinated, without bothering about the words. He didn't say, 'I'm a stranger here myself.' I knew he was no stranger.

'The Central Hotel.'

His thin face screwed up in protest.

'Ach, ye dinna want a taxi, son. It's nae distance. Jist roond the corner.'

His concern was immediate and genuine. Like this, I thought, he must have leaned over his chidren, chiding them gently, teaching them the lessons of life, the dangers of putting out money unnecessarily.

He was at least twenty years younger than I, had perhaps never earned anything like my income, but his native protective nature was instinctive. I was in no hurry. My overnight case was no heavier than a bulky brief case. The imagined need for a taxi was the ingrown habit of years of self-indulgence, as instinctive to me as was his response to it.

I took a better look at him. A joiner? Painter? Bus conductor? Warehouseman? I couldn't guess. I am no Conan Doyle. But he was a typical citizen of Glasgow. I watched his face as he directed me.

'First on the right. Then a wee bit doon the street turn left. Then straight on. Ye can't miss it.'

He didn't use his arms as so many people comically do in setting you right. He gave me credit for knowing what was 'right' and what was 'straight on' without a physical demonstration. The economy of his nature extended to his own movements. Beyond the slight bend forward at our introduction, his spare lean frame had remained still and upright.

'Five minutes away from here then?' I asked.

'Ay, at the most.'

It took me five minutes exactly. I was the better for the walk and the brief encounter, insignificant in itself except that it showed me that the breed hadn't changed. He was like the men I had known years before, played football against, met in the army. He would have agreed whole-heartedly with Monsarrat's description of his city because it was true. He might even had added some harsh details of his own. They would certainly have been accompanied by unexpected laughter and good humour.

Glasgow people have few secrets either from strangers or from each other. They love their city, and share it. They know all their city's faults, its squalor, its undercurrent of violence. The huge tenements, rabbit warrens of humanity, the homes of most of the people you meet in its bustling streets, are its blot, and yet its benison.

For as long as memory goes back Glasgow families have lived almost in each other's lap. Life flows over from family to family, from man to man. The women are neighbours and friends, in and out of each other's house at any hour, sharing luck or misfortune, always at hand when needed most. The children, playing in the streets, know all about each other from the beginning, the good and the bad.

These people have no 'side'; you would be smartly taken down a peg if you tried it on. The long streets of high houses have differing economic levels, with families better fed and clothed, perhaps, than others only two parallel streets away, but their involvement with life and people is the same.

The song 'Glasgow belongs to me', which used to be sung drunkenly in music halls by the comedian, Will Fyfe, could soberly be avowed as 'Glasgow belongs to us' by almost all its citizens. It is certainly what they feel. Glasgow is theirs. In the way that New York belongs fiercely to the polyglot New Yorkers, Glasgow is polyglot too, but fiercely Scots, the centre of an industrial belt that keeps its million people on their dancing toes.

It is more truly the heart of Scotland than any other city, with a beguiling cosmopolitan quality about it that is more Latin than Nordic. If its climate were different the people would eat and drink on the pavements. They associate themselves with their streets, with their cafés and restaurants, bars and dancing halls and fish-and-chip shops, with the stir and spectacle of life all around them, like people in Spain or France or Italy. They come together anywhere.

In the past their great meeting place, now alas no more, was their famous tramcars. They loved their trams, gaudily coloured to denote their routes; yellow-and-white, yellow-and-green, and red-and-blue. They rattled through the long streets like flower-laden floats in a

Riviera procession. They were used by men and women not only to get from one place to another but to continue their never-ending social exchange of gossip or news or just plain larking. The trams were an extension of life in the tenements. No one was a stranger on a Glasgow tram, inside or upstairs. You might enter alone; at once you could believe you were in a pub or at a 'social', and be drawn in to the goings-on.

The silent, taciturn Scot? Not in Glasgow. Particularly not in a Glasgow tram. There it was like calling out through a window to friends in the sunny street. Talk begun between two people sitting together, could quickly lead to a discussion right along the inside of the tram; there were no secrets, especially with a conductor moving up and down, putting in the humorous remark here and there as he caught the drift of the talk. You have to go to writers and broadcasters like Molly Weir and Jack House, both with the privilege of having been brought up in Glasgow, to understand the true flavour of this remarkable city and its irrepressible people.

In the lore of Glasgow trams, that public social intercourse takes a large place. The way a people laugh, and the things they laugh at, or linger over, are an indicator to the character of themselves and their city. All my friends have their own true stories of Glasgow.

One miserable rainy day Bobby Williamson, on a visit to his group of lending libraries, got into a tram. He had been trudging through the wet and muddy streets most of the day. The conductress was a homely, middle-aged woman. Bobby himself was fifty. She gave him a smile as he passed her and she came to take his fare. As she gave him his ticket, she put his change in his hand, and closed her own hand over his protectively. Her concern for him was the concern of a mother. 'Sonny', she whispered, 'turn up the cuffs of your trousers. They're dangling in the glaur' (trailing in the mud).

Could it have happened anywhere else? I know of no other city where the human family is so often revealed as such. Sonny! That affectionate, protective word again. Uttered almost with a caress in it.

In this day of human isolation, it was encouraging to me to discover that Glasgow people were still as involved with one another, trams or no trams. But the affinity with trams dies hard, the stories still abound. Everybody who grew up and lived in that period of the colourful trams remembers them with nostalgia and a lingering sad affection. They were houses on wheels, gypsy caravans, for all the city's people. Glaswegians had the same passion for their trams as the people of San Francisco.

In San Francisco they get out at the terminus and push the tram on the turntable for its return journey. Everybody shares in the pleasurable task. But the San Franciscans still have their trams. When, as everywhere else, the proposal came from bureaucracy to scrap their trams, the sensible men and women of San Francisco stood firm. Scrap the trams? Over their dead bodies! *They* weren't going to give up their trams! They didn't. In Scotland, yes, even in Glasgow, they let their well-loved trams go the way of all other British trams. But the stories, revealing so much, linger on.

The same Bobby Williamson told me of a December day when the filled interior of one of these Glasgow trams was listening with neighbourly good-humour to the confidences of two women, conveniently half-way between back platform and the driver's separating glass panel. It was no effort to overhear. The dialogue was the property of anyone with moderately good ears. Bits of it were lost in the passenger movements of coming and departing, but on the whole a very good time was had by all. The discussion ranged from children's measles to some new exotic kind of bra. It was terminated only by the conductor holding the tram at a stop and calling out to one of the women:

'I thought you said you wanted to get off at Jamaica Street?'

She was the one sitting on the aisle. She brought herself, dazed, back from woman wonderland, half turned, half rose.

'Jings!' she exclaimed. 'Are we there already?'

'Ay,' said the helpful conductor, 'and I'll be getting what-for if I'm much later at the terminus.'

She rose, smiling hugely towards him as she came down the aisle.

'No' you!' she teased, unhurried. 'Ye'll soon make up the lost time.'

And then turning back towards her friend, but progressing slowly towards the exit, she called out: 'Let's have a real crack on Wednesday, Jessie. I've so much to tell you.'

The bus waited patiently.

'Oh, no' Wednesday, Ella!' cried the other woman from her seat. 'I'm having my hair done on Wednesday.'

'OK,' said Ella easily. 'Make it Thursday. I'll see you on Thursday.'

In her progress she had nearly reached the exit platform, and was opposite the last man in the seat before the doorway, a wrinkled middle-aged mechanic with a small tool kit held on his knees.

He put out one hand to arrest her progress.

'Ye can't see her on Thursday,' he reminded her. 'Thursday's

Christmas Day.'

Ella stopped in her tracks. A bright wide-mouthed laugh lit up her whole face as she looked back at all the faces turned in her direction, witness to her folly.

'So help my bob!' she spluttered. 'So it is!'

These discussions in the old trams reflected the life of the city, the nature of the city. Glasgow may be big, bouncy, go-ahead, full of tenements, thousands of which are now going into limbo like the trams themselves; but it is also a city that has all the beauties of nature at its doorstep and much of the postcard glamour of Scotland.

The Clyde is at its heart. You turn down a street and, again like New York, there at the end of it are the unbelievable ships pushing their funnels and masts into the blue sky. You can take off from the end of the street for the beauties of 'doon the watter', and the magnificent isles and lochs. Or you can take off for Canada. They are still taking off for Canada in their thousands. But many more are enjoying the marvels of their own country, skiing on their own slopes, sailing in their own lochs, climbing their own mountains.

3

David Hastie is a hill climber. Or was. But being a father of two little girls and a busy journalist he has little time now for the climbing he loved. He works now in Edinburgh, but he started in Glasgow, as did Max McAuslane, his editor, and Max's deputy Phil Mackie. So too did Alastair Dunnett. All have Glasgow in their hearts, but they spend their labours among the cooler magnificence, the more detached men and women, of the capital city. Glasgow is only an hour away, but for them it is a world away, the world of their upbringing, their earliest memories, their lifelong loyalty. You can tell, talking or drinking with them, that the warmest involvement of their life is their never-ending love affair with Glasgow.

It was from Glasgow that Alastair, as a very young man, set out with his friend Jimmie Adam on an open sea voyage by canoe from the Clyde to the Outer Isles. They knew little of sailing and nothing at all about canoeing. It was the adventure of Scotland that they wanted to experience, and they thought that their own exploits might yield some good stories. They planned to gain expert knowledge about the state and possibilities of the neglected Highland areas and to pass this on to a larger public.

As they set off, each in a thirteen-foot canoe, one of the harbour men gave his opinion that it was 'too late in the year'. He proved to be right, but luckily they did not know that then, and in any case youth is afraid of nothing. They achieved their purpose, sometimes in frightening conditions, in three months, and Alastair's book of their adventure, *Quest by Canoe,* makes as exciting reading today as it did when first published.

In Glasgow, in 1941, Max McAuslane got the chance that showed him to be a man of foresight and resource. Both qualities would prove invaluable to him in his rise in his profession. He was a young newspaper reporter awaiting his call-up into the RAF on the Saturday night of 10 May when Rudolf Hess made his historic flight from Nazi Germany and crashed at Eaglesham, near Glasgow.

Max worked on the *Daily Record,* and on the Sunday morning, preparing for next day's paper he read a memo from their companion paper, *The Sunday Mail,* stating that a German plane had crashed at Eaglesham on Saturday night too late for their edition to print. At that time no one was aware of the identity of the unknown flyer. Neither Max nor his news editor paid much attention to the message. German planes crashing, or being brought down in this country, was old rope.

John Simpson, the news editor, went out to lunch. Max carried on at the news desk. When the phone rang, it was Eric Schofield, his managing director. Schofield, who lived near Eaglesham, had been out for a walk with his dog on this glorious Sunday morning. He told Max that the local gossip was that the German pilot of the crashed plane had asked for the Duke of Hamilton.

When Simpson returned to the office, Max gave him the news and suggested that they get out to Eaglesham. The two men then collected a photographer and walked out into the sunshine. Probably a fruitless outing, but you never know, and it was a smashing day anyhow.

At Eaglesham there was much gossip. There was also a crashed ME 110, a German fighter plane with a limited range. No ME 110 could carry enough petrol to make the flight to Scotland and back to Germany again. Here certainly was mystery. Guarded by the RAF, no close inspection of the plane was possible, but Simpson got the photographer to photograph it. Max McAuslane, thinking he might get more fruitful information elsewhere searched for the ploughman who had been first on the scene. Max proved to be right.

He still remembers vividly the hot sun on his back as David McLean, head ploughman of Floors Farm, leaned against the white-washed wall of his single-storey house, and told him all about it. McLean, a bachelor in his mid-forties (one more Scot who was looking after his mother and sister), was getting ready for bed at 10.45 ('by the alarm clock') on the Saturday night, when he heard the roar of a plane flying just over his house.

At the same moment, four hundred miles to the south, wave after wave of German bombers were crossing the coast to inflict on London the worst raid of the war. London was fighting for its very existence, but up here in Scotland the noise of a single plane shattered the night. As it screamed over McLean's house, he braced himself for the bang of a crash.

There was no explosion; only a sudden eerie silence. McLean looked out through the tiny window, at first could see nothing, and then in the moonlight caught a glimpse of a white drifting parachute. He was out through the door and into the night. The parachute was dragging the pilot across the grass, but as McLean reached him, he released himself. The ploughman told Max McAuslane of all that followed; of Hess giving his name as Hauptmann Alfred Horn; of his insistence that he should be taken to the Duke of Hamilton for whom, he claimed, he had an important message; of McLean taking charge of him and leading him into his small house. After all, McLean had been a private in the Cameron Highlanders in the Great War, and this was only one more German in his life, and a prisoner at that.

It all made a wonderful story for Max McAuslane who, to his dismay, found that the photographer had used all his plates on taking shots of the ME 110. Pictures of McLean and his mother and sister against the whitewashed wall were the ones Max wanted most to accompany his graphic story.

Like everyone else, he was still unaware that the pilot was Hess. But from all that David McLean had told him he could measure that something very unusual was afoot. He wrote his story, which had to be submitted to the censor, and then decided to take the story personally, thinking that the attitude of the censor might give him a clue.

The censor's attitude was quite definite. Nothing doing! The story was rubber-stamped in a manner that meant it was unlikely it would be released for publication at any time. When Max asked for an explanation, he was told the story was 'Rubbish!' He knew then for a certainty what he had surmised: the news was very important indeed.

195

Newspapermen aren't easily put off. Back in the office Clem Livingstone, the editor, contacted a private radio monitoring station run by Polish refugees in Scotland and asked to be told of any unusual broadcast coming out of Germany. His move was rewarded early on Monday evening. The station reported 'Berlin Radio announces Rudolf Hess missing'.

Out to Eaglesham sped John Simpson again, with photographer. Max McAuslane came quickly into the office to start writing the whole story in readiness for the final edition. The *Daily Record* was making preparations in the expectation that the news would break sometime, and they would be away ahead of their rivals with all the available facts.

Recognition of the captured pilot Horn as Hess was essential. John Simpson was armed with several photographs of similar-looking dark men − Cary Grant, Tyrone Power, and so on. And one of Hess. He would confront David McLean the ploughman with these. Not only McLean, but his mother and sister.

A simple telephone code was arranged between the office and Simpson. If one of the McLeans identified the pilot as Hess, Simpson would simply report, 'Thumbs up, once'. If two of them identified him, it would be 'Thumbs up, twice'. If all three McLeans agreed on the Hess photograph, the message would be 'Thumbs up, three times'.

The result was never really in doubt, as Max and Clem Livingstone knew. As now the *Daily Record* knew. Max had completed his story, the dummy front page was all in readiness. It wasn't going to be submitted to any censor when the time came. The bold headline was RUDOLF HESS IN GLASGOW. At 11.20 that night, a brief message was issued from 10 Downing Street that Rudolf Hess had landed in Scotland.

All the *Record* had to do was to add one word to the front page headline: RUDOLF HESS IN GLASGOW − OFFICIAL, and the presses started to roll with a story so complete that every other newspaper was left at the post.

That early resource of Max McAuslane is still very much in evidence today, not only in his Edinburgh job, but in his Edinburgh home. Chris, his wife, is a girl from Skye, and their conveniently placed home is often like the Waverley Station, with innumerable relatives passing through on their way north or south. I have dropped in on a Saturday night in summer and found at least ten people and babies using the McAuslane house as a motel.

But I liked best the occasion when, going back with him for a quiet

196

drink, I ran into fourteen people in the house, all relatives. There were two nephews who had just returned from hitchhiking across France; another nephew who had arrived back from an archaeological 'dig' in Israel; Chris's sister-in-law from Yorkshire, a niece from Sunderland and another sister – with family – who had come down from Skye. On that enchanted evening, one corner of the crowded room was occupied by people conversing in English with Yorkshire intonations, and in the other corner it was exclusively Gaelic. In fact it was like a Highland Ceilidh.

4

David Hastie, tall, lean, puckish-looking, already greying at thirty-eight, with a page-boy style cropped close to his head (so that, in spite of his frowning distaste, I call him 'Hamlet'), lights up Glasgow for me with stories of the city and its people some of which are drawn from life, others are the manufactured stories of bar-rooms and hairdressers. But they are so closely akin, in their broad humour and their hint of violence, that the pub ones could be the truth and the real ones could be the cooked-up. All have probability in them. The basic elements in his stories reveal startlingly the nature of a people and its city.

This one is truth. It came out of David one day over coffee, when Bobby Williamson and I were quizzing him about climbing. Quite suddenly he remembered someone known as Sunshine, a climber friend of his. 'Oh, I must tell you,' he began, and was off. And David tells a story with his mouth, his eyes, his hands – things coming out of him like sparks or rockets, they spring to life so quickly out of memory. It is a performance that has to be watched as well as listened to.

It was a Friday night. Sunshine was off for a weekend in the hills. A tram had stopped for him at Shawfield Park. Sunshine, a huge individual himself, looked like a gorilla with his gear hanging about him. He was also burdened with a pair of skis.

He lumbered along the tram to the driver's end. He wanted to leave his skis on the driver's platform. It was the beginning of a long conversation piece to which all the passengers were privy. The tram remained stationary throughout.

'Ye can't put your skis here!' declared the driver.

'I always put my skis here!' retorted Sunshine, and repeated. 'I always leave my skis in the front of the tram.'

'Well, ye're no' going to leave them here this time.'

'Why not?'

'Because I say so!'

'Oh, you do, do you?' exclaimed Sunshine, becoming slightly heated.

'I do!'

'And who the hell do you think you are?'

'I'm the driver of this tram.'

'So what?'

'And I have to stick by regulations.'

'For God's sake man — what regulations?'

The driver paused and then let him have it between the eyes: 'The regulation that says only one article can be put in the tram on the platform beside the driver.'

'Well, what the hell's wrong with my skis?'

The passengers waited with interest to hear the municipal ruling.

The driver said triumphantly: 'There's already an object on my platform.'

'What object?'

Standing slightly aside, the driver pointed to — of all things — a drum.

'What the hell's that doing here?' asked Sunshine.

'That's the object in the front platform of the tram,' said the driver. 'The single object I'm allowed to have in the front of the tram.'

'OK,' said Sunshine, with fight in his voice, 'if I don't get my skis in the front I'll put my foot through the bloody drum.'

In alarm the driver exclaimed, 'You can't do that!'

'Oh, can't I? You'll be surprised.'

The driver saw that he meant business.

'Wait a minute, wait a minute,' he said hurriedly. 'We might come to an arrangement.'

'What kind of an arrangement?' demanded Sunshine.

'Well, I've got an idea,' said the driver.

'You'd better out with it quick,' said Sunshine, 'or my foot goes through that bloody drum.'

'Well I can't take the drum out the front of the tram,' said the driver, 'but what about you putting your skis on the conductor's platform at the back?'

A tense silence.

'Why the hell didn't you say that in the first place?' asked Sunshine amiably. He promptly manoeuvred himself and his load and trundled along to the back of the tram and eased down his skis on to the platform.

A voice from somewhere in the body of the tram, either the top or the bottom: 'Thank God that's settled. Now I can get on to my bloody dancing.'

A hint of menace in that story? Yes, indeed. The menace and violence is often there in these Glasgow stories whose humour underlines a swift willingness to defy authority and a readiness for a fight. Glasgow has lived with its razor gangs for many a year, and the people's homely friendliness does not preclude their knowledge of what goes on at the fringes of the city and can even erupt in its centre.

Glaswegians are in this respect, again like the Americans. They do not run away from a fight. When I lived in America, I was constantly startled by the forthright, aggressive attitude of its males. It may have been part of the make-up of a young country, a hangover from covered-wagon pioneering days, not so far distant, when you had to fight to survive. But there was no doubt that this primitive and violent outlook remained with American men. They never avoided a fight; they were always spoiling for one. The Scots, from as dark a past, have inherited their own type of belligerence. Sunshine, thwarted, might be ready to have a bash at anyone – the driver of the tram, an impatient passenger who might butt in, even a policeman.

5

David Hastie produced another story, a palpably 'manufactured' one this time, yet with the same basis of probability. It could *almost* have happened; and behind its humour there was again the violence. It dealt with the Rangers-Celtic rivalry, one of the many stories that pass among Scottish football fans all the time.

This one was about a lone Rangers supporter who, coming late one Saturday to the match, mistakenly got to the wrong end of the arena and found himself behind the Ranger's goal among the massed and fervid Celtic supports harassing the Rangers goalkeeper. David used the word 'hooligans' instead of 'supporters'. For the moment I'll give them the benefit of the doubt.

Realizing his mistake, the Rangers man kept mum until his team scored the first goal, and then he let out his bleep of triumph. Instantly, among the silent Celtic crowd around him, the eyes of a hundred enemies turned in his direction. He was a marked man. Celtic equalized and pandemonium raged. His early slip was forgotten or forgiven. When Rangers took the lead and he couldn't hold himself in, the glares towards him were fiercer, the fists began to grip. Fortunately, Celtic once more equalized.

At half-time, in the old days of football, a mass of dedicated club supporters would slowly press through the crowd and change goal ends; and it was an alarming sight to watch the armies, with banners, rattles, and bottles, sing their way, or curse their way, to the other end of the field, yelling threats across the pitch to their rivals moving in the opposite direction. But nowadays, with the press of people, and the police restrictions, these mass migrations have mostly ceased. And our poor lone Rangers supporter was still left wedged among his Celtic foes to stick out the second half of the game.

This time he was behind the Celtic goal and he could see all the moves of the Rangers every time they came within scoring distance. He knew he was still a marked man, and – for once – was glad that the game, roaring on to its end, looked like being a draw.

Then, in the closing minute, with Rangers making the running out on the left, the winger sent over a perfect cross. Their threatened isolated supporter could see that it was ten-to-one that the ball would land right on the head of the Ranger's centre-forward and be in the net in a couple of seconds.

He did not wait for the goal or the crowd's yell. He took off. When the arena erupted with the roar 'Goal!' he was already on his way to the exit, pushing, thrusting and kicking to get there. But so, too, were fifty Celtic fanatics who had marked him.

Close on his heels, they chased him down Copeland Road, through Govan, along Paisley Road and down to the Clyde, yelling for his blood. Fear lent him wings, and he kept ahead, but slowly they gained on him.

The river Clyde was dead-end for him. He'd be a cornered man. But by the Grace of God, one of the blunt-nosed, blunt-ended Govan ferries was standing out from the quay about six or seven feet away. With a last desperate effort he threw himself at it, sailed through the air and grabbed the handrail. It was an Olympian leap. He dragged himself up and staggered on to the deck.

He turned to face his pursuers. The captain of the ferry stood quietly beside him. The triumphant lone Rangers supporter, escaped by a miracle, opened his mouth wide: 'Awa' ye crowd o' bloody green-nosed Papist bastards!' he yelled.

And turning to the captain, he muttered: 'By Christ, that was a close yin!'

The captain: 'Ay, closer than you think. We're just pulling in.'

And another Glasgow story from David, with what you feel must be the authentic truth of a relationship. About a young man who was becoming more and more reluctant to take his girl out on a Saturday afternoon.

'I believe,' she expostulated, 'that you like Rangers better than me.' It seemed to be a time for no compromise.

'Ay,' he said, 'I like Rangers better than you.' And then, to put her on the lowest strata of his affections. 'And if you want to know, I like the Celtic better too.'

6

Violence? 'It can be pretty bad,' says Tom Wilkie-Millar, talking not so much about Glasgow as Edinburgh, where for ten years he acted as a police doctor, called out at all hours while still attending to his own practice and patients.

'The razor boys are the worst. A razor in the stiff peak of a man's cap is very effective. You just pull off your cap and dust it in your enemy's face. That'll do it. Or razor blades stuck in a potato with a handle or a strap attached, for swinging. Or a bicycle chain wound round the wrist, with the end loose. A useful weapon; you can hit with it, or flail with it.

'There are all kinds of weapons. I remember a young lady who didn't like what was being said to her by a man. She pulled off her stiletto-heeled shoe and cut his face from ear to lip.' Knuckle dusters? The worst one he remembers was made of thick glass to fit in the hand, over all the knuckles. Let into the outside edge was a cut-throat razor.

The Glasgow gangs of the 1930s sprang up from the sordid living conditions, unemployment, incipient hooliganism, and the weakness of local magistrates. When a magistrate imposed a nominal fine, of say £5, the victim's pals would shop around to raise the money, ten bob from the butcher, ten bob from the grocer, and so on. Probably quite willingly given.

But from this grew the idea of 'protection', a spreading racket then in the United States and one that could pay off over here. Early targets were the flea-pit cinemas. When offered 'protection', a proprietor, thinking he was safe, might laugh at the idea. The boys then got busy, tearing up the cinema seats, chucking bottles at the screen.

Inevitably they became gangs, and rival gangs. No longer the race-course gangs of other days, but gangs on the American lines. There may have been few guns but there were plenty of razors. The man who tackled the problem with vigour and determination was the Chief Constable, Sir Percy Sillitoe, who later became head of MI5. He got behind his men with new methods, inaugurating combat techniques, baton throwing so that an escaping thug could be caught – smack! – on the skull.

The High Court Judges, not only in Glasgow, but over in Edinburgh, began to impose sentences that kept many a hoodlum out of circulation for a long time. They are still doing it.

It is a revelation to read a Scottish newspaper and discover that punishment – yes, that old fashioned word elsewhere – still means punishment in Scotland. In the High Court in Edinburgh in 1971 Lord Grant, the Lord Justice Clerk, handed out a total sentence of twelve years (in one case seven, in the other five) to two young men for perjury. Both were twenty-one years of age.

The perjury was committed at a High Court trial in Glasgow, and Lord Grant declared: 'We get this time and again in Glasgow. I personally, and my fellow judges, have warned witnesses of the consequences that will follow if they commit perjury. I have seen so many miscarriages of justice in Glasgow that I cannot but take a most grave view when the witnesses responsible are brought to book.'

And when he passed sentence the Judge said: 'I hope that people like you who are tempted to commit perjury will keep in mind that seven and five years are by no means the maximum sentences that may be imposed in cases like this.'

The island of Islay, in the Inner Hebrides, is only twenty-five miles in length and nineteen miles across at its widest point, and every mile is beautiful, every view a rapture. The favourite is the distant hilly range of the Paps of Jura.

Islay was the headquarters of the MacDonalds, the Lords of the Isles. If its past was romantic, its present is of great importance. Important because of its bird life, which attracts many visitors; but important in another way. It is an island of purest water and plentiful peat, and here some of Scotland's best malt whisky is distilled.

The delicate operation of blending whisky — the malts, made from barley malt in the pot stills, with grain whiskies in the patent stills — is carried out on the mainland of Scotland, a great deal of it in and near Glasgow; and blending is one of the fine arts.

Glasgow business men are as shrewd as any in the world. Glasgow's distillers have probably no equal anywhere. Stanley P. Morrison is one of them. And if I mention that Stanley Morrison also happens to be a Rangers supporter, I do so for two reasons: to emphasize that most Glasgow men are Rangers or Celtic supporters, and to remark that, although he may, in his heart, be as fervent as the poor ill-fated Rangers supporter fleeing for the Clyde a few pages back, there is no other resemblance whatsoever.

Stanley Morrison has been in the whisky business for forty-nine years, he is a BSc, an authority on every side of the business, and he directs — aided now by his two sons, Timothy and Brian — the expanding group which carries his name. In a handsome Regency house in Royal Crescent, looking out on garden and trees, yet only a stroll from the heart of Glasgow, his segment of Britain's immense export trade in whisky operates.

It operates in an atmosphere of friendliness and quiet. I go into the airy, welcoming hall on a day when I am to have lunch with Stanley Morrison, and while the telephone girl tells someone that I have arrived, I pick up the single golf club leaning in a corner between two walls.

The club is an iron. A Walter Hagen Number 5. And at sight of the name a host of memories sweep over me. Hagen will ever stay with me as the most colourful golfer of his time. I saw him first when I was a very young man, and I followed his fortunes, often literally, and enjoyed his golf and his showmanship and his genial humour on many a golf course afterwards.

I picked up the Number 5 iron. It had a special grip on it that my fingers closed over as if I had played it a hundred times. Its balance was perfect; the temptation was irresistible. In the empty hall, I played it back and forth for a few times in my hands and then swung it into an imaginery ball. The kiss of it over the surface of the thick carpet was sweet indeed.

At that moment, not putting his visitor to the trouble of finding him, Stanley Morrison came down the stairs to welcome me.

'Not bad,' he said; 'not bad at all.'

'What a club!' I said. 'Where did you get this grip? It's special isn't it?'

'Ah!' His tanned face broke into a smile. 'I'll tell you later. Isn't it a help?'

'Even *I* could play better golf with this.' And then: 'I've got such sentimental memories of Hagen. I saw my very first Open in 1923, and Hagen became a kind of God to me. That was at Troon.'

He nodded. He too was remembering.

'I was there,' he told me. 'But Hagen didn't win that one.'

'No. Arthur Havers. An Englishman, right out of the blue.'

'And he never did much else ever again. That was a funny break for him. But he was a splendid player.'

I was still holding the club. He could guess what I was feeling.

'Have another swing,' he said.

I looked at him, the expert whisky man who had been in the business so many years. The boss of this establishment. He was a few years younger than I, tanned, well-built, wearing a crisp white shirt without a jacket, belted at the waist of a pair of immaculate dark blue slacks. He might have been about to saunter on to a golf course. Comfortably informal in dress and manner, yet with complete authority and know-how written all over him. I doubt if I could have seen his like in an Edinburgh office, but many a leader of a big American business could have doubled for him.

The thought struck me: whisky and golf, the two great products of our country. How right that they should be fused together in this house, for I already know what a keen and excellent golfer Stanley Morrison was and how magic the word Troon was to him as to myself.

For him Troon was his escape from Glasgow at the weekends. All week he stayed in the city, using the top floors of this Regency house as a delightful flat. He 'lived over his shop', I had heard him say, but with a style and comfort – and imagination – that made fun of the words. For upstairs there were cosy living rooms, large bedrooms, a completely modern kitchen and dining room. And, a golfer's dream: an empty room for practice driving and pitching golf balls into a net!

8

Troon meant to him his large stone house adjacent to the golf course, space to store his golf equipment and accommodate his friends. It meant also the sea, the bracing wind, a break from all the problems of distilling, blending, bottling and marketing.

Our lives must have crossed so many years before when, ardently young, we were in the same gallery, perhaps, that followed Hagen. A Number 5 Walter Hagen brought it all back.

That week in Troon, in that long-ago summer, sealed my fate. I had just come back from America, where I had emigrated after the Great War. I was on holiday. I'd had a week at home in Edinburgh and heard that the Open Championship was on at Troon. For a new experience more than anything else, I went through to Glasgow and put up at a cheap hotel with an equally young American friend. Every morning we took the train from St Enoch's to Troon.

And so I was caught up in something that to a young man was one of the most agreeable fevers of my life, and which has stayed with me ever since. Whether I should have been as enthusiastic if I had been roped in with the crowd, like a lot of sheep, I cannot say. But then, thank heaven, that impediment between player and admirer was practically non-existent.

We marched down the fairways with Hagen, amused by his wise-cracks, making way for him to come through the gallery round his ball so that we could watch his next shot. Within yards of him we could hear his brief consultation with his caddy, watch the choice of club, the superb shot, the perfect pitch to the pin.

In his bright blue pullover, white knickerbockers and 'co-respondent's' black-and-white shoes, Hagen would look at the lie of the ball and the flag in the distance, and share his thoughts with the crowd. 'Gee, this one needs a spade,' he once muttered, but the glint in his eye showed the resolve behind the quip.

He may have heard someone murmur, 'Macdonald Smith's 3 under 4's at the ninth.' There was a great bush telegraph in those days, as reliable as the elaborate modern score recording, and this made for a pleasant rapport between player and spectator which is almost unknown today, except in the case of Lee Trevino.

Macdonald Smith was another great showman. In the evenings, after the day's round (or two rounds in those days), he would entertain any hangers-on who remained round the practice area to an exciting golfing exhibition. He had a whole range of tricks, shots and stunts. The most popular one was to get a volunteer to keep a ball down lightly on the ground under the toe of his shoe. Mac Smith then took a full swing with a driver (they were shallower in the face in those days), the volunteer would miss a heartbeat, but the ball would be taken cleanly from under his toe and sail 250 yards away. The foot was untouched. I've never seen the trick done since.

As we went upstairs to have lunch, Stanley Morrison reminded me of another Hagen trait, his immense self confidence.

'He was always sure he would win! Do you remember how he used to ask "Who'll be runner-up?" A lot of people put that down to arrogance. But it wasn't.'

'A certain amount of tactics in it?'

'Yes, and no,' Stanley Morrison explained to me. 'Hagen knew that often enough he'd win, and he was really professionally interested in who would be there beside him.'

We laughed together over the most famous Hagen story of all. Walter liked his drink and a game of poker with friends far into the night. One of them had to admonish him on the night before the final round of a championship: 'Walter, it's two o'clock in the morning and you're on the first tee at nine. All the others have been in bed for hours.'

'Ah,' said Hagen slyly, 'but are they sleeping?'

No man did more for golf, and for the professional golfer particularly, than Walter Hagen. He had a style and confidence, and a bountiful attitude to life, that broke down the barriers of snobbery then enclosing the British golfing scene. When he first arrived in England in 1920, he came as holder of the US Open Championship for the second time. He was here for our Open. He drove from London to Deal in a large opulant car, and as a matter of course went to change in the Royal Cinque Ports clubhouse. It was forbidden territory to a golf pro. So was every other golf clubhouse in Britain.

When he was directed to the professional's shop and saw how Britain treated its golfers, he struck a blow for them that changed the social pattern of the game. He parked his limousine outside the clubhouse and sat in it, using it as a dressing room.

A lot of furious English snobs were delighted that Walter made no showing at all in that year's competition, but with his supreme confidence he said he'd be back again to win. And Walter, king of them all, kept his word. Two years later, in 1922, he won his first Open at Sandwich (only a few miles from the lordly Deal that had spurned him); and he would go on to win it three more times: at Hoylake in 1924, at Sandwich again in 1928, and at Scotland's Muirfield in 1929.

So we talked about golf and people and Glasgow and whisky and the Rangers, and people we both knew in London, over the best roast beef I have ever tasted. The sun came out and suddenly the trees in the garden through the windows shimmered and shone. There wasn't a sound of traffic to disturb us, and in the relaxed atmosphere I took up far more of my host's time than I should. I remembered the description that Monsarrat had quoted about Glasgow being 'a dear green place', and I felt that perhaps St Ninian had not been so far out.

Glasgow has innumerable faces and it was a satisfaction to me to be able to enjoy this one. The trades that keep us all going and were of top importance, and the men who guide these trades and their methods of working, are too often obscured by the ugly and strident other images of industry.

I had watched the skill of Scottish craftsmen, 'nosing' their way through the various malts and grain whiskies to produce the perfect blend in the golden stream cascading into the blending vat. And I hadn't forgotten that as far back as the thirteenth century alcohol was called *aqua vitae,* water of life, and that the monks had distilled in Scotland spirit for medicinal purposes.

With my coffee in my hand, I wandered round the room, admiring the trophies Stanley Morrison has won as a well-known amateur golfer, and the photographs of him golfing with Henry Cotton. There is only one way to learn golf: take lessons at the very beginning from the men who know the game.

It is mistakenly assumed that all Scotsmen are natural golfers, that they only have to pick up a club for the first time, and their game unleashes itself. Nothing is further from the truth. Scotland is full of bad golfers, the men who have believed their own myth and never bothered to take lessons. It is an agony, and almost a crime, to watch the most beautiful courses in the world hacked to bits by native golfers who haven't bothered, or been too lazy, or too mistakenly stingy, or too cocksure, to be taught by the willing and able professionals who could change their game, making it a pleasure instead of a purgatory.

Stanley Morrison is one of the many wise ones who, knowing his own business, knew that other men understood theirs, and that he could learn from them. He learnt a lot and made sure that his sons would begin the same way. There are photographs of the same Henry Cotton, for whom Morrison's admiration is absolute, teaching Stanley Morrison's sons when they were boys. He certainly taught them something, judging by the trophies in this room.

I asked about Tim, the keenest golfer, probably, in the family.

'I'd hoped he'd be here,' said his father. 'He went off to New York a week ago. Business, of course. But he should have been back by now.'

Business, yes, but Tim, as always, had taken his golf clubs with him.

He arrived back just as I was about to take my leave. He had pulled off his business deal in the USA all right. I saw the smile pass between father and son. He had also found time to play, probably against other business men, in the Long Island golf tournament for visitors.

'Look,' he said, and drew a beautiful silver tray from his baggage. 'I won!'

9

I went back to the Central Hotel by taxi, an unwrapped bottle of Rob Roy whisky in my arm, slipped into my hand as I left Stanley Morrison. Glasgow, city of surprises, had another one for me as I went in through the door from the station, which led me past the porter's desk.

It was years since I had seen the face of Rob, but I remembered it well. He was older, the hair greyer, but the welcoming smile was still there.

'It is Rob, isn't it?' I said.

He came round to shake my hand.

'Ay, that's right. The same as on your bottle.'

There was something in the way he said it that put me on to what was behind his words.

'Not Rob Roy?' I asked disbelievingly.

He grinned.

'Not exactly. My name's Robert MacGregor, so gradually they've come to call me not just Rob MacGregor but Rob Roy MacGregor!'

There was a time, long ago, when I was on a mission to Glasgow and had greeted him almost daily. I had called him Rob; he had never, like the reticent Scot he was, presumed to tell me more about himself. I had never had the sense to find out.

Rob Roy MacGregor, the red-headed freebooting cattle raider of Highland legend. The scourge of Scotland around 1700. It was almost too good to be true.

My first instinct was to present Rob with the bottle in my hand. But it was a present from Stanley Morrison and I couldn't do that. I went up to my room, filled a small medicine bottle and returned to the hall.

'Have a drink on me,' I said to 'Rob Roy MacGregor.'

Later I had a drink myself and raised my glass silently to the genial Stanley Morrison. I did not know that I should never see him again. Months after these words were written Stanley died in a clinic in Switzerland.

XVI

1

I sat for five hours on a hot May day at the General Assembly of the Church of Scotland, packed with ministers and elders from every district in the country. At this particular session they were there to discuss a matter not of religion but of simple justice. The public galleries were full. Two thousand people altogether filled the great Assembly Hall.

For two hours the doors were locked. No one could leave and then return, having heard only part of the debate. A resolution would be made only by men who had listened to everything said on this particular issue.

Five months before, the Rev. Leonard Bell had been sacked from his job as editor of the Church magazine *Life and Work* by the Assembly's Publicity and Publications department. He had served the magazine for five of the ten years indicated in the contract he signed, which stated that his post would be 'reviewed' after five years.

Mr Bell claimed that a decision to end his appointment could only be made by the General Assembly which had appointed him, and not by the department. He was represented by Mr Harold Keith QC who handled his case with admirable restraint. He called on the Assembly to declare that the notice to end Mr Bell's contract was ineffective. Mr Bell had carried out his duties to the best of his ability since he was appointed five years before, and there was no evidence to show that the Assembly had authorized the department to end his appointment.

It is well worth while to stay with Mr Keith QC, a little longer in the light of what happened. The case of Leonard Bell had aroused considerable interest and private discussion during the past months in Church and Press circles. He had suffered a heart illness which necessitated hospitalization, and the long period of waiting for the Assembly's hearing must have been an anxious one. He was an editor who had endeavoured to inject a wider-interest reading content into his magazine, a move which had pleased many and annoyed others. But none of that was relevant to this particular issue.

'Mr Bell was in the normal habit of attending meetings of the Department of Publicity and Publications and the relevant sub-committee,' explained his counsel. 'Some change in the normal course of events took place in April last year, and after that he did not formally attend meetings of the department or the magazine committee.'

He had been asked to 'stand by' at a meeting on 3 December although he was not invited to attend it in person, and he was later told that it had been decided to terminate his appointment. 'Mr Bell was not given grounds why his appointment was being ended and had not been asked to make any statements.' The treatment seemed to be contrary to the rules of 'natural justice', said Mr Keith.

I was particularly interested in the case. I had been an editor myself and had had a free hand to make a success of my papers, or hang myself. I could not run a successful magazine or a newspaper by committee. One man's personality and flair should shape the image and character of his production. If he is right, you exalt him; if he is wrong you fire him for being wrong. And he knows why you are firing him.

But more than that, I wanted to see how these men of the Church, these rank and file ministers and elders with their brief cases who had travelled here from every corner of Scotland, would handle themselves. The Church of Scotland was suffering the same emptying of pews as all other denominations. It had problems enough without having this dramatic one thrust on it. And dramatic it was. The Press was fully represented. The television lights were filling the beautiful hall with a golden haze.

But at the start of the proceedings the acting Moderator suggested that this particular debate should not be televised, and gradually the lights had gone out, dimming the large room with what I thought was an ominous symbolism. If justice had not only to be done but had to be seen to be done, we should perhaps have to peer through this gloom to perceive it.

As it was, the dimming of the lights was a blessing for one person at least, the Rev. Leonard Bell. Although he could have had no doubt about the rights of his claim, he had been through a sore time, and television lights (and cameras) on his strained, pale face would have been a further unnecessary ordeal. The silent Assembly heard his QC quietly state his case. There were no histrionics. Silently and intently the Assembly heard him through.

Then, over a long period, which ignored the lunch-time break and everything else, and the doors remained locked, the ministers and elders of the Scottish Church had their say. Somewhere, I imagine, there is a record of what each said; it would be well worth reading. It was a satisfaction to me that the implications of the case were clearly understood and that while various people introduced the question of the quality of the magazine under the editorship of Mr Bell, all understood that this was not the matter being debated. 'I don't care if he is the worst editor in the world,' said one, not necessarily subscribing to that view, 'this is a matter of simple justice.' A man who was an ordained minister of the Church, and had ministered to his own congregation for many years had suffered, no justification had been given for his sacking, he had been allowed no say for himself. I cannot remember if anyone said that it was a disgrace to the Church, but the mounting judgment that the Church could have no part in such an injustice, was unmistakable.

When finally, after a tense and memorable session, the resolution was put to the Assembly that the sacking was 'ineffective', that Mr Bell should continue as editor of *Life and Work,* and that a special committee should be set up to investigate all the facts and circumstances surrounding the background to Mr Bell being given notice to quit his job, only a handful of men rose in disagreement.

And then the remaining assembly rose in an overwhelming body to express its approval. It was a sight to see. I was glad I had missed the sunshine of a May day to see it. And I was glad for the Church of Scotland.

Leonard Bell died of a heart attack nine months later.

2

Up at Gleneagles, the show-piece hotel of Scotland, things hadn't changed much since my last visit many years before. It was a one-night stand for me; a large group from London were holding their banquet there and, invited as a guest, I'd booked to stay overnight and move on into other country in the morning.

It was September, holiday time. The place was packed. An example to the countless Scottish hotels which in spite of living on tourism, couldn't care less, Gleneagles knows how to make you welcome. A bowl of flowers in my room when I went in; with my name on a card, and a message from the manager; 'All good wishes for a very happy and comfortable stay.'

So easy to give you a favourable impression of a place or a country if you know how. You don't have to invent examples of how Scotland doesn't know. This letter, for instance, in that never-sleeping watchdog, the *Edinburgh Evening News*, from J.A. Jenkins of Bath, Somerset:

> 'I intended to pay another visit to your glorious country for three weeks, so the day the postal strike ended I wrote to the Scottish Tourist Board for information and leaflets as advertised. No reply.
>
> 'A month later I telephoned and was told things were behind owing to the strike. Fair enough.
>
> 'Another month passed and nothing, so I again wrote outlining the position and asking for action. Still no reply.
>
> 'When I wrote to the Irish Tourist Board the information was forthcoming by return.'

I went down to get a breath of all that gorgeous Gleneagles hill air before changing for the evening. Tinkly Palm Court music came from the lounge. It might have been Frinton in the thirties, that never-never yesterday. Yet this particular brand had an old familiar and expert flavour, and I glanced in, hoping against hope. The lounge was crowded with well-dressed people.

And the man leading the small band – piano, violin, sax – was indeed Michael Burberry, and I was glad I had pounded my way half across Scotland more from a compulsion of friendly duty than inclination. The boys with him, who had just come to the end of a number, were not the ones I remembered from the past. But Burberry was just the same. Well, maybe a little older. Maybe even a lot older. But he had been a young starter when he played in London, and he had always looked young and fit, being a fresh-air-and-exercise faddist to offset the hours he had to keep and the languid, half-dead mob who danced to his music.

213

He had lived the game all his life, and loving it had kept him young. He was so damned good at it. Now he was wiping his sax in the old way, his eyes down, and looking at him across that crowded room, time fell away and I remembered the pleasure he had given me and some of my friends, not only in London, but later at the Marine Hotel, North Berwick, in the reign of that young and inspired hotelier, Peter Hiller (Wendy Hiller's brother), who made the Marine one of the best — and best-known — hotels in all Europe.

Whenever we had a special publishing project in mind, Keith Briant and I would hare off from London to that secret lair in Scotland, and there would join us Our Man in New York, or Our Man in Paris, for a few days of planning. Swimming in the sea, golfing on the immaculate links, or locked up in one of Peter's suites, with service at hand when we needed it, the plans would be prepared and agreed, the project launched, and in the event millions of pounds might be made and, equally important, millions of people entertained and perhaps even enlightened.

Michael Burberry's part in our activity was simply that he provided the music for dancing in the evening, or for afternoon tea in the big lounge, with its enormous windows letting the sea and the sky become part of the room. Burberry would always greet us with what was then our favourite melody, *Deep Purple.* I can hear it now. In the evening it would be the same. Sometimes we ate in our suite while the talk went on. But sometimes we went in to the dining room. And Burberry would fade out on *See You in My Dreams,* or *Tiptoe Through the Tulips,* nod to his boys, and right into our hearts would flow the sweet, silly music of *Deep Purple.* We were young, the melody belonged to that unique time of make-believe, and Burberry understood.

It was years since I had seen him. A waiter came now to my elbow to see if I wanted a table, but I was watching the slim grey-haired man with the sax. He raised his eyes and saw me. And behind him I was aware not of Gleneagles, but of the old Marine, and people who were dead, and Hiller somewhere — where? — and his old hotel, every room in it, filled with the flowers he loved.

It was good to see the look on Michael Burberry's face. Then he half-turned away and said a word to his companions. And at that moment the magic was almost broken for both of us. They were younger men, perhaps unaware or forgetful of that greatest musical composition every perpetrated. Their faces showed their doubt. Then Burberry put his sax to his lips, started them off, and in seconds they were giving out expertly with the music of *Deep Purple*. To me it was still sweet magic. And I'd have my own quiet session with Michael Burberry later that night.

3

I went out of the hotel, wading through Bentleys, Rovers, and a few Rolls Royces, to have a peaceful view of the distant range of hills. Long pink and yellow antirrhinums were bedded across the billiard-like green lawns. Putting greens, tennis courts, a glimpse of the popular golf course. Bulwarks against boredom.

As I wandered back, I met the friendly shrewd eyes of an attractive woman. Not young; but not too old. Wearing the right clothes with the right voice. Quietly chic.

'Astonishing hotel, isn't it?' I said.

'Well, I mostly live here. It's convenient; saves all the bother of a house. Then after about three months I get in a rut and just have to get up and go somewhere for a change.

We fell into step together. I was silent and thoughtful. I love hotels, the bigger and more impersonal the better. I love to see their administration functioning. I love most of all the anonymity they give me. But if, like my companion, I get away from them at the right time.

Our direction led along a line of parked cars. She gave them a glance.

'I like to see what people are buying,' said my unusual new friend. 'What's the car they're all going for! It gives you a picture of what's going on.'

'Of course,' I murmured, my eyes on her with an increased respect.

'In a car park like this you've time to weigh them up and see what people are putting their money into.'

'And at a place like this,' I said.

'Exactly.' Then she shot me a swift, devastating look. 'You're laughing at me!'

'No,' I assured her. 'I'm not laughing at you. But I'm very, very interested.'

'Why?'

It would have been too personal to tell her that I found her intelligent, lively outlook extremely attractive. So I merely said: 'Well, I'm not all that interested in cars, either as a status symbol, or really in the cost. I like driving them, but if I can't afford one type, I equally like driving another.'

She said, a little sharply: 'But you like to make sure you get value for your money?'

'Of course; but not to the point of lying awake at nights. You can figure yourself right out of living if you think too much of getting value for money.' Then I added the axiom that had got me through my life to this strange moment: 'The value of a thing is what it's worth to me.'

She thought about it, quite deeply to judge from her face. 'Yes, you've got something there. But you're wrong, you know. The value of a thing is its intrinsic worth − to you or someone else!'

Then she told me about her cars. She was now driving a Triumph, her second. She'd given up the MG. Her son had a Wolseley.From there she slid easily back into money. She used to play the stock market. She had a flair for buying low at almost the right time, and I did not doubt her casual admission for a moment. I asked her where she had got that from.

Her father, she said, had been a banker. Her mother seldom came down to breakfast, but had something sent up to her room. So this daughter sat with her father at the breakfast table every morning, the talk often turned to money, and gradually she absorbed the information he told her. It must have been a beguiling companionship for a banker father.

'One thing that always stuck in my memory,' she laughed gaily, 'was my father's dictum: "See that you always have money in hand".'

She had made my evening. Of all the encounters! If only some Scottish business men had the brains and the insight of such a woman, what a country it might be!

4

Melon en Barque; Crème St Germaine; Suprême de Volaille Maréchal; Petit Pois au Beurre; Pommes Byron; Gâteau Nenuphar; the usual several wines; coffee afterwards, and the meaningless talk across the table, total strangers mixed up with slight acquaintances, and the one or two old friends. And then the coffees and drinks continuing in the Gleneagles lounge or the bar far too long afterwards, the midnight jokes, the loud laughing, the secret longing to be away from it all and in bed.

What punishment the human race devised for itself. A lot of the voices were Scottish, and no doubt true Scottish hearts beat beneath the stiff white shirts. But this could have been Harrogate or Bath, and equally sterile. This wasn't the place or the occasion to expect stimulating conversation. Yet it emphasized the lack of it, and the general hollowness had its own message for me. I realized that I had not heard much serious discussion anywhere in the course of my travels. It was true that I had been on the wing, seldom in one place or with one person to have long heart-to-heart talks. But length of time in itself isn't the prime essential for confidences or the revelation of a true spirit. The odd exchange, the revealing smile, the very manner of a person, as well as what he says, can speak a definite attitude. I had been picking up impressions all my life, and living by it; and I could not surely be altogether wrong in feeling that the Scottish silence wasn't now all reticence, which I understood, but a silence which only they themselves understood, and was a mutual compliance, like the handshake of a freemason, or the glance of a fellow partisan, or the soundless words between doctor and nurse who know the condition of a patient.

Seldom had I heard anyone talk about books or music or art, and when I had broached the last subject among a few people, looking at the lovely Anne Redpath original on the lounge wall of the Open Arms at Dirleton before going in to the dining room, they had laughed in disbelief at my admiration of it. *That* should have made the luncheon talk a spirited thing, and I tried to draw it out, but as with so many other topics it was a non-starter.

When I mentioned some controversial book, which even as a news item had made the headlines, they hadn't read it or heard about it; when I compared my previous evening's TV viewing with someone, they had been watching Frankie Howerd or one of the other strange comedy series; I had been alone with something pretty marvellous on BBC-2. Yet all the good new books are displayed in the book shops, *The Scotsman* and *The Glasgow Herald* have excellent review pages, and both BBC Scotland and Scottish Television present lively and informative discussion programmes. Are there no deep personal feelings about these things which people want to try out on one another?

There's the usual chatter about the weather, about football, about who has died or who has had a baby, about the local rates that are always going up and the 'Yanks' who are always being talked down. For a country that has probably sent more of its sons to North America than any other, the ignorance of Scots about the 'Yanks', their way of life, their ideas, and the Americans' alleged ignorance of soldiering (and, presumably, fighting) is a tragic joke. You dare not tell many Scots the simple fact that without the United States we would not have won the Second World War – any more, for that matter, than you can tell the English. Almost the one thing the two peoples now share in common is a resentful awareness that they are no longer the masters of their own fate.

5

The typists and shop girls used to go out to lunch with books under their arms. They'd sit on a bench in the park, with a packet of sandwiches brought from home or bought at a store. Now window shopping, with all its modern attractive temptations seems to have taken the place of the lunch-time book. The big stores are wide open, like an eastern bazaar, every counter and every floor a fairyland of enchantment.

The news-stands are stacked with the same pornographic paperbacks you see at every airport or railway station in the world. Perhaps in this, more than in any other single phenomenon, Scotland has become part of the world beyond its borders, the world of colourful, sexy dust-jackets, the appeal of bedrooms and bare bodies. To watch the silent faces peering at these paperbacks, weighing them up, delving into them, in the city of John Knox, must cause the good presbyterians a lot of concern.

It worries me that politics are almost taboo, or a bore. Throw out a line of bait in the golf club locker room, or in a train, or even at that most likely place, a pub, and nobody takes you up. A mumbled cliché, full stop. All these top politicians flailing at each other in newspapers and on television, and never a murmur about it between men and women whose lives will be ruled by the outcome of the commotion. At one time I even wondered if people were afraid of being overheard, if their opinions were something they'd better keep to themselves. ('You never know who's listening just over your shoulder').

I had seen something of universal silence in Germany in the thirties. The first time I ever mentioned Hitler in a restaurant, I thought my German friends would drop dead. One's eyes fixed on me warningly, another murmured 'Sh-h!' and put his whole hand over his mouth, the other glanced quickly behind him. There was no Hitler in Scotland, but there certainly was some other kind of bogey man.

I really was being fanciful. Who wouldn't in that late-night Gleneagles gathering of waffling, beautiful people? I looked up suddenly as if someone had touched me. Across the table Sandy Trotter was gazing straight at me. Sandy then was Chairman of Scottish Express Newspapers, an old friend, and one of the nicest men in the game – or out of it. Perhaps he sensed something of what was going on inside me. I shall never know. Our eyes met – bang! – right in the centre of the table. His were completely expressionless. My eyes fixed into exactly the same unrevealing look. A poker-faced exchange, between professionals, of all that we have seen and known of human nature in a life-long all-in-wrestle with it.

Once before on my excursions, in a setting even more formal than this, with much footling talk filling up the evening, I had encountered an exactly similar exchange. Across the table from me was Willie Merrilees. Willie is a born story-teller and he had kept us all amused. The table had bubbled with laughter. But there had been moments of boredom and pronouncements of incredible inanity. And once, catching his eye, there was the same expressionless exchange between us that could have meant anything. But whatever it meant, words were unnecessary.

Willie Merrilees is certainly a professional in human behaviour. He has now retired from police work, but at that particular social function he was still Chief Constable of the Lothians and Peebles police force, a man who has fought crime ruthlessly nearly all his life; one of the best-known and best-liked men in Scotland. Except, you might think, by those he has put away.

Yet when the Governor of Edinburgh Prison was leaving on his promotion to HM Inspector of Prisons, he sent Willie a beautiful Scroll with the inscription: 'This was given to Mr William Merrilees, OBE by The Governor and Inmates of Edinburgh Prison in Appreciation of his Kindness and Understanding shown to Inmates over the Years. His Gifts have been Generous and very Acceptable. J. McIntyre, March, 1970'.

A Scot who began, in the old fashioned way, with every dis-advantage. He was born in a single room in the tough Leith district of Edinburgh, sharing the room with five other members of his family. His father earned £1 a week as a sawyer, and his mother went out to work to help make ends meet. Willie started work at the age of thirteen, in a rope works. There, in an accident, he lost all the fingers of his left hand.

There were few pain-killing drugs in those days, and the pain, he admits, was 'savage'. So he took off for Leith docks in the early mornings – regularly about 4.30 – to bathe his hand in sea water.

He got a job in a shipyard, married on the strength of it, was thrown idle by the slump after the first war. He spent some of his spare time teaching children how to swim; he had already saved several lives in the docks at Leith. But he was unlucky when he wanted (and wanted badly) a job as a swimming instructor with Edinburgh Corporation.

The Lord Provost, Sir Thomas Hutchison, however, must have been a very far-seeing man. He recommended Willie to the Chief Constable. Willie was five feet six inches tall, had no fingers on his left hand, and his formal education had been limited. His chances might have been regarded as slim. But to his own astonishment he was recruited, and very soon showed the stuff he was made of.

It would take a book to tell the story of Willie Merrilees, his ways with criminals, his rise in his profession (they would not let him retire when his retirement came due), and his good works in connection with children and old people. And fortunately, the book has been written, by Willie himself, and published by John Long. I give it this mention gladly for it told me something of what goes on behind the splendid architectural façade of Edinburgh.

And – I love to see all the ends meet – it reveals that Willie was the man who probed the scandalous Edinburgh night-life which I mentioned pages and pages ago and left tantalizingly in mid-air. Despite threats, and offers of large bribes, and a risk that could have imperilled his career, he went ahead with a force of seventy-eight of his police officers, and raided a call-girl joint 'frequented by prominent people in Edinburgh, including members of the town council.'

He knew that night would make or break him. It certainly did not break him. It would take a lot to do that to Willie Merrilees. He risked everything in doing his policeman's job, and came through. And he set the tea-tables of Edinburgh abuzz for many years to come.

6

A long note from Stephen Scholfield, the Canadian writer, who is sending back to Canadian newspapers some of his feelings about Scotland. 'Use any of this you like,' he says. 'It may contradict or confirm some of your own impressions, and it might add up to something of the picture.'

On a green hill by the Annan river he saw a long line of white stones marking the graves of Canadians, Australians and New Zealand soldiers who had trained in the district. On Saturday afternoons Mrs Murdoch, a local housewife, puts flowers on them, two or three at a time. No son of hers lies there, and no relations. But she remembers the boys who used to come to her house. 'They loved potato fritters. I had an awful time to get enough fat to fry them in. Sometimes I had to go next door to Mrs Lindsay and ask for a loan of margarine for the airmen. That one there, Jimmy, he used to dig into the sugar something terrible. And it was rationed so strict, you know.

'Sometimes we cooked up everything and afterwards, when the boys had gone, my husband would say: "It's about time I had my supper." I had to tell him, "I canna gi'e ye it. I've got nothing left."

'And he would say: "I don't see why ye gi'e the airmen your best food. They're getting better food thin you." And I'd say, "Ay, but they're somebody's bairns, so far away from home." '

The old airfield is over the hill, where runways still stretch across the fields. Grass sprouts through long cracks in the concrete. Sheep graze here now, and highland cattle. Patches of heather colour the hill which slopes down to the river winding gently through the quiet Dumfries-shire countryside.

7

John Gibson, expressing in his newspaper television review his surprise that Scotsmen can still get up and go out into the world – and take a chance:

'They make enthralling television, those programmes about men who've got up and gone far, far from home to seek their fortunes or simply to earn a living doing something different. But they don't half make you feel puny as you sit there, dissatisfied and maybe a little ashamed of your own lot.

'I'm talking about a new BBC-1 series called *Across the Great Divide* which will be catching up on Britons who have settled in North America.

'For a start they introduced Duncan Pryde, a Scot who emigrated from Glasgow sixteen years ago. Orphaned by the German blitz, Pryde had a mundane job in Glasgow and was looking for something to get away from it all. He found it in an ad in the evening paper.

'The Hudson's Bay Company were looking for somebody to trade with the Eskimos in the Arctic. Pryde took it and before long he was doing his rounds by dog sled, speaking Eskimo in seven dialects, sharing their troubles, their food and their wives. The custom up there, you know.'

8

Voltaire said: 'The rules of taste in all the arts, from epic poems to gardening, come from Scotland.'

Charles Lamb confessed: 'I have been trying all my life to like Scotchmen, and am obliged to desist from the experiment in despair.'

Samuel Johnson disliked us and did not hesitate to say so; Byron, Buckle and Cobbett could take us or leave us; and Henley was out of sympathy with 'the poor-living, lewd, grimy, free-spoken ribald old Scots peasant world'.

Sidney Smith was of the opinion that if you wanted a Scot to see a joke you must perform a surgical operation on him.

And the Englishman, T.W.H. Crosland – poet, obsessive hater of Scots, and author of *The Unspeakable Scot,* – wrote:

> 'A Scot is the one species of human animal that is taken by all the world to be fifty per cent cleverer and pluckier and honester than the facts warrant. He is the daw with a peacock's tail of his own painting. He is the ass who has been at pains to cultivate the convincing roar of a lion. He is the fine gentleman whose father toils with a muck fork. He is the bandy-legged lout from Tullietudlescleugh who, after a childhood of intimacy with the cesspool and the crablouse, and twelve months at "the college" on moneys wrung from the diet of his family, drops his threadbare kilt and comes south in a slop suit to instruct the English in the arts of civilization and the English language. And because he is Scotch and the Scotch superstition is heavy on our Southern lands, England will forthwith give him a chance, for an English chance is his birthright.'

XVII

1

When we came to the road up to Manorhead, the going was rough. The last stretch was a pot-holed dirt track filled in here and there with granite chippings.

It cut through the hill, going on upwards. Below us Manor water flowed in the gully cradled between the hills. It was shallow water, gurgling over the stones, and even in summer it looked cold. Even in summer it gurgled, for it wasn't often that the rains held off long enough to dry up the stream.

We had planned an easy drive through the beguiling border country and a picnic somewhere in the hills, away from everybody. You had to be on your own to enjoy this soft and tremendous landscape of country leading to the hills, especially in the bright sunlight, where the colours were all blues and whites and greens, beckoning on to the purples of distant heather.

It was fine sheep country. Rolling, folding country, climbing ever onwards. There were lush green valleys laced with glinting streams, yielding glimpses of prosperous farm houses, white-faced in the shelter of their trees. The sky was an intensely blue sea with high prowed galleons of clouds sailing through it, powder grey, sparkled at their fringes with a dazzling silver.

There wasn't a soul in sight. And as the hills closed in on us, cutting off the distant view, we were blissfully engulfed in the solitude of a remote world.

A world that had its own problems. And the last stretch of the road up to Manorhead was certainly one of them. We knew nothing about it then, on that first meeting with it, nine years before. We had no knowledge of what the track led to, or where. In that distant summer we had come to Scotland from the lunacies of London, for a few days' golf and relaxation.

At the closed iron gate we got out and surveyed the track ahead. It was narrow and tight, with an impossible surface. It turned and twisted out of sight behind the elbows of hills. There was no board indicating its destination, and no threat of death and destruction to anyone daring to use it. The Highlands, where lairds and lords still want to keep their countless acres free from alien feet, are loaded with them.

'Oh, let's go,' I said, eager to push into the unknown.

'But the car...' Sheila reminded me.

It wasn't the oldest car in the world. But it wasn't the newest either. With a bit of coaxing, I fooled myself, it would surmount this track. *Someone* used it! There must be some kind of habitation up the hill: a shed for vehicles, a shelter for animals, perhaps even a house.

I pushed the gate open, drove the car through, and Sheila closed the gate behind us. At least we could go on till we saw what was ahead or until the track beat us.

It was uncomfortable and slow. If a farmer's tougher vehicle came down from the hill there would be an embarrassing impasse and useless apologies from us. Quite soon we called it a day, manoeuvred the car into a small grass clearing in the side of the hill and knew that here we'd stop. We chocked the car wheels with small boulders which would hold us there till we were ready to kick them out, ease the hand brake, and roll forward for our return journey.

But that would be long delayed. Here we were and here we meant to stay. There was just enough space on one side for us to put down a rug and make a home. And lie gazing at the sky. It was gorgeous. I remembered the line from Walter de la Mare's poem *Autumn:* 'And clouds like sheep stream o'er the steep grey sky where the lark was.' Here the sky was blue and the clouds were snowy white.

This was the real borderland. Three centuries before, beneath all this beauty, had been bloodshed and brutal treachery, pillage and burnings and cattle stealing. By the English or Scots against each other; by the rival Scottish gangs raiding one another. Friend or foe. What did it matter?

It was country familiar to Sir Walter Scott, who used every inch of it in his historical novels. To the south west of us was the rise of the 2,000-feet high Deer Law, and beyond that, unseen from our resting

224

place, lay St Mary's Loch, dearly loved by Scott, and the lonely Tibbie Shiel's Inn. No one was in sight. Not a single plane disturbed our silence. Only the 'murmur of innumerable bees', the trickle of water over the pebbles, the faint bleating of sheep, bent and busy with the short grass on distant slopes. We missed the lonely call of the curlew, for the curlew was still down near the sea and would not be back here until her breeding season.

In the early afternoon we stirred, got up, and went our separate exploring ways. Crossing the stream, Sheila climbed the higher ground with her camera; I went up through the gorge to follow a trickle of a burn, crystal clear, which caught the colours of the sky, the heather and the golden bracken. Both of us spied for the first time the shepherd's house at the head of the track.

She got back to the car first and started tea. I sipped at my first cup, my eyes still on the ever-changing colours of the hills. Almost to reassure myself that it was all still ours and ours alone, my glance went back down the steep rough road.

'We've got company,' I murmured.

Sheila followed my gaze. She reached for the binoculars, German made and relic of German War number one. She raised them to her eyes. It couldn't have been to see what kind of company. I could see them and enjoyed the sight of them with my own unaided eyes. But I knew well why she wanted the glasses, and why the enlarged vision through them brought the smile-lines round her mouth. This was a sight to see.

She silently handed me the glasses. They brought the trailing line of climbing children sharply clear. There were three of them, trudging up the track slowly in single file. They were coming towards us. Two girls and a boy. The older girl, her fair hair bright in the sunshine, was leading. The boy, smaller and younger, a few yards behind his leader, was less distinct. He kept weaving in and out of the shadow thrown on him by the leader as he tried to come up level with her and then take her place in the lead.

From the slim streamlined look of Goldilocks, I surmised that he'd never have a chance. The last — there's often an endearing last in a group like this — was little more than an infant. About three years old, I thought, my eyes on her small figure struggling sturdily after her older brother and sister, trying to keep up with them, hopelessly behind. And feeling the heat, the climb, and the eternal juvenile frustration that always affects the youngest. Her hair, as fair as the taller girl's from this distance, fell about her face. She was flushed and bothered, flailing her tiny arms about her to keep off the flies.

'Have we any cake left?' I asked.

'Plenty,' Sheila said, without taking her eyes away. 'And lots of biscuits and sweets. And orange juice.'

'That's item number one!'

2

At that time, nine years ago, we had a grand-daughter of just about the smaller girl's age. We knew the problems of heat and hill and unprivileged infancy. There's one in most families, trying to be up with the older children, being shooed off from expeditions, mockingly bullied, but mostly aware (I hope) of sure protection when needed. So it was still the little one in the rear we were watching when the first two rounded an elbow of the hill and came suddenly upon us.

At sight of us they stopped, only a few yards away, almost on top of us. The bright sunlight was full on them. They had come up from the east and the afternoon sun was now high in the south-west. It wasn't every day they came upon two strangers having a picnic in this spot, with a car perched oddly on the grass beside them.

We could tell that at once, not by any strained shyness, but by their still, quiet pause. They were like the surprised animals of their own countryside, their look one of curiosity and interest. This whole place, the grass we sat on, the hills around us, the stream below, was their possession and heritage, their own undoubted hallowed ground.

But in the surprise there came a quick-grown delight. We were an acceptable novelty, a break in the routine of what we guessed to be a little family homing it to the shepherd's house up Manorhead.

I judged the girl to be about eight, the boy maybe six. She was quite beautiful, with corn-coloured hair and deep brown eyes, almost amber. They narrowed now against the sun's glare, alive and warm. And with an eagerness in them that I could only think came from a love of life. She stood still in the sunshine in her skimpy cotton frock, her long slim legs as tanned as her face, her feet bare, and showed her pleasure at our intrusion. The brown shoes she had been carrying she now let drop on the grass. She had come to stay.

'Hello!' I said.

226

'Hello!' she said back, with a wide smile and a flash of teeth.

The boy had moved up beside her. He surveyed us with the same straight look, and his elder sister's instant acceptance. But where her face had slimmed down and already showed the shadows of high cheek bones, his face was still the round face of a boy. The man wasn't there yet, but he wasn't far away. And the way his hair had been cut, closely machined up from his neck and his ears, leaving an unruly mop on top, straggling forward thickly over his forehead and down towards his eyes, revealed the shape of many a countryman's head of almost any age.

'Hello!' he said, his voice beginning high and dropping where the girl's had risen lightly on the last syllable. His legs and feet were bare like hers, and as brown. His white shirt open to the waist and grey shorts were sufficient covering on that warm afternoon. They waited till the youngest had come into the circle. Then all three slumped together on the grass with an 'ah!' of pleasure.

For the child it must have been a welcome break in the long hot walk. Her face was the round red face of the baby, hot and bothered. The same family look was there, but she had more blue in her eyes, and her hair wasn't the corn-colour of her sister's, but paler, almost white in places, falling over eyes and ears. Her gaze, wide-eyed and straight, was puzzled, silently questioning. Who were we? What was this all about?

We reached for the orange juice. She had to come first. One tiny grubby hand came out to take the plastic cup, the other continued to scratch at the multiple red insect bites on both her legs. Scratch, scratch, scratch. The eyes watched, the mouth opened to drink and eat, but never to speak. That first encounter, so many years ago now, passed without a word from her. There was no need to talk. Her radiant sister was doing all the babbling for her, and for her brother as well.

Sheena Coltherd stands out clearly in our life from those first moments of meeting. Alive, vital, lovely, making interesting movements with her hands and arms as she prattled on, restless with energy, rising on her slim legs to point out a tree shelter for the sheep, a path on a distant hill that led to St Mary's Loch, or merely to move in joy to tell a story. A fascinating child-woman full of high spirits, showing her warm friendliness with us all, there in the bright sunlight.

Now and then she would laugh to joyous scorn something John said that made nonsense to her in all her eight years' knowledge of life, or throw a proud and watchful glance at little sister Lesley. We were enthralled, our golden day complete. The discovery and unexpectedness of her, the surprise of the meeting, the delight of the grouping on the

227

warm grass, filled us with happiness. Of course Sheena knew that at once, as all little women of her intelligence and charm do, and she was slightly heady with the miracle of it.

She never stopped her gay and giddy chattering. The biscuits and sweets were handed round, the orange juice vanished, accepted gracefully by all, by Sheena and John with a polite 'Oh, thank you' at each offering, by Lesley in interested silence, her eyes still taking us in, her infant defences unbreached.

If they were headed for tea or supper as at that hour they might, and someone could be anxious about their absence, a word of query was enough for Sheena.

'Oh, my mummy knows us!' She laughed gaily and twirled on her feet. She did not know that with those five words she had started to fill in the picture of a happy family. A splutter of laughter: 'And we know her!'

John gurgled with pleasure, sharing in that moment a whole family album of familiar jokes, escapades, mishaps, crises of living. Little Lesley contentedly munched her biscuit and scratched her legs.

Were there any other brothers or sisters?

'Goodness, no! Do you not think we're a big enough handful?'

I could imagine. Yet, I thought, for all the mischief in them, entirely manageable. And again I glimpsed something of a close cooperative family adventure.

'And you live up here?'

Her eyes wide open at the foolishness of the question.

'Of course! Where else?'

'Is it the house at the end of the road?'

Joyously: 'Have you been up?' And in a rush: 'Yes! have you been up to see my daddy?'

Her father was the shepherd. She thought that perhaps I had something to do with farming and had been paying a call. When Sheila told her that we had only spotted the house from this distance she said at once:

'Oh, you can come up with us. Mummy will want to meet you.'

3

Of course we went; we needed no persuasion. Sheena danced around us as we got up from the grass. She tossed her shoes to John. 'You can carry these now,' she commanded, and he grinned and aimed a mock punch at her. But he caught the separating shoes adroitly in mid-air. Lesley got staunchly to her feet, and my heart was with her.

I said regretfully to Sheena:

'We can't really get the car round again to give you a lift.'

She laughed scornfully.

'We always walk the whole way. You'll just have to do the same!'

'Then I'll give Lesley a piggy-back.'

'Oh, her!' But full of womanly affection. 'You'll find her a weight!'

She was too. She let herself slump completely, as a cuddled cat does, and she was a dead weight on me. But its first impact vanished as the other two ran madly ahead, came back and tagged closely at our sides, skipping and jumping. John had caught the mood, and the two young voices surrendered the happy secrets of the Coltherd family. 'My daddy does...mummy can't bear to....She's always baking the....My mummy says...do you know what – guess!...we're going to have electricity! They're going to put up the electric poles quite soon...and Daddy says we can have a real electric radio...Lesley found a dead....But Mummy wants a fridge...a fox got at two of the sheep...you should see Mummy when...Daddy's going to fill in the road...sometime....'

The distance was nothing. The track wasn't all that bad. We could have come right up in the car after all, with a bump or two. Lesley ceased to weigh a ton, but her arms around my throat had begun a slow strangling movement.

The sight of the shepherd's home was a pleasure, and a relief. The usual low, one-storey house with white-washed walls, and typical Scottish blue-slated roof. Approached across a wooden bridge over a stream that rippled down over the boulders and pebbles to feed Manor water in the valley. A glimpse of small outbuildings, separated from the house by an earth yard, dry and hard and cracking in the summer heat, but a quagmire, I imagined, in the winter. Two or three cows on the other side of the gate, turning blank eyes on us. The hills rising right behind and, seemingly, all around us. A line of washing.

At the eastern window facing our approach a woman's face appeared. It vanished, but there it was, a few seconds later, as we went in through the gate and round the back to the door, where Chrissie

Coltherd, the children's mother, came to greet us.

Slim, bright-eyed, completely unruffled although caught in the midst of her household activities. I had a flashing glimpse in my mind of any average suburban housewife, surprised by unexpected visitors, whipping her apron off, swiftly stuffing things under the kitchen cushions, patting her hair as she hurried to the door. Mrs Coltherd had done none of these things, or even thought of doing them. Her dark hair was a bit tousled, there was flour on her hands, her blue apron was still around her. She was serene in her Scottish assurance of herself and her home.

'Hello!' she said. 'They've all landed themselves on you, I see. They would!'

A soft Lothian voice, but quick and sure in utterance. There was nothing slow about this woman. Her movements through the kitchen were quick and definite; her mind worked quickly. She laughed a lot, but neither laughter nor easy conversation with the two strangers thrust unexpectedly upon her had interrupted her preparations for the family meal. She was deftly energetic. She would have to be, with this brood, a hard-working shepherd husband, and the loneliness and handicaps of her remote dwelling.

She was swamped at once with highly-fanciful descriptions from Sheena (and not so fanciful from John) of how we had all met and why *we* were there. She listened and laughed, flashing us an eye, but continued her activities.

'I hear you're going to have electricity soon,' said Sheila, one woman to another in the eternal domestic scene.

She stopped in her tracks. Only this, the high light of a new way of living, could pause her for a second or two.

'It'll be a godsend,' she exclaimed. And then, mentally crossing her fingers. 'If it ever happens!'

'An electric radio, mummy!' Sheena cried out.

'A washing machine!' said her mother.

At once the competing claims for the new electricity were bandied about the room in high good spirits. In the midst of it, Chrissie went quickly out of the room, came back with a small bottle and dabbed a spot of Dettol on most of Lesley's insect spots while the child was putting a saucer of milk on the floor for the cat. Lesley jerked up her head, knew it was too late to protest, became absorbed in her task.

We ought to be going, I said. We had intruded, Chrissie had made us welcome, but her hands were full. She was a woman to watch with admiration. She had made none of the usual feminine apologies for the state of her kitchen. She knew we understood.

'I expect you couldn't get a word in edgeways,' she laughed at us.

I noticed how the children proceeded at once to carry out an individual household chore, part of their Scottish upbringing, as it had been part of my own and my sisters' and brothers' routine. The job first: brushing the boots, or seeing to the food for the dogs or hens, and so on, before the meal with father and mother, and the family fun.

'When do you really expect the electricity?' Sheila asked; and I was glad that she had delayed our departure. If anything could cover up our untimely dallying, this was the one ripe topic.

'Goodness knows!' And then heartfully, 'but I hope it will be before winter.'

'Radio in winter'll be grand!' cried Sheena in delight.

This was a family living in anticipation of blessings to come. They had blessings enough around them, and well they knew it. It was a joy to stand there (Chrissie had rightly not asked us to sit and make ourselves comfortable; we shouldn't have, anyway. Well, maybe we might), and be part of the happiness and contentment around us. But I had seen no sign of the legendary 'poles' for the electricity cables anywhere in the valley or on the way up; and I wondered how long it would really take to bring the Coltherd's their new blessing. I hoped Chrissie's 'before winter' would prove to be true, but I had my doubts. Life for her must have been a strenuous affair bringing up her little family. The things she must have had to do without! The comforts and household helps that millions of women take for granted. So many years without them; with the nearest shops miles away, and deliveries doubtful – and certainly precarious – in a tough winter. I thought of snow drifting across these hills and filling the valley. Where was the nearest doctor?

And suddenly I realized that by sheer chance we had landed ourselves on the Coltherd family at the very time when for them it was almost the point of no return. We were glimpsing them, enjoying their friendship, just at the end of their period of 'doing without'. They had become as they were, the lovely eldest girl, the sturdy boy, the indomitable silent little Lesley, the happy, energetic wife, the bonded family, out of years of difficulty and struggle unimaginable to most women. I had no idea what a shepherd earned back in that year 1962 when we stood in the kitchen for the first time. It would have been even less, without doubt, in the years before. Whatever it was, all of it and probably more would be needed to make ends meet.

I had not been looking for the Coltherd family. We had stumbled upon them, or rather they had stumbled up the hill upon *us*. The golden-haired, high-spirited girl, the competitive younger brother, the insect-bitten, heat-bothered baby. But they had led me to a rediscovery of the kind of life that millions of Scottish people knew, understood, and lived. Down the centuries. Hard, frugal, living with nature, fighting for survival. Of course they had the benefits of the twentieth century; a farm truck could get them bumpily into Peebles, a grocer's van could risk its axles bringing out their necessities. But in a sense, they had had to depend on their own strength and stamina, their character, their will to live in the little house up the hill.

Without realizing how much, their lives were about to change, were bound to change. When the poles were brought up the valley, and fixed into position, and the cables were strung up and connected with the white-washed house, and the fridge was making life a bit easier for Chrissie (or the electric radio was thrilling the spell-bound Sheena; and without doubt she'd get her radio sooner or later), the routine of the family would change. The larger world, which never until this time had been able to penetrate these stone walls, would bring the comforts of civilization and the news of what was happening beyond these hills, in the towns and cities and countries across the seas.

It was odd to stand there, for a moment only a fragment of a family of the past, and be aware that change was on its way: an order in some local Council office, a note on somebody's desk pad – 'Coltherd's electricity'; perhaps a phone call to some timber yard about 'these damned poles, Alec'.

'Here's dad!' called out Sheena.

I was glad I had delayed. Mr Coltherd was coming through the door, with his boots off and already placed outside. Sheena went straight to them and picked them up; the boots were her job. But the door was open to the summer warmth and she stood framed in it while she brushed, still a part of the scene.

Mr Coltherd had the same Christian name as his three-year-old daughter, but his 'Leslie' differed in the spelling. I took to him at once. Like his wife, he showed no surprise but accepted us as all part of the day. He would, himself, become a natural part of any situation. He would always be in place. He was quiet in his speech and movements, used to the silence of the hills, the care and control of his sheep and the understanding companionship of his dogs as they worked with him.

Like his wife, he was much younger than I had expected. I had forgotten the ages of his children in relation to the word 'shepherd', imagining the older shepherd of memory and legend, perhaps sporting a bit of a beard, with slightly stooped shoulders, and the 'lowp'-ing walk that comes from lifting the feet in a certain manner over the heather. Almost bounding across it, in fact, in short regular lowps, or leaps.

Mr Coltherd would have been amused if he had known what I was thinking. He was nothing like my picture. But he would have smiled slowly and surely, the smile as deliberate as the rest of his movements, and coming from an inward measuring of values. He supplied the strength and solidarity that made the little group complete. And he was a handsome man by any reckoning.

By my own reckoning too he must be more than ready for his evening food and the company of his bairns rather than strangers. So I said, quite definitely this time, that we ought to be on our way.

'Why don't you come up another day?' Leslie Coltherd suggested. 'That is, if you're round about here?'

'Oh, yes!' Sheena and John called out.

And Sheila crowned it by saying we might be in the same place down the hill the next day. Could we give the children a picnic and take some coloured photographs of them?

5

That first meeting gave us the feeling that we were a small part of the Coltherd family and their corner of Scotland. Sheila sent them the photographs when we got back to London. At Christmas she sent cards or a box of chocolates or toffees. We had three grandchildren of our own and the next few years would bring three more. What with them, and their tiny friends, we were very involved with children. Inevitably, tangible contact with the family at Manorhead grew fragile, although the memory of that first day did not fade, and has never faded.

About three years later I had a chance of being in Scotland for a few days, and Sheila came with me. We drove to Manorhead up the hill, bumps and all. Chrissie's face appeared at the window. She smiled and waved and came out to meet us. She was just the same. Leslie was out on the hills; Sheena was now at the school for older children in Peebles, and would come home much later. John and Lesley were at the same little school six miles down the hill. They would be leaving there in about twenty minutes, and the school bus would bring them as far as the end of the tarmac road.

'We'll pick them up at school,' I said, 'and bring them all the way.'

It gave us an opportunity of renewing acquaintance with the girl who had been only three at our first meeting. So we waited outside the small stone school, with its cemented playground (as in my own day) and dry-stone walls. The school was also the County Library. We could not see through its windows, but inside the children were singing a hymn, and that meant end of day.

When the straggle of boys and girls appeared I spotted John and caught his eye. His face broke into a smile and he waved; then he bent to say something to the girl with the fair hair beside him. Six-year-old Lesley could not of course remember us, but no doubt the earlier meeting had been mentioned in the family. And she'd have seen the picnic photographs. She looked towards us. I was surprised to discover that her eyes weren't the blue I had thought but a pale grey, like her father's. They were interested and enquiring, and she smiled straight at us, accepting.

So it was a joyous journey back up the hill, and although we could only stay for a very short time, and did not see the shepherd or Sheena, we had put our foot in again and made contact. As we did on another occasion a few years later.

But now, after living with Scotland for the last two years, I felt the pressure of the Coltherd family sharply against my mind. And I realized, through my tangle of experiences and impressions, that it had been there, vaguely, for some time and for some reason that eluded me.

What had touched it off? Something I had heard or read? Someone I had met? I telephoned Sheila who was in another part of Scotland and told her I was going to Manorhead. We had been parted a great deal by my travels, but this was something we had to do together. Somewhere along the line I needed reassurance about the Coltherds. They had been out of our lives too long.

I went back to my notes, some typed, some handwritten, some with only a few words that might light up a whole dialogue with a person, some so detailed that they were experiences or talks almost verbatim. I sat with the pile of paper on my knees and waded through it, seeking a clue.

And after a time I came upon my meeting, so long ago, with the man from the Forestry Commission. Vividly I remembered standing in front of a deserted farm cottage and hearing him say: 'All these places used to be full of farm workers. I knew most of them. But mechanization's taken over. These cottages rightly belong to the men and women who lived in them.' And almost simultaneously I could hear the last sad line of Marion Angus's poem:

> And heather creep, creepin'
> ower the bonnie dryin' green.

Something had nagged at the back of my mind since that day. I was certain of it now. The empty farm cottages. That 'mechanization'. It had shocked me then, and the worry must have stayed. Could it possibly have happened to that happy family up at Manorhead?

I told myself I was being foolish. Mechanization affected the field workers, not the sheep country. Leslie was a shepherd. There was nothing that he and a couple of dogs did that could be handled more effectively by any other method. Good shepherds were the salt of the earth. You couldn't survive without them. But I wanted to be sure.

As we went over the wooden bridge leading to the white-washed house, I saw at once that my fears had indeed been foolish.

Through the far gate, leaning over the stone wall and watching my movements as I got out of the car was the unmistakable head of a new Coltherd. The tousled fair head and bright eyes of a little boy of about three, had the sure stamp of John and the Coltherd girls as they had been at our first meeting long, long ago. Near him was a small well-used van. I had never seen that before. And beyond him, cap on head, bent low over a single sheep he was tending in a walled pen, was Leslie Coltherd himself. He looked up from his preoccupations, puzzled for a moment, then smiled a welcome.

'I've got an awful memory,' he said, not in excuse but in explanation. 'I can hardly tell one face from another.'

The washing was out on the line and once more Chrissie saw us from her window and waved us in.

'He didn't remember me,' I told her.

'Oh, him!' she laughed, her dark eyes flashing amusement. 'He doesn't remember anything. Except his sheep. He can recognize every one of them a mile away!'

'And how's the family?' asked Sheila.

She could ask it with confidence. The atmosphere was the same, that of complete contentment.

'Oh, we're all fine,' sang Chrissie. 'I'll give you all the news; but I'll have to throw it at you. I'm in an awful hurry, but I'll tell you all about it in a rush.'

Was there ever a time in our few visits to her when she wasn't doing a dozen things at once? But I sensed a special urgency now and waited with interest to hear what was afoot in this constantly surprising shepherd's family.

The new little Coltherd had come silently in and was at his mother's side, weighing me up with his blue eyes. His face wasn't impeccably clean, his thin cotton trousers were grubby, his hands were dirty.

'I've got pockets,' he said. They were the only words he uttered throughout. He had the silence and the watchfulness of his sister Lesley when she had been his age. But no insect bites. And he was as much at home in his untidyness as was his mother in her dark, energetic freshness. But there was a special gleam about her this time, and we had not long to wait for the big news. In a few minutes she was going to drive herself into Peebles to have a hair-do. She addressed herself to Sheila, and I wanted to know why the urgency and why the hair-do. But I was still watching Graeme, struck by the resemblance to his little sister. I could have told myself that time had stood still.

He came across the floor and stood beside me. He had waited, as animals do, and then without any urging had accepted me. I showed him a quick flick trick with a coin that usually baffles children. I move a coin fairly adroitly between two hands in such a way that it must obviously end up in the right (or the left) hand. 'Which hand?' I ask, holding the closed hands in front of them. And generally they choose the wrong one. Surprised, they clutch quickly at the other hand, and there is nothing there either. I always show them how to do it, and they get the coin anyway.

But this little boy's eyes followed the coin, not the hands. He knew where it was, and got the sixpence. But he was completely foxed when, on putting the coin into his pocket, he discovered another sixpence already there. As his split trews pocket had been gaping open quite close to my hand, I hadn't needed to be a member of the Magic Circle to slip it in.

6

Time hadn't stayed still at Manorhead. It had brought its changes and rewards. A silver trophy stood on the sideboard. A week before Mr Coltherd had won the Samuel Barr Memorial Trophy for the shepherd with the best conditioned sheep. I had noticed two big tents in a field on the way up, and there, on the previous Saturday, had been the judging. I wished we had been there. For thirteen years Leslie had been shepherd on this lonely hill-land and I could imagine his modest pleasure at the award.

Electricity had come to the Coltherds, and television and a deep freeze and a washing machine. Now, seventeen years after their honeymoon, Chrissie and Leslie were going away to enjoy their first holiday alone together. No wonder Chrissie was aglow. We had landed in on her hectic preparations for their departure a few days later. They were going to stay with a relation at Dovercourt in Essex.

The arrangements that had to be made! The family were being left behind. A hired couple were coming to live in and look after the animals while they were away. Sheena would stay on at the house. She was taking an extra year at Peebles High School. It was easier for her to stay on here and be picked up by the school bus down the road, and go in to Peebles and come back that way. John, Lesley, and little Graeme were going to a near-by granny.

Sheena had been a bit rebellious about that extra year at school (I could imagine!), but her far-seeing father had insisted, as he had also insisted that she should later take a shorthand-typing course. She had her eyes on a job as an air hostess, and was irked at having to continue at school while all her old school friends were already working and earning money. I could understand. It was the old Scottish desire to be standing on your own two feet as soon as you could, making your living.

But neither she nor her mother had been idle. All the home comforts, and the luxuries, had had to be earned. With three of her children now well on their feet, and a new freedom to make her own contribution to the family's funds, Chrissie had been working as a waitress at week-ends at a Peebles hotel. Sheena had been with her mother, but working in the kitchen.

'She preferred that,' Chrissie laughed, 'because it was more lively with plenty of backchat going on!'

In those few words she recreated in a flash that younger, barefooted

Sheena of the high spirits and the gay, incessant chatter, dancing up the hillside.

The dirty boots were still discarded outside the door, waiting for whichever child did the cleaning, but inside all was lovely. On top of the deep freeze there were wire trays containing a large luscious circular sandwich cake Chrissie had baked, and a whole variety of smaller cakes. The rooms were impeccable. Their small modern bathroom had aquamarine walls and a thick pile blue carpet; and a wall heater. If things had been rugged in the early days before the 'poles' brought-up electricity, the tight little Coltherd family had tackled their battle in their own way. This was the old self-help on which Scots had always prided themselves.

I felt at home again in this room, with its inevitable clutter from a family of six, two dogs, a big ginger Tom and a wee grey kitten and, at the moment, an irrepressible mother. Chrissie was laughing and telling Sheila of the great day when, with £200 in her purse, she went on her shopping spree to Edinburgh during a special BARGAIN WEEK and bought her fridge, washing machine, electric kettle, electric fire, the famous 'electric' radio, and an electric iron. And then wheedled all the necessary plugs out of the stunned salesman!

'Oh, it's all so lovely here,' she finished, flushed with her bounty. 'We have so much now. Everything that anybody in a town like Peebles has, only we have the hills as well and the lovely country and the animals. I wouldn't change for anything.'

We knew something of her romance with Leslie. He had been born in Canada, his father had been killed in a train accident, and his mother had brought him back to Scotland. Chrissie had met him when he was seven.

'I thought he was detestable,' she had amiably told us once, 'the most detestable boy I had ever met.' Her own father was a shepherd and in the course of time Leslie Coltherd came as a young shepherd to help him. The rest ran true to form. And as she told us, I thought: this really is the end of the story. God's in his heaven, all's well with the world. It would have been difficult for me to have found a family, Scottish or otherwise, nearer to nature, nurtured in the beauty and hardships of farm life.

Chrissie was ready to rush off. We watched her, in the small van, taking all the road bumps with panache. Then we followed her, with more caution, to pick up Lesley at the school. Once more we waited outside, heard the end-of-day hymn, saw Lesley come out. She recognized us. We had no difficulty in spotting her, although time had worked its changes. Here was a trim young woman in a red anorak, blue tartan-style dress beneath, white ankle socks and shoes. Her fair hair, unmistakable at a glance, had been cut short.

'Far too short,' she said when we commented about it. 'It was right down to my waist, but Mummy had it cut short. I wish it would grow again.'

It was an early indication of her decisiveness. At this stage in her development, she had taken the place of the earlier lively, chattering Sheena; but although Lesley talked, and was willing to go on talking, she was thoughtful, self-possessed. Her talk was straightforward, no nonsense, with the purpose of a reflective mind behind it.

7

She sat between us on the front seat of the car, eating the biscuits we fed her, and watching the hills. We stopped at the road end, before the hill track, to wait the coming of the Peebles school bus. Now and again she would give us a laughing glance, or a straight look to see that we were as serious as she was, but mostly her eyes scanned the hills. She was doing what she had done all her young life, reading the country like a book, watching for any movement, anything different. Utterly confident in herself, in us (I hoped), in the place where she belonged.

'There's a heron over there,' she told us quietly. We followed her gaze but could not see the heron. She was worth knowing, this young woman. I tried her on television, a sure beginning with the young. I wanted to judge her against her age group of the cities. What about *Blue Peter?* I should have known better.

'It's not often I see it,' she said, 'because we don't look at television until we've all finished our regular jobs when we get home.' And with one school at the village six miles away, and the other in Peebles, *Blue Peter* had long since gone off the screen by the time the young Coltherds got up the hill and did their chores.

'My favourite's *Tom and Jerry,*' she said, knowing to continue on the subject. We were off. Very animatedly. From there to pop music. 'I'm not so keen on pop. I don't like the noise and all that carry on. I like songs and music and things with real tunes.'

But if she did have to choose a pop record?

She answered without pause: 'It would be *Twenty-five, Twenty-five.* There's more harmony in that than that hippy stuff.'

I wondered what her father's favourite was. What would a shepherd deep in those hills all day choose to listen to in the way of popular music?

'Albatross,' she said, without hesitation, and added with quiet knowledge, 'but not sung by the 'group who do sing it.'

Remembering the delightful singing at my own Scottish school when I was a boy, conducted by Mr Love, I asked whether there was much singing at Lesley's school.

'No, we don't have any singing,' she said.

'No Scottish songs?'

'No.'

'What about poetry?'

'No, we don't have poetry either.'

'Not even Robert Burns?'

'No.'

I was floored. Particularly because of the singing. I remembered *Bonnie Mary of Argyle, The Harp that once through Tara's Halls, On the Banks of Alan Water, Cherry Ripe* and a whole host of other melodies. Singing had been one of the joys of our young lives, a real relief from the drab background of our existence. Poetry too we had loved, stood up in class and recited, caught in its music and romance.

'What about religion?' Sheila asked. 'Do you have a hymn in the morning?'

'Oh, yes,' she said, 'we have prayers and a hymn.'

But she did not elaborate and Sheila did not press her. In her own time and her own way Lesley was very forthcoming, and we saw that this was a very special child. I looked at the unchanging hills around us, the valley that had been the same for hundreds of years, the clouds, grey and silver, scattered over the blue sky – all was the same, but we were all living in a new world and this little girl was going to be very much part of it.

'Our teacher says there ought to be classes for older people who're having difficulty with decimals instead of the pounds, shillings and pence they've used all their lives. It's going to be easy enough for me and little Graeme, who'll begin on decimals and go on from there, but what about these older men and women?'

I thought of the people I'd seen standing in front of the boards in stations, wondering what 21.45 meant or 17.11 and making troubled calculations within themselves or counting silently with their fingers against purse or handbag.

'There it is again,' she said suddenly; 'the heron.' And was pleased when we spotted it.

Further up the bank I had noticed a red, dented, much-used cycle leaning against the turf.

'Oh, that's John's,' she said, with a derisory laugh, and all the maturity of a woman towards her three years older brother. 'He leaves it there when he cycles down for the morning school bus, and he'll pick it up again when he arrives.'

'What! Over that rough road?'

'Oh, he's daft,' she said affectionately.

I wondered aloud about John's future.

'I don't think he's sure,' Lesley said, 'but he works well with my dad. He'll want to have something to do with a farm.'

'And you?'

'I don't really know,' she confessed thoughtfully, 'but I know I'll always want to work in the country. Maybe with animals.'

She was a shepherd's daughter and she knew all about the country, about the sheep and the lambs and the dogs, about the bull far down the road that I'd seen in a field when coming up the road, where I had been warned by a notice: 'Beware of the Bull.'

'It's not a bull, you know,' Lesley said, 'it's a bullock.'

Then she went on to tell us how, when a ewe loses a lamb, you can only give her a lamb that needs a mother.

'You take the skin off the dead lamb,' she said, matter-of-factly, 'and wrap it round another lamb that needs a mother. The ewe will accept it as her own and you only need to keep the skin on for a little while and then take it away.'

She had done it herself with a little lamb they had tried to save, bringing it into the warmth of the house, 'giving it brandy and all that carry-on', but the lamb had died. Her expression 'all that carry-on' was simply an expression she used constantly to mean all the things that have to be done in certain circumstances. There was a warm-heartedness in this girl and plenty of compassion, but she was well acquainted with nature and its ways.

She passed ruminatively on to giving us information of changes to come. Nearly 900 acres of the hill-land were being taken over by the Forestry Commission. Thousands of trees would be planted.

'They'll all give cover for foxes to breed here,' she said,

241

'and go for the sheep and the lambs.'

8

I had thought that time might pass slowly during the long wait for the bus, and had half expected that after a few words with Lesley she would want to make her own way up the hill. I'm glad she didn't. She was a stranger to us except in the memory of past association, and we were almost complete strangers to her. I doubt if I have ever spent so pleasant and rewarding a half hour. I can't remember what I was like at her age, or how I appeared to other people, but I certainly had not the happy self-possession of this girl nor her knowledge of the country, of people, seemingly of the world as far as she knew it. But then I hadn't been a little Coltherd, brought up in the happiness of her home in the hills.

We could hear the school bus coming, and we all got out of the car and waited. When it rounded the bend, only Sheena and John were aboard. They peered towards us through the window. Then they exchanged a quick remark, and started waving. Impossible to describe the clamour and chatter, the road bumps and accompanying giggles, as we went slowly up that rough path which long ago had led us to this family. Sheila drove and I tried to recognize in Sheena the eight-year-old, her fair hair shimmering in the sun, who had monopolized our first picnic. Her colouring had changed; this young woman was darkening towards a resemblance with her mother; the girlish babble had gone; but the smiling eyes were the same, and the Coltherd resolution. My swiftest thought was that Sheena would never have to think much about a career; some young man would only be too eager to ask her to marry him. I did not say so, of course, and we talked about jobs and shorthand not only in the car but when we got out and went into the house.

Leslie Coltherd had finished for the day. He was wearing a dark green pullover, and I got a glimpse of warm brown socks in his slippers. He was completely relaxed and had just had a cup of coffee from the Rayburn cooker. Lesley slipped away and presently came back in a bright red jumper and brown corduroy slacks.

The Coltherd family only lacked Chrissie who would shortly return, radiant with her new hair-do. We thought it better in a situation that would produce family criticism or family ribaldry, or even family admiration, to make ourselves scarce. And I had already heard from the shepherd the news about John that I'd hoped for. He was going to be apprenticed in a year's time to a neighbouring farm. 'A very good farmer,' said his father.

As we went down the hill, I put up the car window. There was a chill in the air. Soon winter would close in on the hills and the valley. It would have to be a hard, hard winter to daunt that little lot.

XVIII

1

I wanted to get away from Scotland for a day or two. Too many
impressions were crowding upon me, and I needed to sort them, and
myself, out. Nothing could make me happier than that last meeting at
Manorhead, confirming everything I had ever known, understood, and
lived in Scotland. But for a brief interval I wanted to turn it all over in
my mind from a distance. At this rate, I was fast becoming a resident
Scot again, and soon any attempt at objective judgment would be
blurred by familiarity and propinquity.

I hadn't given myself time to reserve a seat in the train for Kings
Cross so I got to the Waverley early and found myself a place at the
carriage window before the crowd arrived. Everybody is travelling
nowadays; the whole world is always going somewhere. I had bought
nothing at the bookstall; I wanted no Scottish newspapers that day, no
books on Scotland with their beautiful coloured jackets of hills and
glens, all about history and touring.

For reading I had brought an old favourite, Hemingway's *A Farewell
to Arms,* a bit tattered since it was a first edition from 1929, and
certainly shouldn't have been risked the further ill-usage of a railway
journey; and an old copy of *The New Yorker* magazine. The train was
still only half empty, with fifteen minutes to go before moving out of
Edinburgh. I settled myself comfortably to forgetfulness of the world
and to the life I had been chasing these last two years.

Vain hope. I riffled through the pages of *The New Yorker,* smiled at
one or two of the cartoons, mentally noted a feature I would read later,
and then landed on a gaily-coloured full-page advertisement. It was

temptingly designed to attract the American tourist to come to Scotland, filled with pipers and caber tossers at the Highland Games.

Every September these Games bring thousands of people to the Highlands. They have become a kind of national symbol. The Royal Family holiday at Balmoral, and when the Braemar games are on they are in attendance. I have two old friends up there who have been their hosts. Frances is the American-born wife of Captain Alwyn Farquharson, the Laird of Invercauld, a vast estate rolling all over the Cairngorms. The Queen and her family and friends go out with the guns over this ground, and from almost every corner of the world friends of the Farquharsons turn up to enjoy the hospitality and intimacy of Invercauld, the turreted house which, with Braemar Castle, can be seen standing in the grounds well back from the Braemar-Balmoral road.

The sporting atmosphere of Invercauld is only one aspect of its appeal, and of the Farquharson interests. Frances has always absorbed herself in the life of the small community and the surrounding country. Her personal efforts to develop and enrich the cultural life of Scotland reach out far beyond the Scottish border.

At Braemar she created a small but lively Festival for visitors in the summer season, redecorating the old disused village chapel in an effective soft pink and yellow motif. And her Braemar Gallery seeks out and offers for sale the work of Scottish artists and craftsmen in every medium – engraved glass, china, appliqué pictures, hand-printed materials, and so on. I have seen garments and materials made from wool, grown, spun and dyed in Scotland; and here I have picked up a few excellent oil and water-colour paintings by artists whose work is now much in demand.

People from many countries visit Scotland for the scenery and the Games. Women particularly enjoy the picturesque and romantic aura of these gatherings. Set among the mountains and the glens, with the skirl of the pipes and the swirl of the kilt, with brawny men and lovely lassies in gay tartans on view, I can well understand how they surrender to the visual appeal of Braemar or Aboyne and the other meetings.

As a spectacle of movement and sound and colour, and a contact with history (when the Games were for the relaxation of the warrior rather than the titivation of the tourist) the Highland Games have their special appeal. But they are not anything like the heart of Scotland.

You can get too much of a good thing, and a whole day of piping and dancing and tossing the caber, especially when over-organized, is more than enough for me. And I don't feel a traitor for saying so. I dislike the commercialism, and the professionalism of contestants who sometimes travel from meeting to meeting like Miss England or Miss World. If the Games were a spontaneous coming-together of the clans and the people how different it all might be.

Long ago I agreed with the sentiments of A.G. Macdonell, expressed in his book, *My Scotland:*

> 'Games can be very dignified and very noble. So long as they are instinctive celebrations of the people of the soil, rejoicing for a moment on the ground where they work for the rest of the year and from which they gain their food, and their drink, their shelter, and their clothing, they are a kind of thanksgiving festival. The new age has changed all that. It is true that it has not transplanted the Games from their native soil. The new age is much too clever to make such a mistake. The preservation of the Highland Games in the old setting of glens and mountains and lochs is made part of the publicity arrangements of the new age whereby it hopes to lure ever-increasing numbers of tourists. The only part of the Highland Games which the new age has not changed is the soil.'

2

There was some commotion going on a few compartments away, the coming and going of people, voices raised in the forced heartiness that often accompanies farewells. I got up, not only to stretch my legs before the train pulled out, but to investigate. And as soon as I was in the corridor, and saw the group of men and women and children, I could almost guess. At once I wanted to retreat back into my corner.

But I went on up the corridor, becoming one of them for a moment while I pressed through, came to the door, and saw the overspill on to the platform. It was indeed a send-off. Passing the compartment I had seen the suitcases in the luggage racks, the overnight bags stamped P & O LINE and the brightly-coloured labels on everything: SYDNEY. Even at a glance I could mentally separate the two or three people who were departing from the many friends who would presently disentangle themselves and stay behind.

I dropped down on to the platform and stood close to a young man.

Those on the platform were the less involved; the friends, not the family; not even the very close friends. But they had come for old times' sake. All the others in the corridor or the compartment were sharing their handshakes and their embraces to wish the departing god-speed; and their kisses that might be the last for many a day.

'Emigrating?' I murmured to my companion.

'Australia,' he said, his eyes not coming away from the window.

'How many are going?'

He shot me a quick look.

'Two old pals. One with his wife and kid; the other on his own.'

I remembered the compartment.

'But there's another wife and kid there.'

'His. They're staying behind here till she sees how he gets on.'

He didn't want to talk. Especially to a stranger, who wouldn't understand.

I went down the platform to go in by the far door. I did not want to press through that shattered little group again.

Oh, God, I thought, this is where I came in. There hadn't been a crowd like this when I – and *my* pal – left Waverley so long, long ago, but we had no wives and we were only gambling our own lives and futures. We had gone in a creaky tub of a boat – four in a cabin – that took fourteen days to get us from Glasgow to Quebec. And when you went in those days, you were practically gone for good.

Now you could get back from Australia in two or three days – if you had the money. These two families weren't pulling up roots and going 13,000 miles away from their home and loved ones because they had the money. It was because they hadn't. They hadn't got the jobs that would give them the money to live comfortably, or they wouldn't be breaking up like this.

As I sat down, viciously closing *The New Yorker* with its gaudy Highland Games, pipers an' a', I remembered what Professor Robert Grieve, chairman of the Highlands and Islands Development Board had said: 'A major factor in the high level of emigration must be Scotland's central belt which is so unattractive, so slipshod, and so decayed, that if people do not leave this particular environment, then they darned well ought to!'

It was almost on time. The bustle up the corridor increased as people made for the platform. The wife with the little girl in her arms was the last to go. I could hear her broken cry 'Oh, Tam... Oh, Tam...' and then mercifully the little crowd started singing, *Will ye no' come back again?*

For the moment it drowned despair, but all despair was in its lament:

> Will ye no' come back again?
> Will ye no' come back again?
> Better lo'ed ye canna be,
> Will ye no' come back again?

Better loved you might not be, but even love needed a job, and money, to sustain it. The singing rose. I had sung the song, and had it sung for me, in many strange places. But the Waverley Station in Edinburgh is for me the place where it is at its saddest.

A door banged shut. The train began slowly to move. I did not want to look out of the window, but the woman with the little girl in her arms had run forward, so that she would see her Tom longer. She was still running alongside the train as our window passed her. The tears were streaming down her face.

I turned away from the parting and the heartache, thankful that I was in the train and not left there on the platform to watch the weeping.